I0810679

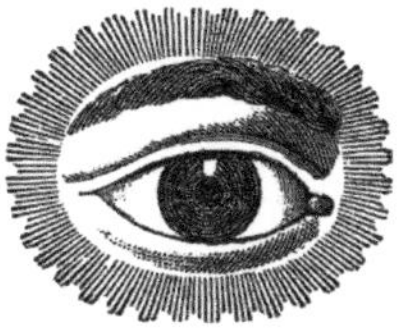

ENCYCLOPEDIA of EARLY TEXAS HISTORY

A Compendium of TEXAS ANTIQUITY *for the* INQUISITIVE MIND

STEPHEN P. BILES

Charleston London
THE History PRESS

Published by The History Press
Charleston, SC 29403
www.historypress.net

Front cover, left circular inset: "Fabulously Quirky Lady with Binoculars—Vintage Steampunk Image." *From the Graphics Fairy, thegraphicsfairy.com.*

First published 2014

Manufactured in the United States

ISBN 978.1.62619.454.0

Library of Congress CIP data applied for.

Notice: The information in this book is true and complete to the best of our knowledge. It is offered without guarantee on the part of the author or The History Press. The author and The History Press disclaim all liability in connection with the use of this book.

I dedicate this book to my wife, Elfie, who supported me so lovingly during this effort. I also appreciate my daughter and son-in-law, Sarah and Cameron, who frequently encouraged me as I worked on this project. Finally, I offer this book to all Texans, especially our grandson, Erik.

CONTENTS

ACKNOWLEDGEMENTS

The idea for this book began in the 1950s when my parents gave me a wondrous book, *The Story of America in Pictures* by Alan C. Collins.[1] I treasured this book. I made sure it went with us as our family moved frequently from one U.S. Army post to the next. Throughout my childhood, I read and reread the captions and looked longingly at the images of nobles, sailors, Indians, explorers and politicians who represented the variety of people who made American history. I gazed tirelessly at the splendid and ordinary places where Americans rode, farmed, sailed, played and fought. I cherish this book as it, along with my parents, inspired me to look for meaning in the past and try to understand how it affects us today.

Eventually, I studied history. I am imprinted by and forever grateful for the guidance and inspiration from professors at three Texas universities: Midwestern State University, the University of Texas–Austin and Texas A&M University. Forrest D. Monahan Jr. and Kenneth F. Neighbours, two Midwestern State University history professors, shared their dedication and love of history. Thomas L. Philpott, history professor at the University of Texas–Austin, demonstrated how much information lies under numerical data. James F. McNamara, professor emeritus of educational psychology at Texas A&M University, modeled clear thinking and writing when I was his doctoral student.

The Texas State Archives in Austin is one the capital's jewels. Texas State Archives staff members preserve, conserve and curate thousands of precious historical documents that tell the history of Texas. I particularly appreciate the guidance and assistance of John Anderson, archives preservation officer. He led the way to finding archival documents of the people, maps, engravings, pictographs, Republic of Texas currency and Margaret Lea Houston's "summer spread" featured in this book.

Finally, I greatly appreciate the vision and skill of Christen Thompson, commissioning editor at The History Press. In addition to insights she shared about the text, she offered many design and conceptual ideas giving this book its artful feel and appearance.

INTRODUCTION

Encyclopedia of Early Texas History introduces the reader to the wonder and variety of early Texas history. Many people are familiar with some of the big names in Texas history, such as Stephen F. Austin; Santa Anna; the Yellow Rose; David Crockett; Sam Houston; Cynthia Ann Parker; her husband, Nocona; and their son Quanah.

This book features less widely known people, some of their activities and the places where they lived. The topics are arranged alphabetically and represent individuals, groups, places and activities that shaped early Texas history. Whenever possible, an image accompanies the text.

People began living in Texas thousands of years ago. Archaeologists conclude that the flint at the Alibates Flint National Quarries Monument in the Texas Panhandle has been used for thirteen thousand years: "Until around 1870, Alibates

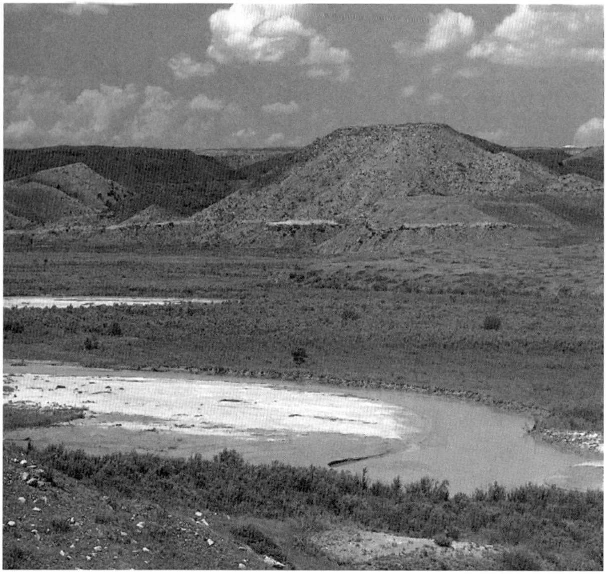

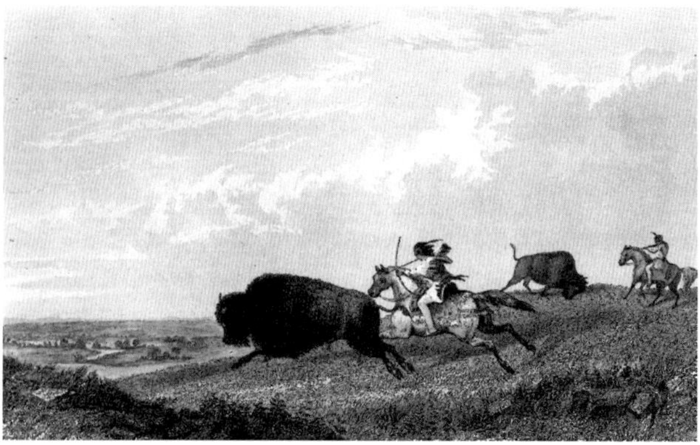

flint was used for projectile points, scrapers, knives, and other stone tools."[2] Early Texans left us thousands of petroglyphs and pictographs in many locations. These incomparable rock carvings and paintings document various aspects of complex life, including work, spirituality, plants and animals of the region.

Early Texas written accounts of history begin nearly five hundred years ago. Spanish explorers, and later others from France, reported about the land, people, plants and animals they found. Texas in the 1500s and 1600s was a thinly populated land of prairie, coast, desert and woods. The land had plenty of game and plants that fed the Native Americans for thousands of years. Gradually, the Native American economy based primarily on hunting, gathering and some farming gave way to intensive farming, ranching and mining. Eventually, the Texas economy diversified, embracing other enterprises.

Politically, Texas fell under the claims and rule of six distinct ways of life. Texans often summarize this change by saying there were "six flags over Texas." Between the early 1500s and mid-1800s, these flags included ones from Spain, France, the United Mexican States, the Republic of Texas, the United States of America and the Confederate States of America, followed again by the United States of America.

Opposite, top: The Canadian River winds through the Alibates Flint Quarries National Monument in the Texas Panhandle. *Photograph by National Park Service staff.*

Opposite, bottom: *Buffalo Hunt* by Captain Seth Eastman, U.S. Army. *Courtesy Texas State Library and Archives Commission, Prints and Photographs Collection, #1/140-3.*

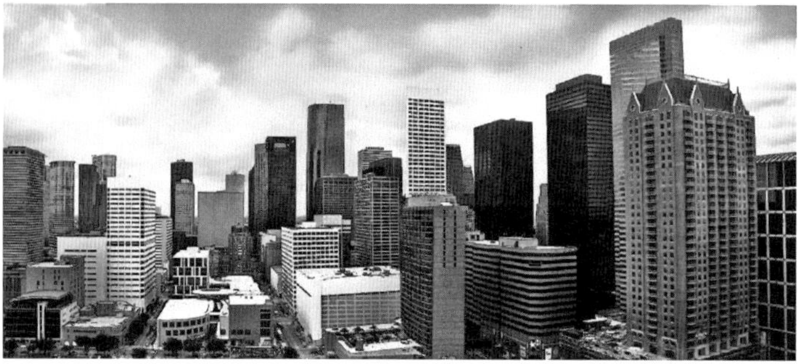

Panoramic Houston skyline. *Photograph by Hequals2henry.*

The Texas economy has also changed dramatically during the last five hundred years. Buffalo hunting and cattle drives have given way to a diverse economy varying from large-scale agriculture to technical research and development. Most Texans now live in large urban centers surrounded by sprawling suburbs.

The 2010 U.S. census reports that six (30 percent) of the twenty largest cities in the United States are in Texas: Houston (4), San Antonio (7), Dallas (9), Austin (14), Fort Worth (16) and El Paso (19).[3]

MARQUÉS DE SAN MIGUEL DE AGUAYO (JOSÉ DE AZLOR Y VIRTO DE VERA)

Marqués de San Miguel de Aguayo was born a commoner into a family with a history of serving Spain's rulers. José de Azlor y Virto de Vera was a soldier and governor who married the daughter of the first marquis. This marriage brought him the title by which he remains most known, Marqués de San Miguel de Aguayo. The married couple moved in 1712 to a large hacienda that included nearly half of Coahuila in northern New Spain.

When Aguayo offered to rid eastern Texas of the French, New Spain's viceroy rewarded the marquis with civil and military authority over the province of Coahuila y Tejas. In 1720, the newly named captain general financed and led the reoccupation of a *presidio*, a fort that Spain had abandoned the previous year. The Aguayo Expedition "so solidified the Spanish claim to Texas that it was never again challenged by the French."[4] The Spanish Cross of Burgundy flag would continue flying over New Spain for another one hundred years.

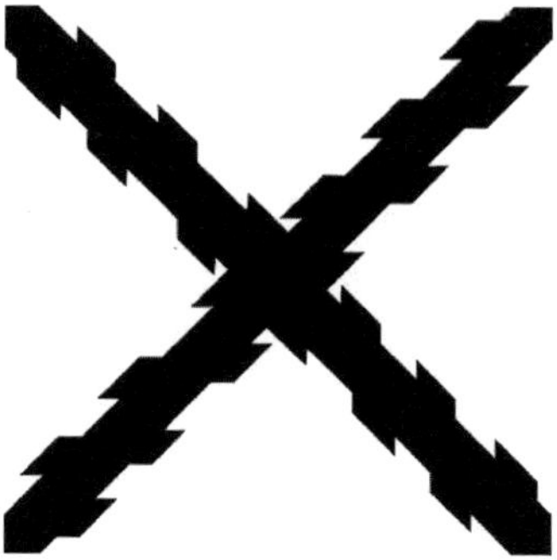

The Cruz de Borgoña (Cross of Burgundy) represents the Cross of St. Andrew. Spanish viceroys used the Cross of Burgundy on a flag called the *Bandera de Ultramar* (Overseas Flag) during Spain's colonization of the Americas. *Photograph by Buho07, vector by Adam Redzikowski.*

Before Aguayo's march into Texas, Spain only had one presidio and two missions. Aguayo saw a need and strove to increase Spain's presence in Texas. Prior to Aguayo's efforts, Texas's Spanish population was concentrated only in San Antonio de Béxar with just 60 soldiers. By 1722, when the marquis' expedition ended, 250 soldiers lived among four presidios, and there were ten missions and a small civilian population in San Antonio de Béxar.[5]

One mission in the San Antonio de Béxar area was named San José y San Miguel de Aguayo.[6] This mission was built to relieve the overcrowding

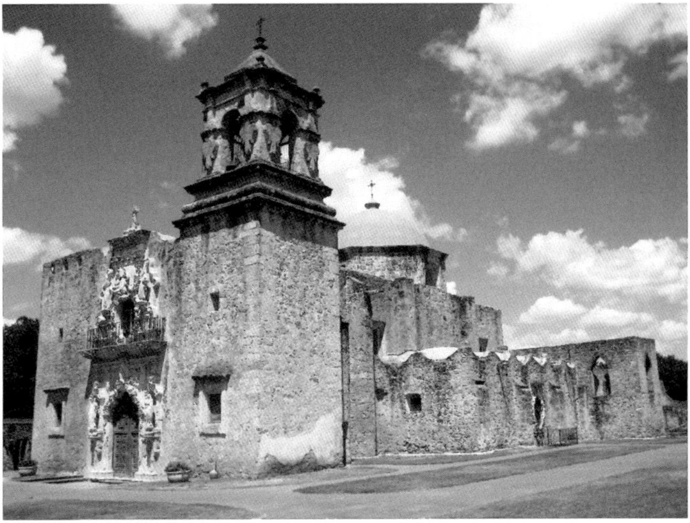

Mission San José y San Miguel de Aguayo in San Antonio, Texas, was named in part to recognize José de Azlor y Vitro de Vera, Marqués de San Miguel de Aguayo. *Photograph by Livenon001©Travis Witt.*

of San Antonio de Valero, more commonly known as the Alamo. The new mission was built to serve the Coahuiltecan Indians. As the numbers grew, the structure expanded to accommodate 350 rooms for the Coahuiltecans, as well as guest rooms, offices, a dining room and a pantry. The 1768 limestone buildings remain intact and are part of the San Antonio Missions Historical Park.[7]

In addition to his fostering reoccupation and new construction, Marqués de San

Miguel de Aguayo is credited with drawing the blueprint for Spanish colonization in Texas. He recommended the king of Spain expand the number of Spaniards in Texas to more securely anchor the royal claim to the territory with a permanent civilian society. He urged the king to settle four hundred families between San Antonio and eastern Texas. He thought they should be recruited from Galicia in northern Spain, the Canary Islands and Cuba.[8]

Aguayo's proposal was accepted and put into practice by Juan Antonio Bustillo y Ceballos in the 1730s (see page 38). The Marqués de San Miguel de Aguayo resigned his governorship of Coahuila y Tejas due to his declining health on June 13, 1722. He returned to his homeland, and the king showed his gratitude by promoting him to field marshal. He died on March 7, 1734.

AGUSTÍN DE AHUMADA Y VILLALÓN, MARQUÉS DE LAS AMARILLAS

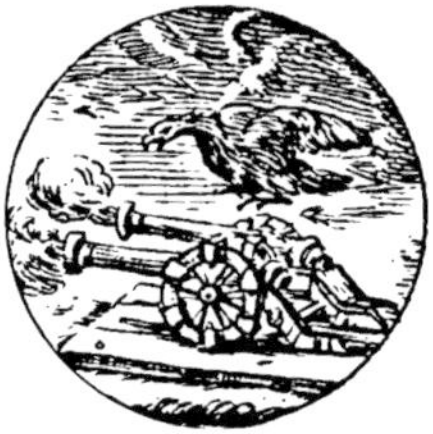

Agustín de Ahumada y Villalón's life spanned the middle of the eighteenth century. He was a Spanish military officer whose victories in Italy brought fame and promotion to become the first Marqués de las Amarillas, a title by which

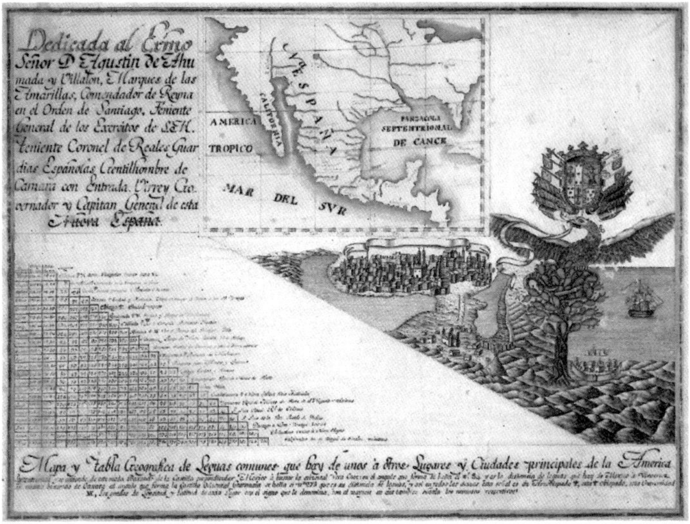

Mapa y Tabla Geográfica de Leguas Comunes que Hay de Unos à Otros Lugares y Ciudades Principales de la América (*Geographic Map and Table of Distances between Principal Places and Cities in America*). This extraordinary map and table is dedicated to Viceroy Agustín de Ahumada y Villalón, Marqués de las Amarillas. The map illustrates the location of Spanish towns and cities in mid-eighteenth century New Spain. *Courtesy Library of Congress.*

he is often known to historians of this era. Spain's King Ferdinand VI commissioned him a lieutenant general before asking him to serve as Barcelona's governor. He was further rewarded when the king appointed him viceroy of New Spain.

Ahumada arrived in Mexico City on November 10, 1755. He celebrated the naming of the Virgin of Guadalupe as New Spain's patron. Indeed, she often became the leading patron in the entire Spanish-speaking lands of Central and South America (see page 231). Ahumada also focused his efforts on cleaning up excessive vices associated with clerical behaviors, such as the selling of holy orders. He also sought to arbitrate among individuals vying to control New Spain's increasing wealth centered in silver mines.

Ahumada devoted a lot of energy and attention to defending some of Spain's imperial outlying posts. For example, he sent aid to the Philippines to combat anti-Christians. He sought to stop French incursions on the Texas coast and English pirates' menacing of ships in the Caribbean.

Within two years, the new viceroy increased the size of the army in New Spain to 2,897 men, primarily housed in Mexico City and Vera Cruz on the Gulf coast.[9] Ahumada used this force to counteract raids that the Comanche Indians were making in Texas. On March 16, 1758, two thousand Comanches rode in black and red war paint as they stormed the San Sabá presidio's walls. Nearly every Spaniard, both soldiers and clergy, was killed. After consulting with church leaders, headmen of friendly Native American tribes and experienced soldiers at San Antonio de Béxar, the viceroy approved a plan to mount a counter defense. He sent armies to regain lost power and control in Texas. In August 1759, Ahumada sent six hundred soldiers commanded by Colonel Parrilla to "sweep the Indian country north of [San Antonio de] Béxar."

Parrilla's forces quelled the fierce Comanche uprising.

The victory yielded only a short-lived peace: "There was a subtle but terrible change on the Mexican-Spanish frontier; the balance of power had turned over, and from 1759, the Spanish were on the defensive." From this time forward, the Spanish founded no missions in the frontier, facing the potentially hostile Native Americans. After the Comanche raid on San Sabá, Spanish soldiers did not have any "serious campaigns against the Comanches."[10]

Toward the end of the marquis' term as viceroy, a volcano erupted in Michoacán, west of Mexico City. All the nearby ranches and villages were ruined, and people abandoned them. Ahumada spent his fortune to help the refugees of this disaster. When he died in Mexico City in 1760, the marquis was impoverished. New Spain's treasury paid for his surviving family's return voyage to Spain.[11]

LUCAS IGNACIO ALAMÁN Y ESCALADA

In the late 1820s, Mexican officials became alarmed about the number of immigrants coming from the United States to Texas. General Don Manuel Mier y Terán traveled in Texas and reported to Mexico's president how concerned he was about the increased number of Anglo Americans in Texas. This concern was taken up by Lucas Alamán y Escalada.

Alamán was one of the best-educated people in New Spain. He was also wealthy and held prominent government positions throughout his life.

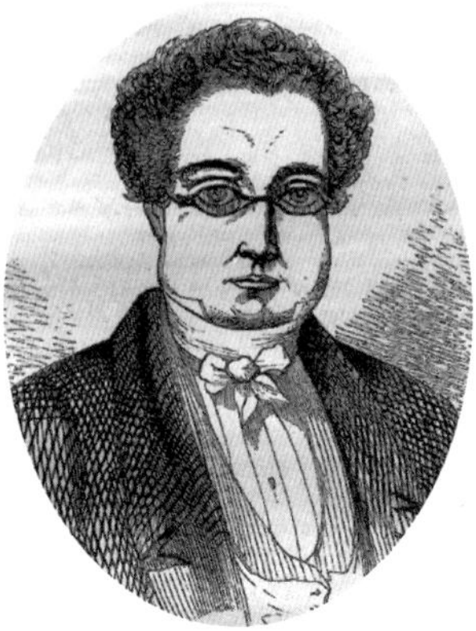

Don Lucas Alamán in an illustration in Fay Robinson's *Mexico and Her Military Chieftains*, Hartford, CT: Silas Andrus & Son, 1848, 267. *Courtesy Texas State Library and Archives Commission, Prints and Photographs Collection, #1998/001-21.*

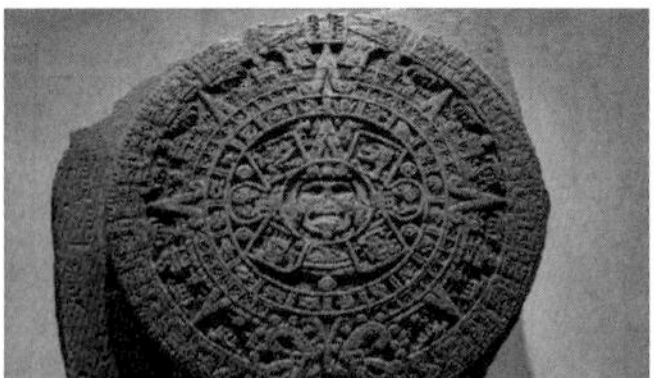

The Aztec calendar stone in the National Anthropology Museum in Mexico City, founded by Lucas Alamán. *Photograph by George and Audrey De Lange.*

He was a member of the Cortes Generales (the Spanish parliament), the minister of foreign relations and a renowned scientist, historian, conservative writer and editor of political newspapers.

Lucas Alamán founded one of the world's premier museums, the Mexican National Archives and Museum of Anthropology. As well, Alamán was an attorney whose clients included the highest members of New Spain's society and later Mexico's families. For example, he represented the family of Hernán Cortés. When Alamán shared an opinion, it was seriously considered. With this in mind, it was significant that Alamán urged Mexico's congress to stop the expansion of Anglo Americans advancing into Texas.[12]

Generally, the Spanish and English had different goals in the New World. The English usually came to colonize, plant new cities, develop an agrarian society, prosper from the exploitation of natural resources and establish trade surpluses, or profit. On the other hand, "the Spanish system was incorporation, not colonization. Spain never intended to send out large numbers of settlers—emigration was rigidly controlled—and except in rare cases, those who arrived expected to live not off the soil but off the resources of a subject native population."[13]

Alamán saw the Anglo Americans moving west from the United States, overwhelming the Mexican population in numbers and influence. The Anglo Americans had different cultural and economic approaches to life. The Anglo Americans moving into Texas brought slaves with them to set up large-scale commodity crop farming like cotton plantations. Few of the newcomers were Roman Catholics, the religion of most Mexicans. Different legal and social traditions came along with the different language used by the Anglo Americans—English instead of Spanish. Over time, these differences meant that the Mexican experience in Texas was no longer secure. The Anglo Americans brought a significant set of challenges that might eventually undermine the control Mexico had in its own land.

Mier y Terán reported to President Guadalupe Victoria that Mexicans had "disappeared" north and east of San Antonio. He said Mexicans were outnumbered ten to one by the *norteamericanos*, the North Americans.[14]

Lucas Alamán advocated for and the Mexican Congress prohibited further immigration of Anglo Americans into Texas. The law of April 6, 1830, had eighteen articles defining the role and scope of Mexico's policy toward immigration and settlement in its northern border area. Articles 10 and 11 especially shocked recently arrived empresarios from the United States, such as Stephen F. Austin and Green Dewitt. Article 10 forbade bringing more slaves into Texas, and Article 11 called for an end of immigration by people from bordering nations, meaning the United States. Austin and DeWitt succeeded in securing an exemption to these articles for their operations. Newly arrived Americans deeply resented the law of April 6, 1830, and it engendered a rift between the immigrants and the Mexican government much like the Stamp Act had done in the British colonies decades before.[15]

Despite the new law, Alamán's desire to stop the immigration of Americans into Texas would not be likely to ever happen. The *norteamericanos* were already established in Texas. The law of April 6, 1830, arrived too late to be effective. Anglo Americans had already gained place and prominence wherever they went.

B

GABRIEL MINIME, SIEUR BARBIER

In the 1680s, René Robert Cavalier, Sieur de La Salle, traveled extensively in North America on behalf of France's King Louis XIV, the wealthiest and most powerful monarch of the time.

In 1682, La Salle journeyed down to the Mississippi River to the Gulf of Mexico. He claimed all the land served by the river's watershed, about one-third of the contiguous states in the present-day United States. Now both Spain and France claimed the same land. King Louis XIV wanted to expand the boundaries of New France.

La Salle returned to France and learned the king was eager to bolster the claim by establishing a permanent settlement at the mouth of

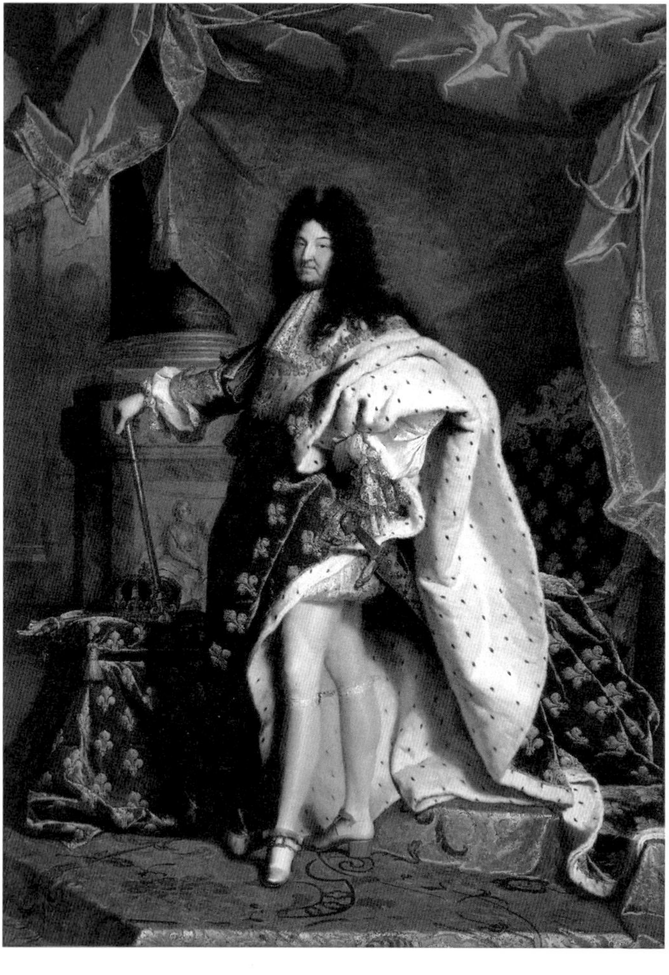

King Louis XIV of France. A 1701 oil painting by Hyacinthe Rigaud. *Photograph byHarpsihord246.*

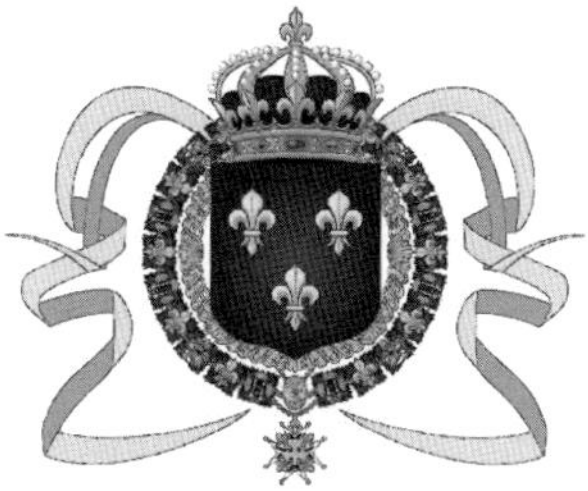

The royal standard of France was used as the flag of New France. *Photograph by Bluebear2. From WikimediaCommons.*

the Mississippi, a river the French called the Colbert. In 1684, La Salle sailed again to the Gulf of Mexico, a body of water the Spanish now claimed for their exclusive use. The French claim of Texas was part of a continent-wide exploration that the French undertook to gain more land and wealth in the New World. A late seventeenth-century map clearly shows that most French claims were in present-day Canada and the northern United States. La Salle's voyages sought to extend this influence southward toward the Gulf of Mexico and its surrounding lands.

From the beginning, La Salle's excursion into Texas did not go well. After losing one ship to the Spanish navy, he sailed quickly toward what he thought was the mouth of the Mississippi River. La Salle and his countrymen went ashore on the banks of a bay. On a slight rise above the bay, they founded a settlement in 1685 named Fort St. Louis.

This fort was not particularly strong or strategically secure in its location. It had no surrounding stockade, and it was not protected by a large garrison of troops. Fort St. Louis consisted of one large building and several smaller ones near a creek. Several cannons faced the bay to

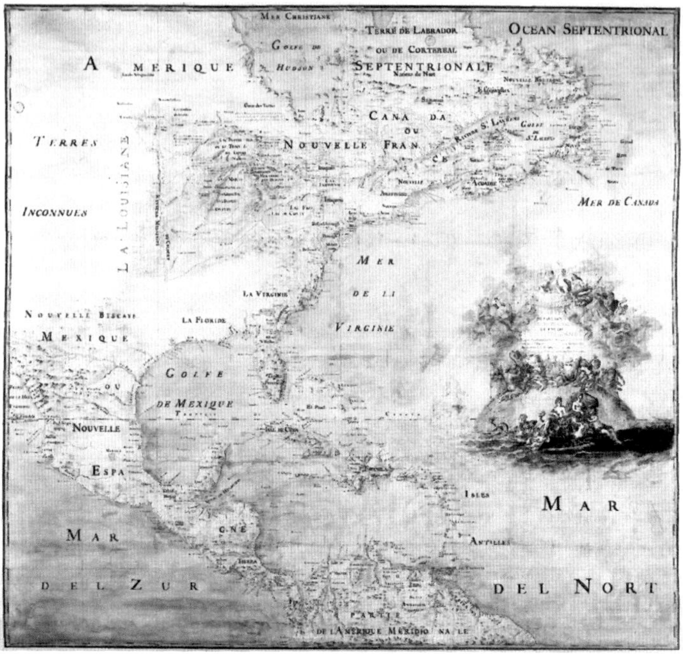

Carte de l'Amérique (Map of America) by Claude Bernou, 1681. *Photograph by Paris 16.*

protect the site from potential strikes from any ships that may approach from the sea.[16] Carlos de Sigüenza y Góngora produced a map with drawings of the fort, lost ship and the bay with its islands. The map was based on sketches made by Alonso de León during his 1689 travels. The map provides a detailed look at the travels of Spaniards in North

America, including what was known about the location of this ill-fated French settlement on the Gulf coast.

The French men and women who came with La Salle to start a colony and establish France's claim to this part of North America did not fare well from the beginning of their experience. The local Native Americans were not welcoming. Indeed, they killed many of the Frenchmen. Sickness also felled many of La Salle's party. Worst of all was the loss of the new colony's essential supplies. In the bay was what a Spanish visitor, Alonso de León, later on called a *navío quebrado*, or "broken ship," the *La Belle*.[17] The *La Belle* ran aground and sank near the bay's barrier island in February 1686. This ship carried "more than one million" artifacts that "represent a 'kit' for building a colony in the seventeenth-century New World."[18] Losing this ship was an insurmountable setback for the colonists. La Salle's party found themselves alone with hostile Native Americans for neighbors, few supplies, hundreds of miles from French settlements in Canada and thousands of miles from France.

Four months after the *La Belle*'s sinking, in June 1686, Sieur Barbier married a French woman who had come on the journey. They had a child born in 1688. Thus, Sieur Barbier and his bride are believed to have been the first marriage of Europeans in Texas. Barbier is considered the father of the first person born in Texas to a person of European ancestry.[19]

On January 7, 1687, La Salle traveled eastward, trying to rejoin his countrymen in the Illinois Country. As he departed, La Salle appointed Sieur Barbier to command Fort St. Louis. Barbier's command was not strong. He had command of only some gravely ill men, children and some women who had journeyed to the New World hoping to find suitable husbands.

In 1688, a Frenchman near death, Jean Henri, arrived at a fort in northern New Spain. He said he was from the ill-fated Fort St. Louis. The next spring, in April 1689, Don Alonso de León, governor of Coahuila, led 150 men to the site of Fort St. Louis. There he found skeletons and total destruction.

A few Frenchmen survived in nearby Native American villages. They told León that Sieur Barbier, along with many others, had been killed by the Karankawas Indians (see page 140). The Indians reportedly captured and took away most of the children and women. After hearing these stories and looking at the ruins, de León's men destroyed the remains of the fort.[20]

One of the more lasting outcomes of La Salle's attempt to establish Fort St. Louis was the Spanish reaction. The Spanish sought to redirect their interests from western Texas to the eastern part of the area. Although this effort at Fort St. Louis failed, the French remained committed to a claim to Texas. The two kingdoms vied for Texas for more than one hundred years: "Virtually every Spanish move in Texas and the borderlands came as a reaction to a French threat, real or imagined." This continued struggle gave rise to the later United States claim that it had a legitimate claim to Texas once it bought the French holdings known as Louisiana. The United States and Spain did not settle this issue until 1819 with the Adams-Onís Treaty.[21]

In 1996, archaeologists discovered the exact location of Fort St. Louis near Arenoso Creek at Inez, Texas, in Victoria County.[22] In addition to the fort's buildings and artifacts, the remains of a sunken ship were found, the *La Belle*.

Amazingly, after more than three hundred years, the ship has been recovered. The Center for Maritime Archeology and Conservation at Texas A&M University is conserving and rebuilding the ship's remains at a one-of-a-kind facility in Bryan, Texas. Once it is restored, *La Belle* will be displayed at the Bob Bullock Texas State History Museum in Austin, Texas.[23]

JUAN ANTONIO BUSTILLO Y CEBALLOS

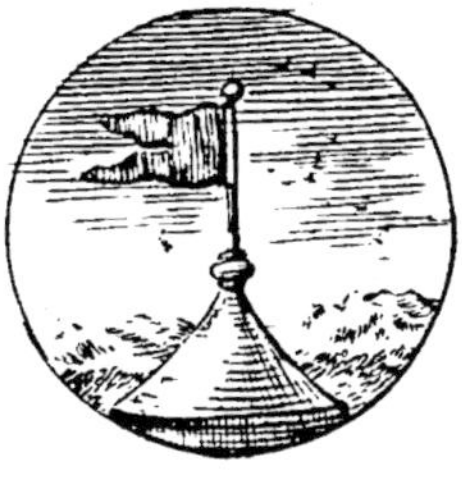

Juan Antonio Bustillo y Ceballos was born in one of Spain's mountainous areas, Burgos, around 1691. He was a servant of the king in Texas from 1722 to 1734. His first post was as the captain of the fort at Nuestra Señora de Loreto Presidio at La Bahía Espíritu Santo. In 1731, Bustillo was appointed governor of Texas. One of his first efforts

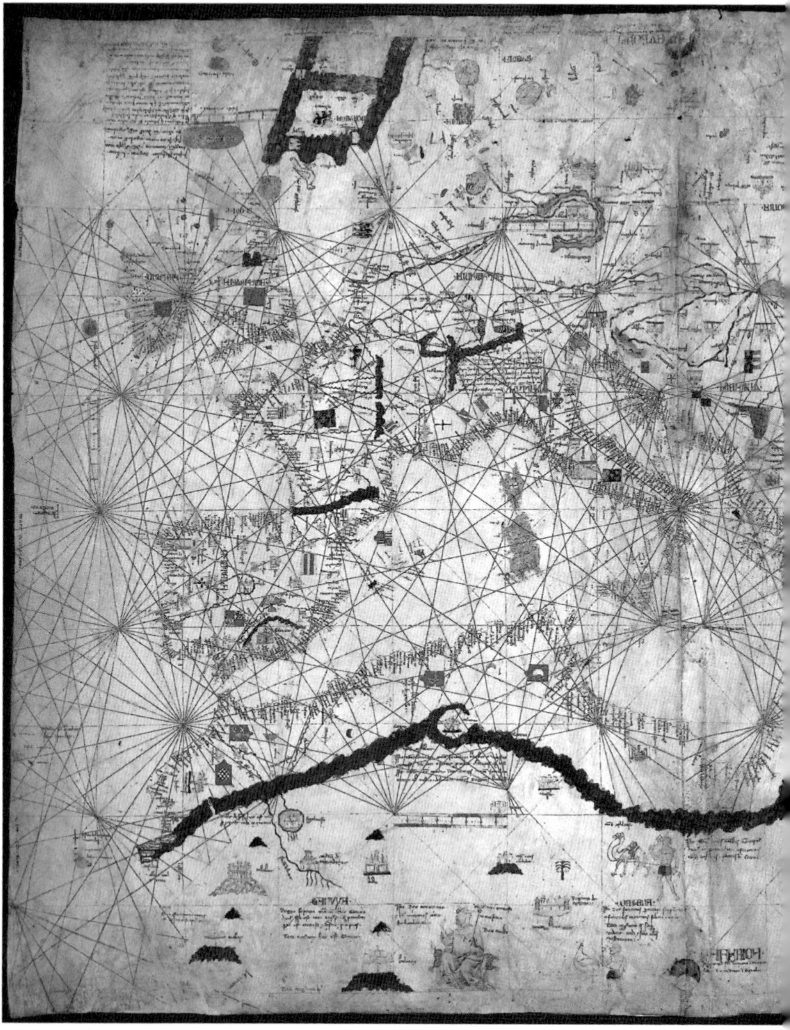

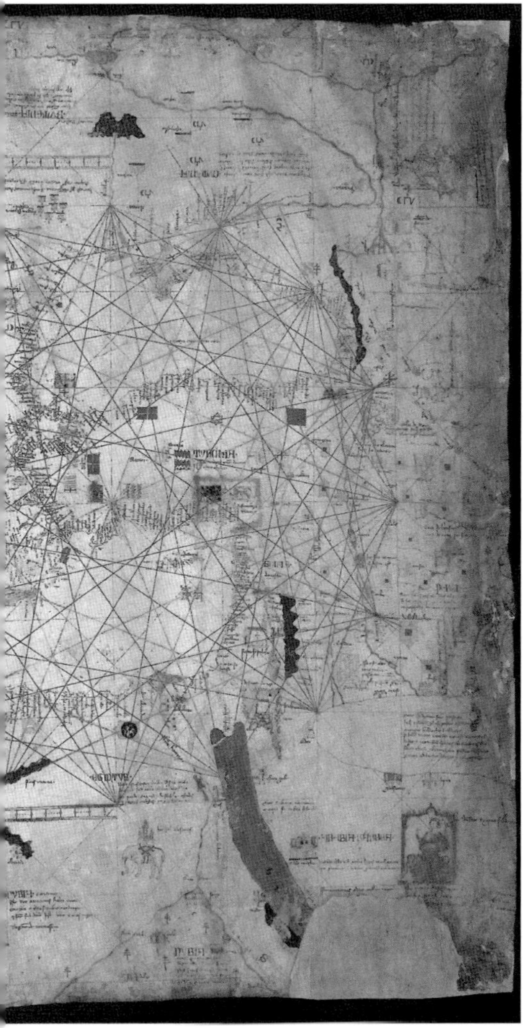

Angelino Dulcert's August 1339 *Carte Marine de la Mer Baltique, de l Mer du Nord, de l'Océan Atlantique Est, de la Mer Méditerranée, de la Mer Noire et de la Mer Rouge* (*Map of the Baltic Sea, North Sea, East Atlantic Ocean, Mediterranean Sea and Red Sea*). The Canary Islands are shown off the western coast of Africa in the lower left corner of the map. *Photograph by Trialsanderrors.*

was working to relocate the missions from eastern Texas to San Antonio.[24]

In 1732, the newly minted governor led a campaign against the Apaches, who threatened the missions on the San Xavier River (now named San Gabriel) and San Sabá River. He led a force of 220 men, including 160 Spaniards and 60 Native Americans, who defeated a group of Apache Indians west of San Antonio. Along with warriors, many women and children were killed.[25] A common occurrence, this battle was merely one of the frequent skirmishes in Texas, which served as the northern frontier of New Spain.

Bustillo y Ceballos oversaw the arrival of settlers from the Canary Islands that Marqués de San Miguel de Aguayo had proposed in 1722 (see page 22). The first twenty-five families from the Canary Islands arrived in Cuba in June 1731. They sailed to Vera Cruz on the Gulf coast of New Spain. Juan Leal Goraz led the colonists on foot for more than seven hundred miles north to San Antonio. These Canary Islanders were the "nucleus of the villa of San Fernando de Béxar, the first regularly organized government in Texas." Some of their descendants still live in San Antonio. One of the popular restaurants on the city's river walk is named in their honor, Las Canarias.[26]

In 1734, Bustillo y Ceballos resigned as governor of Texas and moved back to Mexico City. He served as a member of the Audiencia Real, literally the Royal Audience, which acted as the highest judicial and administrative body in New Spain. His opposition to establishing new missions in the Apache regions was ignored.[27]

ÁLVAR NÚÑEZ CABEZA DE VACA

Whenever people decide to emigrate and forsake their known territory and comfortable life, they usually send out scouts to learn what may be expected. Emigrants want to know as much as possible before they commit to leaving their known comforts and move to another place. People want to know what to expect, the likelihood of succeeding in the new place. A person who thinks about emigrating considers many questions. For example, what is the land like? Is there enough water? What crops would likely thrive, and what livestock would be suitable? What minerals and timber sources are available? Spaniards in the 1500s were especially interested in finding gold and silver. They were amazed at the riches Cortés found in Mexico and Pizarro discovered in Peru. Tons of gold and silver left the new lands in heavily laden ships sent to Spain.

Much of the world was unknown by European adventurers. Some people found this uncertainty an attraction while others were afraid to go far from known lands. A German scientist, mathematician and cartographer, Sebastian Münster, published a compendium of information and maps—*The Cosmographia*, initially published in 1544—that was one of the most-read books of the sixteenth century with one hundred editions. His *Map of America* featured few details as Europeans had not yet explored and mapped this part of the world. Similarly, most Europeans knew what creatures might live in the seas surrounding America. Münster included some realistic and fanciful sea creatures in his large book.

Many Spaniards in the sixteenth century sought the fame and power that only gold and silver could bring. One of these men was Álvar Nuñez Cabeza de Vaca. He was born in Jerez de la Frontera near the coastal city of Cadíz. As with many others who lived near port cities, he was adventuresome and sailed westward to the Americas.

Opposite, top: Sebastian Münster's 1561 *Map of America*, first published in 1544 in *Cosomographia*, is one of the first maps to depict the New World. *Public domain, photograph by Manuel González Olaechea.*

Opposite, bottom: Olaus Magnus's *Carta Marina* published in Sebastian Münster's *Cosmographia* in 1544. *Contributed by Andreas Praefcke.*

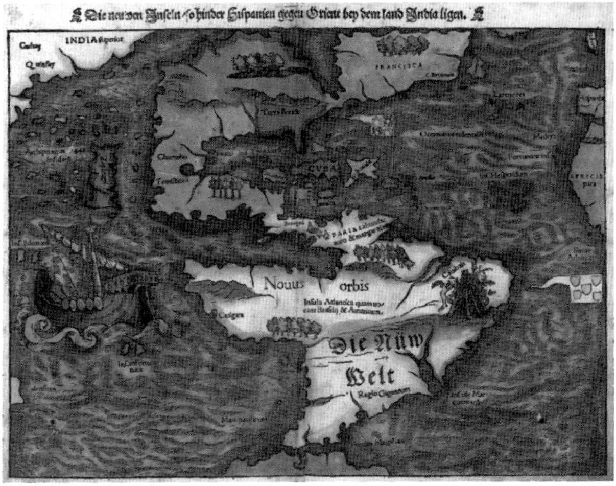
Die new'en Inseln / so hinder Hispanien gegen Oriente bey dem land India ligen.
INDIA superior
FRANCISCA
CUBA
Nouus orbis
Die Nüw Welt

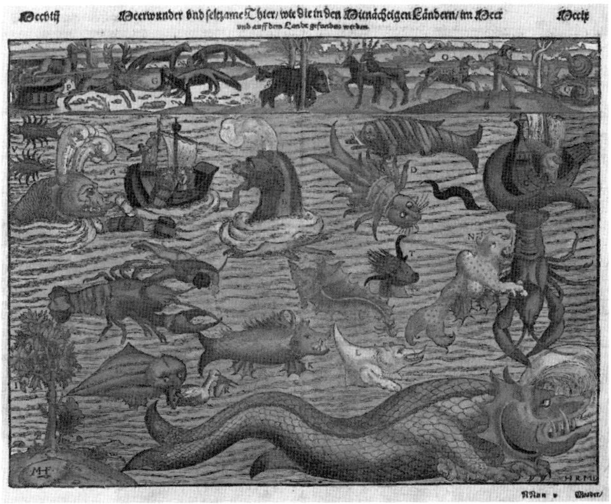
Meerwunder und seltzame Thier / wie die in den Mitnächtigen Ländern / im Meer
und auff dem Lande gefunden werden

At some point, Cabeza de Vaca decided to use his mother's surname instead of his father's. His mother's family name, Cabeza de Vaca, had a higher social standing. Cabeza de Vaca hoped adopting his mother's surname would bring him a more favorable status in the New World.[28] He suffered a shipwreck on the Texas coast and wandered for six years with only three companions before making his way back to New Spain. His route from 1528 until 1536 began in the southern reaches of the present-day United States from Florida in the east to the far western reaches of Texas and the Pacific Ocean, then south into New Spain.

Cabeza de Vaca had many other accomplishments. He was a man of many talents. He carefully observed and wrote about Native Americans. He is credited for writing the first ethnographic studies of the Coahuiltecans.[29] Cabeza de Vaca cared for injured and ill Indians by using prayer and medicine. He surgically removed an arrowhead from the heart of one injured man. He is remembered as the "Patron Saint" of the Surgical Society.[30] Cabeza de Vaca's accomplishments as an explorer, ethnologist, doctor, naturalist and historian are unparalleled.

In addition to these skills, he trekked for years across hundreds of miles of open land with little to sustain him. Cabeza de Vaca also related fabulous tales of the wealth he had seen in cities of gold. In actuality, he was captured and held by the Karankawas and Coahuiltecans in Texas. The cities he described were actually the many-storied adobe and stone pueblos of various Native Americans in New Mexico.

The viceroy of New Spain, Antonio de Mendoza y Pacheco, Marqués of Mondéjar, Count of Tendilla, had little trouble believing Cabeza de Vaca. After all, he was still amazed at the mineral riches found in New Spain and Peru, as were most Spaniards at the time.

Viceroy Mendoza sent Fray Marcos de Niza, a Franciscan friar, to verify what Cabeza de Vaca had said. After hearing the friar's confirmation, Mendoza was convinced and organized the thorough expedition led by Francisco Vásquez de Coronado. Viceroy Mendoza was so convinced that he personally financed about half the cost of Coronado's expedition that began in 1540.[31]

In his late career, the Spanish king appointed Cabeza de Vaca *adelantado*, literally one who goes before or first. As the military leader and governor of Río de la Plata, present-day Argentina, Cabeza de Vaca explored and assessed the new lands and its resources. He unsuccessfully

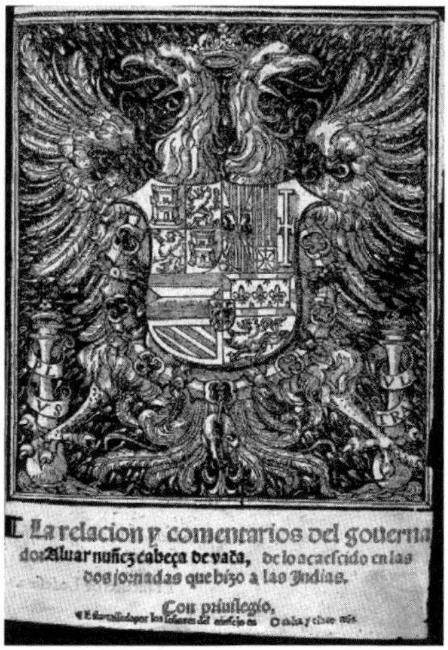
La relacion y comentarios del gouerna dor Aluar nuñez cabeça de vaca, de lo acaescido en las dos jornadas que hizo a las Indias.
Con priuilegio.

The title page of Cabeza de Vaca's *La Relación*. *Public domain, from Internet Archive.*

tried to foster beneficial policies for the indigenous people. He wrote an account of his experiences titled *La Relación de Álvar Núñez Cabeza de Vaca* (*The Account of Álvar Núñez Cabeza de Vaca*) published in Spain in 1542 and again in 1555 in an expanded version. Later editions were retitled as *Los Naufragios* (*The Shipwrecks*). This remarkable book was a memoir and a detailed natural history of what he found during his extensive travels in the Americas and his experiences as an administrator in Río de la Plata.

Cabeza de Vaca was falsely accused of mistreating the Guarani, the indigenous people of Río de la Plata. Subsequently, Cabeza de Vaca was imprisoned, sent to Spain and condemned to prison in Oran, a Spanish possession in northern Africa in present-day Algeria. Cabeza de Vaca's sentence was commuted in 1552. He died in Spain in 1559. His grave's location is unknown.[32]

CHARRO

Hernán Cortés introduced the European world to a new land that he called New Spain.

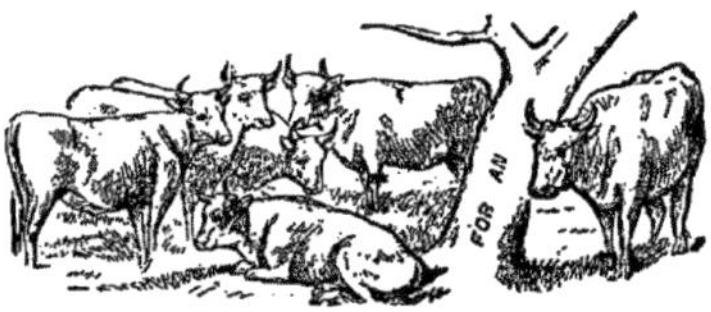

To this new land, he brought his religion, food, language and animals, including horses. Native Americans had never seen a horse and were awestruck. The people of New Spain thought the horses that Cortés and his men rode gave them a supernatural size and power. Horses forever changed the everyday life for most people in the Americas.

The Spanish brought a culture that cared for and respected the horse and the life it gave to the men who rode it. Men who rode horses commanded respect form those who walked. Horsemen were essential for the care of another valued animal that the Spaniards brought: cattle. As a means to understand the power of language, consider that the English word peon means a person of low economic and social status. In Spanish *peón* literally means someone on foot, horseless.

For centuries, Europeans valued the horse and the horseman, especially in the development and spread of chivalry, a word derived from the French word *chevalier*, meaning a man riding a horse. The Spanish word for *chevalier* is *caballero*. Chivalry was based on the roles played by a horseman, a knight. The knight's behavior prescribed an ideal for society as he defended his king, protected the weak and upheld society's values. In the Americas, culture continued to develop around the horse. Similarly, charro culture revered the horsemen whose skills were essential to successfully take care of cattle. A *vaquero*, or cowboy, rode independently and tamed the country while growing the wealth of the cattle industry.

Charro is a term describing the culture, manner, dress and activities of the traditional horseman of central and western Mexico. Charro culture derived from centuries-old practices in Spain. The horseman himself was also known as a "charro." He was a cultural hero known for "bravery and disregard for personal danger; comradeship with peers; and almost mystical loyalty to the hacienda and its brand; the determination to ride any horse that lived; skill with the rope; and utter disdain for any kind of work that could not be done in the saddle."[33] The English language incorporates many words from this charro culture.[34] Examples include *adobe*, *arroyo*, *bronco*, *chaparreras* (chaps), *corral*, *hacienda*, *la reata* (riata), *lazo*, *loco*, *mesteño* (mustang), *pinto*, *rancho*, *ranchero*, *rodear* (rodeo), *sombrero* and *vaquero*. Texans sometimes call the work of the cowboy "cowboying."

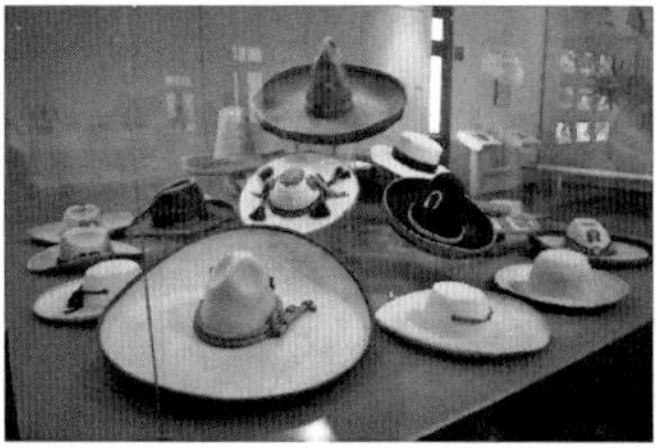

A display of charro hats in the Museum of Popular Arts in Mexico City. *Photograph by Alejandro Linares Garcia.*

Charro culture provides the dominant themes found in the United States for western stories, novels, film, television and art, including such examples as Larry McMurtry's *Lonesome Dove*, the heroes of Louis L'Amour's many novels, Hewey and Walter Calloway in Elmer Kelton's trilogy and John Wayne in Mark Rydell's *The Cowboys* or in Howard Hawks's *Red River*, as well as several of Tom Lea's and Charles Russell's paintings and Frederick Remington's bronze sculptures. Likewise, in Mexico, the charro lives on in countless films, paintings, songs and events.

The charro culture still defines one ideal of how life is to be lived in Texas. Its influence is ever-present in clothes, language and cultural icons. Since 1938, the citizens of Brownsville, Texas, at the southern tip of the state, have held a parade and celebrations to commemorate "Charro Days" with a fiesta. The fiesta coincides with events in Brownsville's sister city, Matamoros, which lies across the Rio Grande. The two fiestas usually begin in late February and last into March, roughly coinciding with the beginning of Lent.

Mythic Texas rested on the charro and his successor, the cowboy. Much has changed during the late twentieth century and the beginning of the twenty-first century. Larry McMurtry began his writing career in the 1960s as a chronicler of the declining status of mythic Texas in books such as *Horseman, Pass By*. Perhaps this title presaged what would evolve. It is the last line of a William Butler Yeats poem, "Under Ben Bulben." Yeats's epitaph concludes with "Horseman, Pass by!"

Larry McMurtry now writes of a more contemporary people in urban settings. He says many Texans "have shaken off the frontier ethic and become mature urbanites… Texans spent so long getting past the frontier experience because that experience is so overwhelmingly powerful."[35] Constance Whitney Warren captured the romance and lasting mythic power of charro culture in a larger-than-life sculpture, *The Cowboy*, completed and cast in 1921 in Paris. In 1925, she presented it "as a memorial gift to Texas, the native home of the cowboy… [as] a tribute to the rough and romantic riders of the range." It stands on the

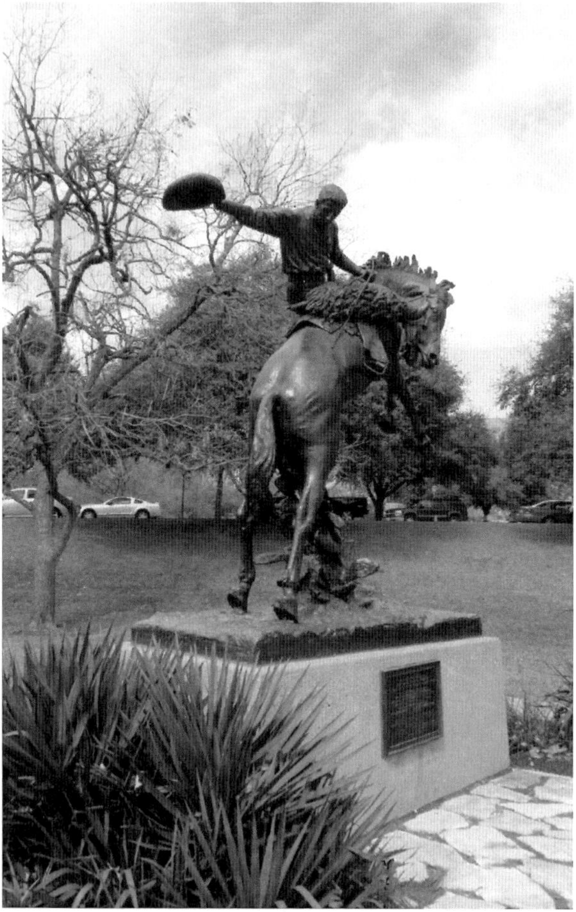

The Cowboy by Constance Whitney Warren, 1921, is located on the grounds of the Texas state capitol. It was cast in Paris by H. Rouard. *Photograph by the author.*

grounds of the Texas capitol in Austin, Texas.

TEODORO DE CROIX

Teodoro de Croix's life is an example of how some of Europe's monarchies reigned over vast lands spread around the globe during the eighteenth century. Croix's life was devoted to serving the king of Spain in various locations including Spain, Italy, Flanders, New Spain and Peru. When he was seventeen, Croix became an ensign in the grenadiers of the Royal Guard and was sent to Italy. Three years later, in 1750, he joined the Walloon Guards, who served as bodyguards to the Bourbon kings of Spain. He was promoted to lieutenant in 1756 and received the Cross of the Teutonic Order when he was in Flanders. This entitled Croix to the noble title of caballero, a title very equivalent to a knight. Four years later, in 1760, he was promoted to colonel in the Walloon Guards.

In 1766, Croix accompanied his uncle Francisco, Marqués de Croix, as he went to New Spain to become its new viceroy. He served his uncle as captain of the viceregal guard and later as governor of Acapulco. His uncle's patronage and his own merit brought more success in New Spain. Brigadier de Croix left New Spain, returning to Spain with Uncle Francisco in 1770. They were joined by their colleagues José Bernardo de Gálvez Gallardo and his son, Teodoro's peer, Bernardo de Gálvez. These two families had a great deal of influence and power in the Spanish court.

The king accepted the elder Gálvez's proposal to separate the northern reaches, the *Provincias Internas*, or "Internal Provinces," of New Spain into a new administrative entity. Gálvez reasoned this would enable the Spanish to "deal more effectively with the Indian problem."[36] Croix began his new position as commandant general on May 16, 1776. King Charles III gave him a "new authority with almost viceregal powers over the provinces of Texas, New Mexico, Coahuila, Nueva Vizcaya, Sinaloa, Sonora, and Baja California."[37]

Croix shared authority over Alta California, now known as California, with Viceroy Antonio María de Bucareli de Ursúa. In 1781, the king separated out California and Baja California to become a separate jurisdiction named the *Provincias Internas de Occidente*, or "Western Internal Provinces."[38]

After a review of the current status in these frontier areas, Croix concluded that his predecessor was incompetent and had not effectively countered the raids of the Comanches and Apaches on the missions and presidios of Texas. He left in August 1777 from Mexico to gain a firsthand look at the situation in Coahuila and Texas. On Christmas Eve 1777, he crossed the Rio Grande and stayed in Texas for nearly a month before leaving on January 22, 1778. During this tour, he found a dispirited population with few aspects of a cultured life. He found no professional men, neither doctor nor lawyer, or public education. Croix said the colonists "live miserable lives because of their laziness, captiousness, and lack

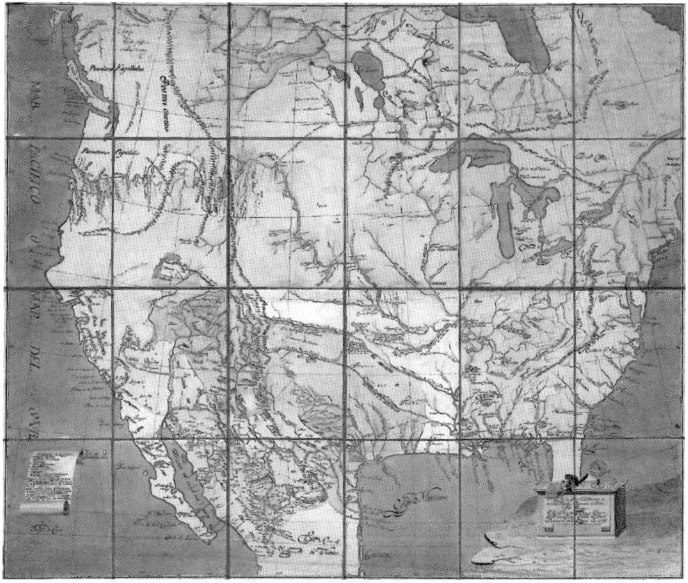

La Mapa de las Provincias Internas del Vierrianato de Nueva España (*Map of the Internal Provinces of the Viceroyalty of New Spain*), 1817. Map by José Caballero, provincial artillery captain of New Spain. From the Royal Academy of History. *Photograph by Hispalois.*

means of support, all of which defects show themselves at first sight."[39]

After the tour of the area, Croix consulted with military officers in Monclova, San Antonio and Chihuahua. The war councils recommended attacking the Apaches. The governor of Louisiana, Gálvez, proposed joining forces in a large-scale campaign totaling two thousand soldiers. The Spanish king was reluctant to send such a large force, and the plan never took hold. Croix remained determined to raise a large enough force to stem the Apache and Comanche raids.

He did succeed in gathering 4,686 armed militia members in a large territory stretching nearly eight hundred miles from the area around San Antonio to the current state of Sonora, Mexico. Staggering logistical dilemmas and long distances between presidios made it very difficult to use these forces in any decisive manner.

In 1784, Croix was promoted to lieutenant general and named viceroy of Peru, where he stayed until 1790. Upon his departure from New Spain's Internal Provinces, "the bulk of his policy was abandoned," and the sparsely settled Texas frontier remained vulnerable with few defenses.

Croix ended his career much as he began it. In 1791, he was named a colonel in the royal bodyguard and a commander in the Teutonic Order. He died in Madrid in 1792.[40]

D

DELAWARE INDIANS

For generations, the Delaware Indians moved farther and farther west in front of the advancing Europeans, who claimed their lands and supplanted their way of life with European settlements.

The Delawares—also known as the Lenapes, meaning "original people"—lived for centuries in the northeastern region of the United States. In the 1750s, they lived in present-day New York and in the Delaware River Valley of Pennsylvania and New Jersey. Some of them migrated west of the Allegheny Mountains to settle in the Ohio River Valley. They were often called Mingos when they lived in Ohio. In 1754, their land was fraudulently sold to some Connecticut land speculators who sought lands in Pennsylvania's Susquehanna

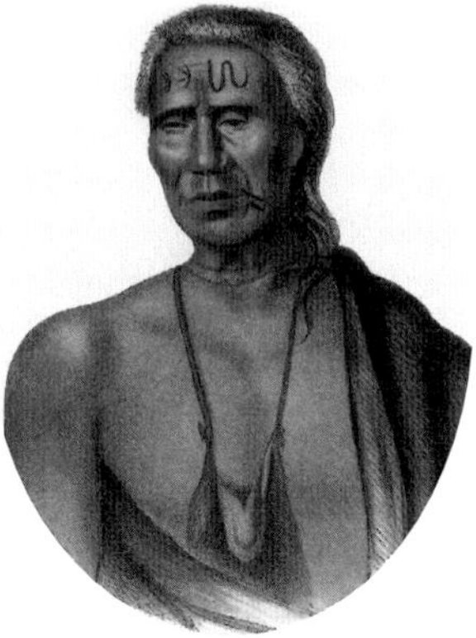

Lapowinsa, Chief of the Lenape. A 1737 painting by Gustavus Hesselius. *Courtesy Library of Congress, Rare Book and Special Collections Division*.

River Valley.[41] The Delawares were protected by the six nations who united in the Iroquois Confederacy. The Iroquois considered the Delawares tenants and referred to them as "nephews."[42]

The Delawares were compelled to move farther westward by the passage of the Indian Removal Act in 1830. Andrew Jackson was the first president whose adult life took place and held roots west of the Appalachian Mountains. He was determined to move Indians out of the way of the advancing settlement of Americans. By the early 1800s, the Delawares had been moved westward and lived on the northern Texas border. George Catlin, a noteworthy artist and chronicler who traveled among the Native Americans from 1832 through 1839 said, "No other tribe on the Continent has been so much moved and jostled about by civilized invasions."[43] After the 1830 law, more Native Americans drifted into Texas looking for a haven. They were not welcomed by the Native Americans already living there or the Anglo Americans who planned to move there.

In a move to rid Texas of bothersome Native Americans

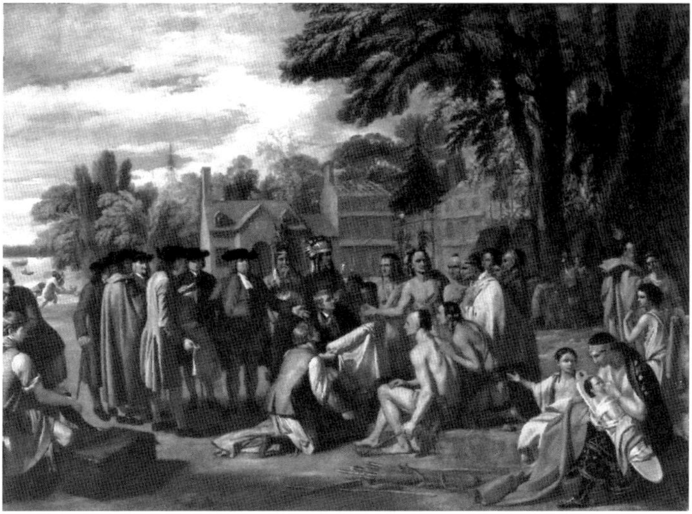

Treaty of Penn with the Indians. A painting by Benjamin West. *Photograph by the Pennsylvania Academy of Fine Arts, Philadelphia.*

living on lands coveted by the newly independent Texans, Generals Kelsey Douglas and Edward Burleson led a force of the Texas militia that pushed the Delawares across the Red River into Arkansas on July 25, 1839.[44] Some managed to stay in small groups and were often appreciated by some Texans. Delawares were often considered honest and reliable. Delawares had an enviable reputation as being intelligent and resourceful. Americans who encountered them in Texas often sought their assistance as hunters, guides and interpreters when dealing with other tribes.[45]

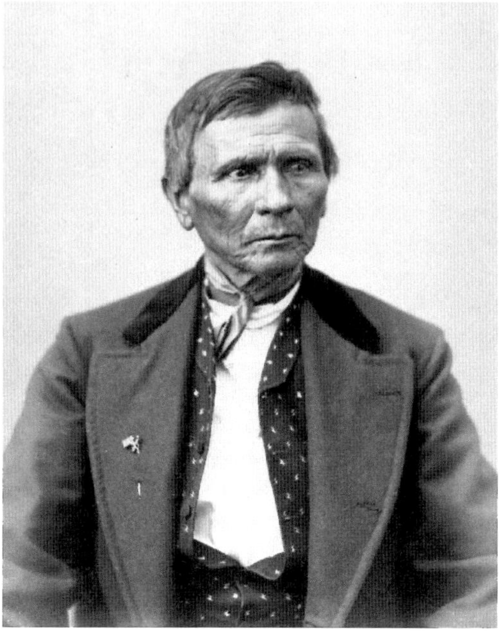

Black Beaver, a Delaware (Lenape) chief, scout and interpreter. *Photograph by Alexander Gardner for the U.S. Department of Interior, Bureau of Indian Affairs, 1872. Courtesy National Archives and Records Administration.*

Sam Houston, following his election as president of Texas for the second time, reversed his predecessor Mirabeau B. Lamar's policy toward Native Americans by concluding a treaty with the Delawares in 1843. Houston then engaged some of their leaders to encourage Comanches to enter negotiations and sign a treaty.[46] Two Delaware war chiefs, Jim Shaw and John Conner, participated in negotiations with Comanches and signed the treaty along with chiefs of the Penateka Comanches, establishing a lasting peace between them and German immigrants in central Texas. The treaty is titled "Between the Commissary General of the German Immigration Company and the Comanche Nation" and was signed on May 9, 1847 (see page 153).[47]

In 1848, John Conner was instrumental in guiding the exploration of far western Texas. This mapping and scouting action was termed the Chihuahua–El Paso Expedition. In 1853, the Texas legislature thanked Conner for his service with a grant of one league of land.[48] Another Delaware, Suck-tum-mah-kway, known by Anglo Americans as Black Beaver, was the central figure in various expeditions and mapping explorations led by Randolph B. Marcy. Black Beaver set forth the definitive routes for both the California and Chisholm Trails, as well as many routes throughout Texas: "In his 1859 guide book, *The Prairie Traveler*, Marcy wrote that Black Beaver 'had visited nearly every point of interest within the limits of our unsettled territory.'"[49]

Many Delaware tribe members now live in Oklahoma. The Delaware Nation is headquartered in Anadarko, Oklahoma. There are also Delaware communities in Kansas, Wisconsin and Ontario, Canada.

E

HADEN AND BENJAMIN EDWARDS

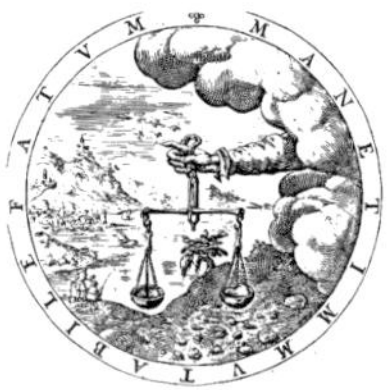

The Spanish, and later the Mexican government, felt a need to increase the population of its borderlands, including Texas. Not only would the population growth increase production, wealth and trade, but it would also dissuade other powers from taking the territory. To this end, missions and forts, *presidios*, were established beginning in the late seventeenth century.[50] In the early nineteenth century, land grants were offered to North Americans who would bring settlers to Texas and anchor Mexico's claim to this land and all its potential wealth. The grantees were called *empresarios*. The most well known of these entrepreneurs are the father-and-son team of Moses and Stephen Austin.

Like Sam Houston, Haden Harrison Edwards was born in Virginia. His father, John Edwards, was one of the first U.S. senators elected to represent the new state of Kentucky.[51] Just as his father had moved west, so did Haden. Like others of his generation, he looked to Texas as a land of opportunity. He traveled to Mexico City with Stephen Austin and spent three years there encouraging Mexico's authorities to grant lands to him and the Austins. While the Austin colony took hold, Haden Edwards was not so fortunate. He had a grant from the State of Coahuila y Tejas for acreage in east Texas to settle eight hundred families.

When Haden Edwards arrived in October 1825 at Nacogdoches, he learned that other men, both Anglo Americans and Native Americans, had claims to the same lands. Many of them were already living on lands Edwards thought were his. He asserted that these lands were rightfully his. He even asked others to show him their grants with the idea that he would decide whether the grants were valid. To seal his bid for supremacy, Edwards called for an election of an *alcalde*, a local judicial officer, similar to a mayor, with some duties similar to a justice of the peace. The Mexican authorities in San Antonio disapproved and appointed a man to represent the State of Coahuila y Tejas in the disputed area.

Haden Edwards left Texas to do some business in Kentucky and asked his brother Benjamin to act in his behalf while he was gone. Benjamin negotiated a treaty with the Cherokees in the area and hoped to find a solution to the problems of the confused granting of titles to more than one person. Stephen Austin advised Benjamin Edwards to seek clarification from Vice Governor Victor Blanco. Blanco's reply was not favorable, and he annulled the grant to the Edwards brothers.

The Fredonia Rebellion flag of 1826. *Photograph by Glasshouse.*

In a swirl of exasperation, Benjamin Edwards declared the "Republic of Fredonia" on December 21, 1826. He sought to divide the lands between "the Red and White," to have equal treatment to the acquisition of land justified by the individual's "improvements."[52] The Fredonians fashioned a flag boldly proclaiming "Independence, Freedom, and Justice." Stephen Austin was so strongly opposed that he sent one hundred men to join the Mexicans sent to quell the rebellion. Austin persuaded the Mexican leader, Colonel Ahumada, to grant amnesty to all who surrendered. Many did. Benjamin Edwards did not. He and several followers fled to the United States in January 1827.[53] Haden returned later to Nacogdoches, where he lived the rest of his life.[54]

American newspapers rallied behind the Edwards brothers

and printed some sensational accounts. Mexico's President Guadalupe Victoria understood from two sources that this episode did not represent a larger plot to undermine Mexico's sovereignty. First, Stephen Austin sent men to take up arms against the Fredonians, strongly demonstrating his loyalty to Mexico's law and administration of its grant systems. Second, U.S. president John Quincy Adams did not support the Fredonians' action. Indeed, Henry Clay—like the Edwards brothers, originally a Virginian—who moved to Kentucky in his twenties, was now the U.S. secretary of state. Clay told Mexico's ambassador to the United States that the United States did not condone or support the Fredonia adventurers.

Haden Edwards is remembered in some Texas place names. Edwards County in south-central Texas is named in his honor.[55] His name is also linked to the Edwards Plateau and Edwards Aquifer, which span across several counties in central Texas.[56]

JOSÉ DE ESCANDÓN Y HELGUERA

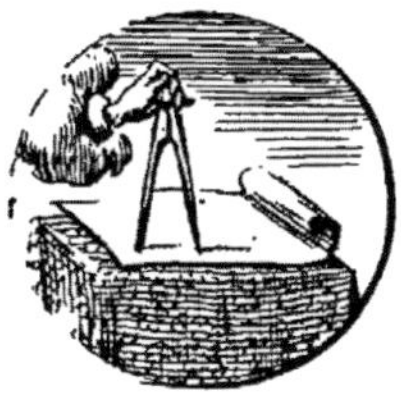

José de Escandón y Helguera lived for the first seventy years of the eighteenth century. He was born in Marina, Santander, Spain, and died in Mexico City, where he was buried in 1770. He was strong, visionary, decisive and usually successful as he planned and planted the beginnings of Spanish settlement in what is now northern Mexico and southern Texas. For more than two hundred years, Spain had claimed the land stretching northward from Mexico City to Texas and for hundreds of miles west to the Pacific Ocean. Despite the claims, there were few permanent settlements. Missions were considered temporary, a means to convert Native Americans, and *presidios*, forts, were built there to guard frontiers. The region lacked civilian life and the towns and cities that came with it.

Escandón left Spain at age fifteen and became a cadet of a cavalry company in the Yucatán. He assisted in quelling an Indian uprising and was promoted and transferred to Querétaro in New Spain. Querétaro was 165 miles north of Mexico City and 650 miles south of the Rio Grande. He was sent to survey and report on conditions in the area between Tampico and the San Antonio River. In January 1747, he sent seven divisions there and used what he learned to develop a large-scale colonization plan in October 1747.[57] Spain's King Fernando VI approved the plan and the viceroy of New Spain put the plan into motion. Escandón was named governor of Nuevo Santander, the name given to the region to be settled. By November 1748, Escandón had 755 soldiers and 2,513 Spanish Mexican colonists in Querétaro. He led these 3,268 people to Tampico on the Gulf coast and picked up more people eager to start a new life on the frontier. Large land grants enticed many to travel north. During the next seven years, twenty towns were founded. Most were south of the Rio Grande. Some settlers ventured as far north as the Nueces River near present-day Corpus Christi, Texas. One of the largest towns north of the river was Laredo, founded in 1755. Little attention was paid to the lands along the coast, as it was feared to be a land of fever and disease.[58] Escandón's success earned him the nickname "Father of the Lower Rio Grande Valley."[59] He is remembered well in Alice, Texas, where a larger-than-life sculpture stands prominently near the city hall.

In 1748, King Fernando VI rewarded Escandón by naming him the first Count of Sierra Gorda and knight of the *Orden de Santiago*, or "Order of Santiago." The order was founded in the twelfth century and named for Saint James the Greater, the patron saint of first Galicia and then all of Spain. Originally, the order sought to protect pilgrims on their way to Santiago de Compostela, where remains of Saint James are believed to be.[60]

In addition to these honors, Escandón and many of the gentlemen who accompanied

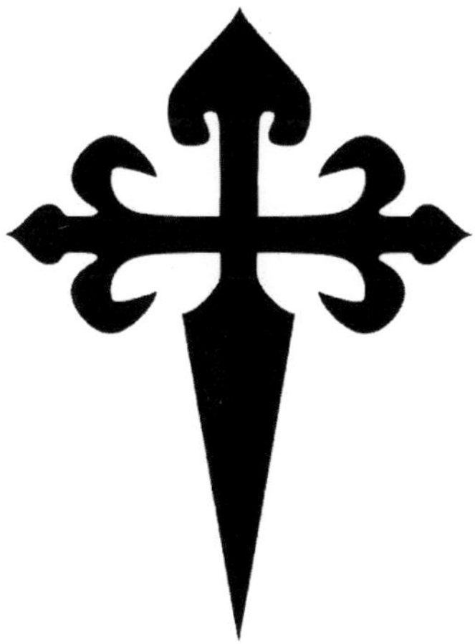

The Cross of Saint James, the military emblem of the Order of Santiago. *Photograph by WarX.*

him were granted thousands, some even millions, of acres of land. This was rather dry land, often unsuitable for large-scale crop production without extensive irrigation. The climate was mild, and the plentiful grasses allowed cattle ready access to grazing lands. Consequently most of the agriculture focused on raising cattle.

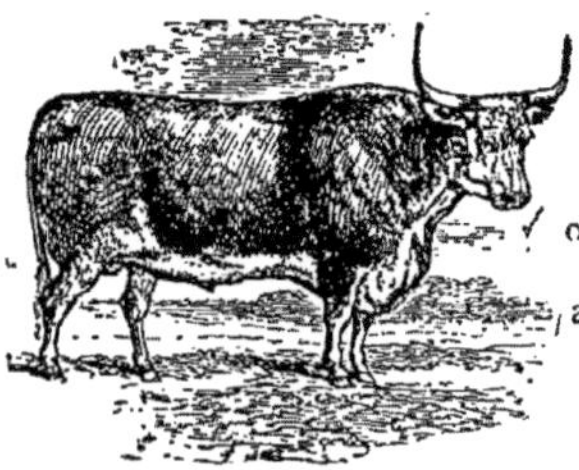

Huge ranches dominated the land. Thousands of Longhorn cattle grew on their own into millions of heads of cattle. With this economy, the colonists did not concentrate in cities. The ranch hacienda was the center of life. Power and wealth was held by the few at the top of a social and economic hierarchy. A middle class of merchants teachers, artisans and professionals, such as doctors or lawyers, did not thrive in this dispersed society of ranches.

José de Escandón y Helguera did well until he was accused of severe malfeasance and mistreatment of Native Americans. Indeed, he was known by some as the "Exterminator of the Pames of Querétaro." He was tried for illegally using Native American labor, even slavery, and of bringing in contraband from the English into Nuevo Santander.[61] In a dramatic scene, Escandón died during his trial on September 10, 1770. Three years later, his son won a petition to the court to exonerate his father.[62]

The Apaches and Comanches never relented for long and soon resumed raiding the new settlements. In 1771, a year after Escandón's death, the townspeople of Laredo fled south across the Rio Grande to reestablish their town as Nuevo Laredo. The Spanish continued to convene and counsel with the Native Americans. Plans continued to be made. Despite this effort, little change lasted for long. The tough people who began the ranching culture in Nuevo Santander clung tenaciously to the foothold and remained in place, primarily south of the Rio Grande. Only a few hundred Spanish-speaking people lived along the north side of the Rio Grande in 1800.[63]

Escandón's effort had three lasting outcomes. First, the beginnings of the charro culture (see page 44) took hold in northern Mexico and Texas. Second, the Spanish system of legal titles to land and water rights set the stage for future laws. Third, the determined and tenacious Mexican frontier attitude and behavior took root on both sides of the Rio Grande.[64]

FRANÇOIS MARIE CHARLES FOURIER

The Europeans who followed Columbus to the New World had many motives. Some came to find riches, others to expand the kingdom of God by converting Native Americans to Christianity. Some came to find a place where they could live a more perfect life, a separate place away from the strife they had experienced in Europe. While sailing across the Atlantic Ocean, John Winthrop, governor of the Massachusetts Bay Colony, said that he and his fellow Puritans strove to build a "city upon a hill."[65]

Many of the early European immigrants to North America were imbued deeply with an understanding and appreciation of Judeo-Christian thought. When Governor Winthrop

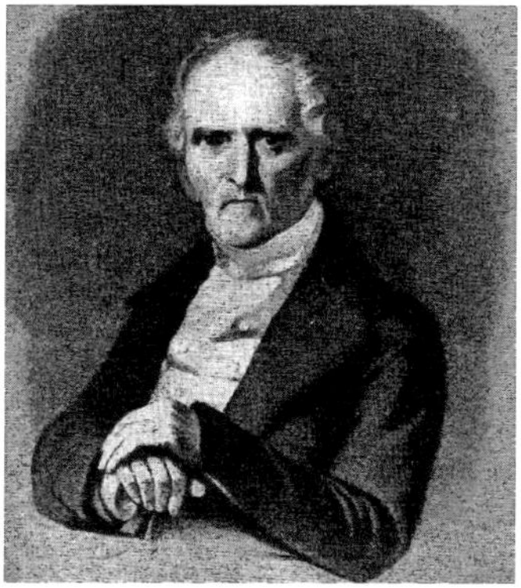

François Marie Charles Fourier. Drawing by Élisée Reclus in *L'Homme et la Terre,* 1905. *Photograph by Vieux Tétard.*

envisioned a "city on a hill," he was citing commonly known scripture. He envisioned the new commonwealth to "my holy hill of Zion," as the psalmist wrote in Psalm 2, verse 6. As Matthew wrote in Chapter 5, verse 14, "A city that is set on a hill cannot be hid." Indeed, the city on a hill is a beacon shining the light of God's presence on Earth.[66]

The desire to start afresh and build a better life was shared by a group of Frenchmen who sought to build a utopia in Texas. This group followed the beliefs of François Marie Charles Fourier. He was a humble man, the son of a draper from the provincial town of Besançon, France, the same birthplace as Victor Hugo. Fourier believed that man is inherently good and needs appropriate direction to use his energy as work for the common good. He thought humans were brought down by the corruption of worldly institutions.[67]

To this end, Fourier spent years trying to raise enough money to start a separate colony of people to live out his dream of a just society based on a collective ownership that distributed its goods fairly to all citizens.[68] Although Fourier died in 1837, his ideas lived and inspired the founding of twenty-nine communities in the United States. One of the most famous of these was Brook Farm on the edge of Boston, Massachusetts. Nathaniel Hawthorne was a member of this community.[69]

In 1854, a follower of Fourier, Victor Prosper Considerant, published *Au Texas* (*To Texas*). This book was popular enough to have a second edition. In this tract, Considerant recruited people to move to Texas to found a colony following Fourier's ideals. The community planned to share ownership and work its farms cooperatively for the benefit of all members of the commune. With land purchased and a deep commitment to this new society, hundreds of Fourier's followers from France, Belgium and Switzerland founded La Réunion colony near present-day Dallas in 1855.

These colonists were utopian socialists seeking to forge a new society based on an economy of willing cooperation. They believed this could only be achieved by living in isolation from the corrupt life led by most other people. The French, Belgian and Swiss colonists landed on the Texas coast and walked 250 miles to their chosen location. Some pushed handcarts on this long walk. They arrived on June 16, 1855, on the south side of the Trinity River in the center of present-day Dallas.

The number of settlers peaked at 350 in 1856.[70] The farming enterprise had many setbacks. Lack of farming experience was a significant problem. Most of the colonists were not farmers and had no inkling of what an agricultural life entailed. Even if they were more prepared and experienced, the community would have still had a rough experience. Where they settled, the land was not so fertile nor the climate as favorable as anticipated. Rains don't fall regularly, and north Texas summers can scorch while its winters can freeze. One of the worst events possible occurred in May 1856, when a blizzard covered north Texas in snow.[71] Financing was not enough to sustain current operations and the continued purchase of adjacent lands for future expansion. The colony lasted only about eighteen months. It disbanded in January 1857. Many of the utopians returned to Europe. About half of them stayed in Texas, leaving many descendants in Dallas and San Antonio.[72]

The colony has two historical markers. The Daughters of the American Revolution placed one in 1924 marking the location of La Réunion at the sixth tee of the Stevens Park Golf Course in western Dallas. A second one is on Fish Trap Road along the side of the Trinity River in western Dallas. This second marker is at the La Réunion Cemetery where some colonists are buried.[73]

The last surviving colonist, Emanuel Santerre, was buried in La Réunion Cemetery in 1939.[74]

FRANCISCANS

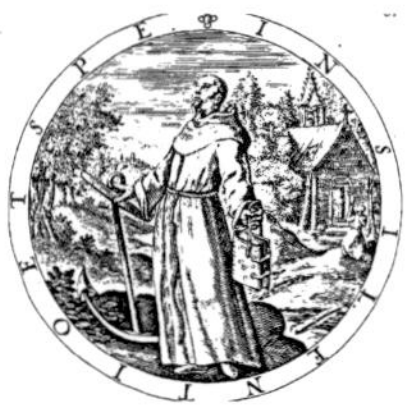

Nearly three hundred years before Christopher Columbus sailed to the Americas, Francis of Assisi founded an order of priests and brothers in 1209 called the Order of Friars Minor.

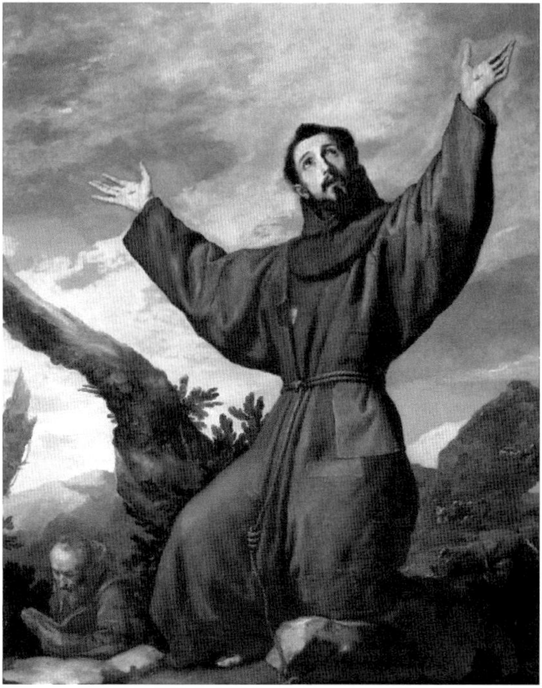

Francis of Assisi. A 1642 oil painting by Jusepe de Ribera. *Photograph by Aavindraa.*

Popularly they were known as Franciscans. St. Francis expected the members of this order to work alongside and for the benefit of the poor to bring them a fuller life spiritually. In 1517, Pope Leo X divided the order into two groups, the Observant Friars and the Conventual Friars Minor. A third order, the Capuchin Friars, began in 1526 and eventually became a separate order in 1619.

Most of the Franciscans in New Spain were Observants. Between 1534 and 1606, the Franciscans took hold in New Spain with six friaries organized into provinces and a *convento*, or *colegio apostólico*, a college similar to a present-day seminary. The Franciscans who journeyed north to plant missions and convert Native Americans represented the variety of provinces and colleges.

Franciscans with ties to the Province of Santo Evangélico, Mexico City, founded a mission to the Jumano Indians in 1632 near present-day San Angelo. This same province sponsored the missions in the El Paso area in 1659 and 1680, as well as the one near present-day Presidio in 1683. Later on, in 1715, more missions in the Presidio area were founded by Franciscans of the Province of Zacatecas, which had charge of the vast area of the present-day state of Chihuahua in Mexico.

Most of the missions in Texas were the work of Franciscans from the College of Santa Cruz de Querétaro, established in 1683. Of the original nineteen priests who founded the College of Santa Cruz de Querétaro, nine served in Texas. The clergy at this college established two more that both sent missionaries to Texas: College of San Fernando de México and the College of Nuestra Señora de Guadalupe de Zacatecas. The College of Santa Cruz de Querétaro founded the following missions:[75]

- Santísimo Nombre de María in 1690
- San Francisco de los Tejas, which became Nuestra Padre San Francisco de los Tejas, in 1716

- San José de los Nazonis in 1716, which became San Juan Capistrano in 1731
- Nuestra Señora de la Purísima Concepción de los Hainais in 1716, which became Nuestra Señora de la Purísima Concepción de Acuña in 1731
- San Antonio de Valero in 1718
- San Francisco de los Neches in 1721
- San Francisco Xavier de Náxara in 1722, which merged with San Antonio de Valero in 1726
- San Francisco de la Espada in 1731
- San Ildefonso in 1748
- San Xavier de Horcasitas in 1748, which became Nuestra Señora de Guadalupe in 1756
- Nuestra Señora de la Candelaria in 1749
- Santa Cruz de San Sabá in 1757
- San Lorenzo de la Santa Cruz in 1762
- Nuestra Señora de la Candelaria del Cañón in 1762

Franciscans established a total of thirty-seven missions in Texas, one in Louisiana and six *visitas,* temporary sites, along the lower Rio Grande.

This extensive undertaking took a toll on the Franciscans. Of the many friars, thirty-two died in Texas after having devoted their life at the missions serving the Native Americans.

In addition to some of the difficulties the Franciscans faced, some of these missions fared poorly over time. One of the more well-known missions, San Antonio de Valero, better known as the Alamo, began as

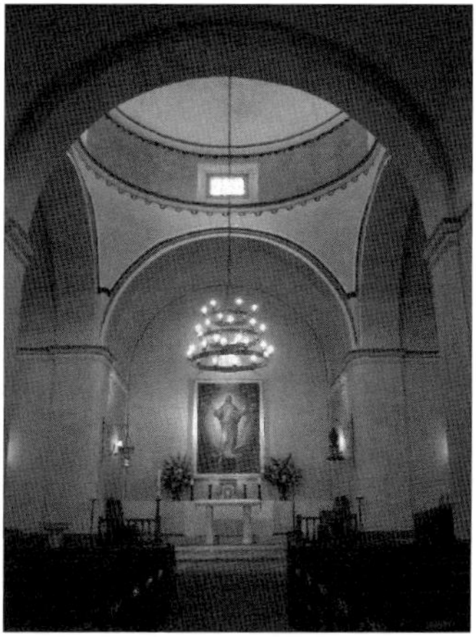

Interior of Nuestra Señora de Purísima Concepción de Acuña Mission (Concepción Mission), founded by the Franciscans. *Photograph by Liveon001 © Travis Witt.*

a small venture, built in 1718 as most other missions were to convert, colonize and defend the northern reaches of New Spain. Construction at the current building site began in 1724. The monks stayed there until 1793, when the government disbanded the mission and distributed the land and buildings to secular purposes. During this long period, there were never a large number of Native Americans. The highest number was 328 in 1756, and that declined to 44 by 1777.[76]

When reflecting on his experiences across the northern region of New Spain, Padre Francisco Garcés, a Franciscan friar, wrote in his diary in 1775–76, "I see that for a century the faith has been planted in these provinces, and that nothing has prospered."[77] Garcés died in a 1779 civil revolt by Quechan Indians at the mission San Pedro y San Pablo near present-day Yuma, Arizona. The Quechans were angry with Spanish settlers who took away their lands in violation of a treaty.[78]

Life for the Native Americans at the Texas missions was difficult. Most of the converts were Coahuiltecans, a collective term for the varied groups of

Native Americans living in the southern reaches of present-day Texas and the northern state of Coahuila, Mexico. The Native Americans were often willing to live there, but some would want to leave. They were in a difficult situation, expected to labor daily, eat unfamiliar foods, accept and worship a new god with a new religion and be subjected to punishment. In short, their entire lives were changing very quickly with little time to adjust. One of the outcomes was a rise in mortality. Native Americans died at alarming rates. Some grew indolent, dispirited and withdrawn. Even if they tried to run away, soldiers would find and return them. There was no way out of this life: "Mission life was miserable…[For some] death was the only way out."[79]

The Franciscans worked in many parts of the world and this internationalism is seen in the variety of Franciscans who came to Texas. In addition to the Spanish-speaking Franciscans of New Spain, there were three French-speaking friars and six priests who came with La Salle. All but one died at Fort St. Louis at the hands of the Karankawas in late 1688 (see page 34). In the mid-1800s, five German-speaking Franciscans worked to assist their fellow countrymen in New Braunfels, Fredericksburg and San Antonio. In this same era, a Polish-speaking friar helped found the first Polish settlement in the United States at Panna Maria, Texas, in 1854. In the 1930s, friars came from the Chicago area and worked to establish parishes among Mexican Americans in San Antonio.[80]

G

PADRE GARZA

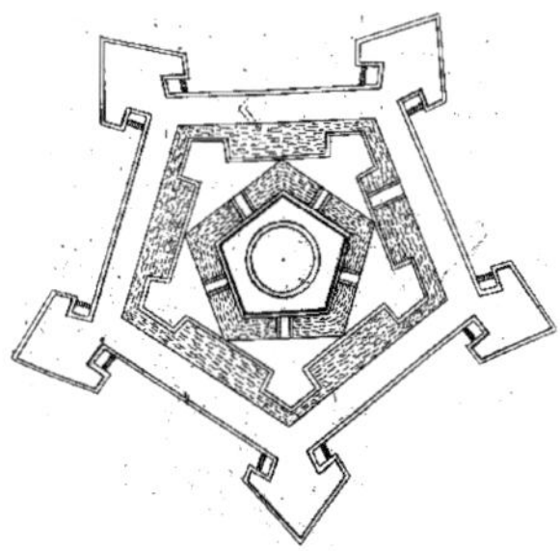

Spanish efforts to populate and secure its hold on Texas alternated between action and retreat. A harsh climate, poor soils, long distances from supplies and other Spaniards in New Spain and the frequently hostile Native Americans all worked against a steady rate of settlement. This pattern lasted for more than three hundred years, from the 1540 expedition of Francisco Vásquez de Coronado until the annexation of Texas into the United States in 1846.

One approach the Spanish took in the eighteenth century was to establish missions and forts, *presidios*, as "barriers against the further advance of the French."[81] By the middle of the 1700s, the French had slowed their advance. They had no fixed base in Texas. Their only colony, Fort St. Louis, was gone by late 1688. In 1766, the Spanish king commissioned the Marqués de Rubí to inspect the frontier and report on his observations.

In 1772, the king incorporated Rubí's recommendations in the "New Regulations for the Presidios." Generally the king called for a retreat and concentration of power in the San Antonio area. Some of the people who had already taken root in East Texas asked Barón de Ripperdá, the governor of Texas residing in San Antonio, for permission to return home. He allowed them to move eastward but cautioned them not to get closer than one hundred leagues of Natchitoches, a French settlement in Louisiana. Barón de Ripperdá agreed to Antonio Gil Ibarvo's request (see page 95) to a site on the Trinity River. Ibarvo named the new town Bucareli in honor of Viceroy Antonio María Bucareli y Ursúa.

From 1774 until 1778, Bucareli prospered on the bank of the Trinity River, about four miles east of the current town of Midway on Texas State Highway 21 in Madison County. The town grew to have 345 people with a church, plaza and wooden houses.

After a few years of prosperity, some Comanches took notice and rode away with some horses. Ibarvo gathered a posse, who trailed and killed the Indians.

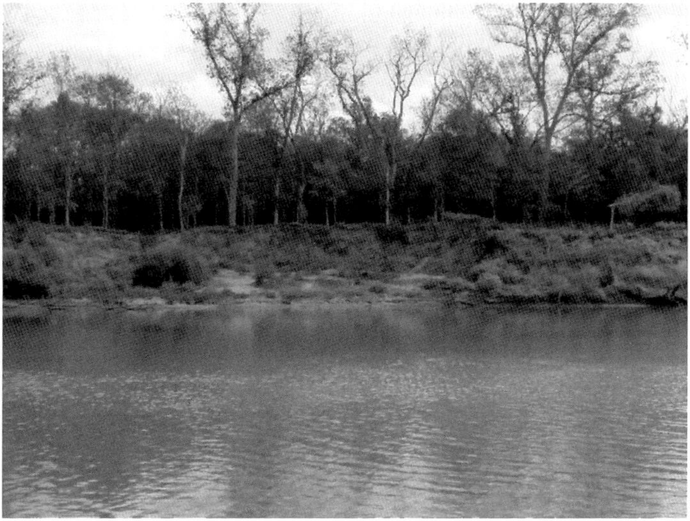

A ford across the Trinity River known as El Paso Tomás (Thomas Ford) at the site of Bucareli. *Photograph by the author.*

Governmental authorities in San Antonio approved yet could offer no additional troops to protect this eastern outpost. A few months later, the Comanches returned and stole 276 horses but did not kill any of the Spaniards. The settlers were unsure how to assess this latest development. Should they stay and risk future raids, even death?

Padre Garza, the priest in Bucareli, helped sort through the options. He wrote a report to San Antonio. He said no one felt able to leave the village's center. People were too afraid to even plant crops or tend the fields in any way.

No one wanted to go hunting alone or even in small groups. They feared any action that would risk being exposed to Comanches. The townspeople lived in fear and dread both night and day. Padre Garza concluded that it was too dangerous to stay in Bucareli. He feared the settlers would be killed in future raids by the Comanches.[82]

Antonio Ibarvo, the Spanish governor's designated leader for this outpost, listened to Padre Garza and weighed the options. He did not want to chance another encounter with a Comanche warring party. Ibarvo decided to move his settlement farther east to the location of the old presidio in Nacogdoches. The five hundred settlers arrived there in April 1779. They prospered and were no longer in the path of any Comanche raiders.[83]

Once the settlers left Bucareli and moved eastward, the authorities in San Antonio accepted the new reality and took no means to punish or bring the settlers back to San Antonio.

The group that heeded Padre Garza's warning and followed Ibarvo's leadership stayed in the Nacogdoches area for nearly two centuries. Some of their descendants still lived there as late as the 1990s.[84]

JARED ELLISON GROCE

Jared Ellison Groce was born in Halifax County, Virginia, on October 12, 1782.[85] He joined several others who were born in Virginia when he immigrated to Texas. His fellow Virginians included Stephen F. Austin, Haden Edwards (see page 59) and

Sam Houston. Jared Groce also shared with these men the desire for new lands at ever cheaper prices. Groce's moves to South Carolina, Georgia, Alabama and Texas mirrored the growth and expansion of cotton plantation enterprises built with slave labor. When Groce came to Texas in 1822 to join Stephen F. Austin's colony of "Old Three Hundred" settlers, he received title to ten *sitios*, each one the equivalent of 4,428 acres, a total of 44,280 acres. He brought with him fifty wagons of supplies and ninety slaves.[86] Some of the slaves were born in Africa and others in the United States.[87]

Groce introduced large-scale cotton production at Bernardo Plantation, with a large house on a hill overlooking the Brazos River, four miles south of the current city of Hempstead. He built a cotton gin there in 1825 and purchased other lands to further grow his holdings.

This first planter in Texas built a large home. It was one and a half stories with four large rooms downstairs and two rooms upstairs. The site also had a kitchen building, a doctor's office, a dairy and quarters for house slaves. He also built a "Bachelor Hall" to accommodate the large number of travelers he hosted. Field slaves' and their overseer's houses, a kitchen a dining hall and a day nursery for the children of field slaves were situated near a lake on the same property, apart from Groce's house. In response to a malaria epidemic in 1833, he divided his lands among his children and moved north

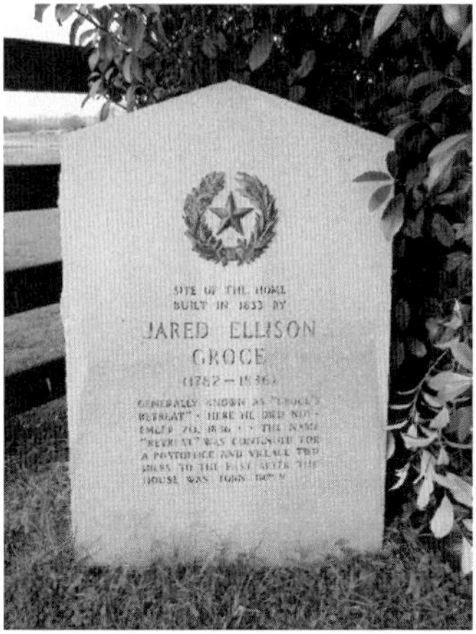

Texas state historical marker of James E. Groce's second home site from 1833, often called Groce's Retreat. On Grimes County Road 323. *Photograph by the author.*

to a new location known as Groce's Retreat.[88]

In addition to his agricultural enterprise, Jared E. Groce participated directly in Texas public life. He, like Stephen F. Austin, opposed the Fredonian Rebellion led by Benjamin Edwards (see page 60). He felt the Americans needed to abide by their commitments to the Mexican government so that they could continue to prosper as handsomely as he was. He supported Colonel Mateo Ahumada's 1827 military campaign to quell the rebellion by providing ferry service across the Brazos River as well as the use of his wagons, teams of horses and slaves. He did not support a resolution to seek Texas independence at the Convention of 1832. He chaired a committee to draft petitions for tariff reductions. He also participated in the Convention of 1833.

Groce's viewpoint changed over the next few years so that he advocated revolution in 1836. Although he was unable to fight due to physical limitations, he outfitted five others to join the newly formed army. He hosted

George C. Childress when he drafted the Texas Declaration of Independence at his new home, Groce's Retreat. Once completed, the document was taken to Washington-on-the-Brazos, where it was ratified and signed on March 2, 1836.

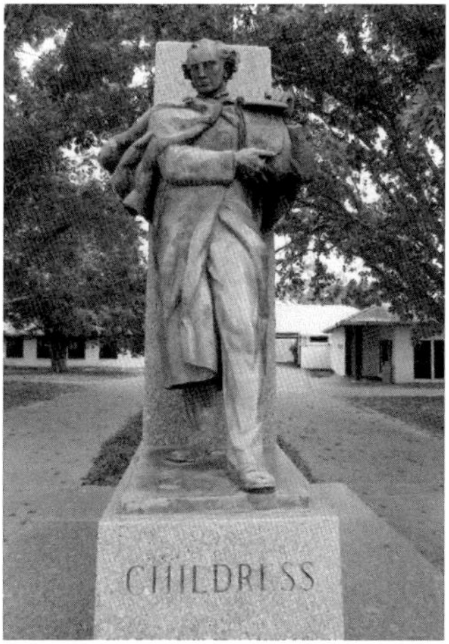

Statue of George C. Childress, author of the Texas Declaration of Independence at Washington-on-the-Brazos state historic site. *Photograph by the author.*

Groce's hospitality was so much that his home even served as the newly declared republic's capitol for a few days, from March 18 to 21, 1836, while the new government rested there on the way from Washington-on-the-Brazos to Harrisburg in present-day Houston. The "twin sisters" cannons brought to Texas from Ohio (see page 194) landed at Bernardo Plantation before they were sent into battle. Following the final battle of the Texas Revolution at San Jacinto, Sam Houston and his army rested there for two weeks with Groce offering food, shelter and medical care.[89]

Groce died on November 20, 1836, just eight months after Texas declared its independence.[90] His economic prosperity and political influence significantly contributed to the advancement of Texas both while a part of Mexico and

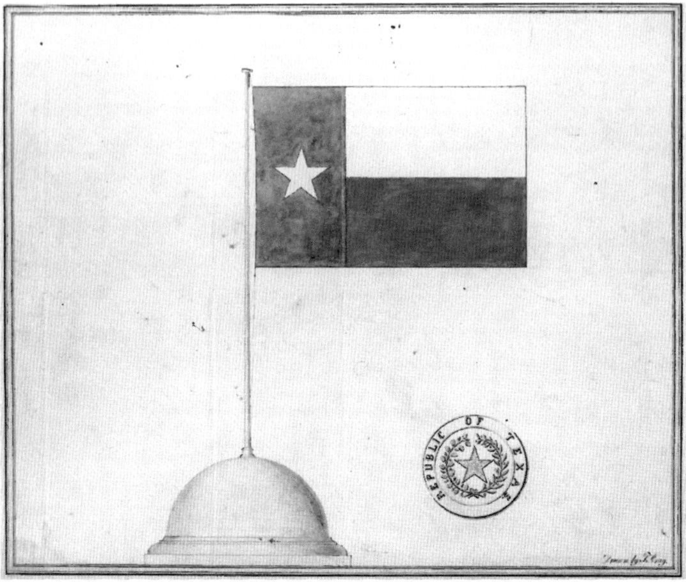

The Lone Star flag of Texas designed by Peter Krag in 1838. It was approved on January 25, 1839, as signed by Mirabeau Lamar, president of the Republic of Texas; John M. Hansford, Speaker of the House of Representatives; and David Burnett, president of the Texas Senate. *Courtesy Texas State Library and Archives Commission, Historic Flags Collection, #1974/066-001.*

when the republic was birthed and took hold. He also modeled large-scale cotton production using slave labor that took root in much of early nineteenth-century Texas.

H

HAPE INDIANS

The Hape Indians were also known as the Ape, Jeape and Xape Indians. They lived on the north and south side of the Rio Grande. They were usually termed to be Coahuiltecan Indians, a collective term the Spanish used to define the various *naciones*, tribes, who lived in the vast area of the state of Coahuila. In Texas, they lived primarily in the area near present-day Eagle Pass and its companion city across the river, Piedras Negras.[91]

As a people among the Coahuiltecans, historians believe they lived as hunter-gathers and found a variety of foods readily at hand, such as the *nopal*, or "prickly pear cactus," and its fruit, *tuna*, that flourish in the region. They also used flour made from the beans of mesquite trees and enjoyed nuts from pecan trees.[92] All of these plants were supplemented with local game and the bison available on their migratory journey to the north. The Coahuiltecans found a way to thrive in the dry, brushy plains of southern Texas and northern Mexico. Their economy and social structure "represent[s] the culmination of more than 11,000 years of a way of life that successfully adapted to the climate and resources of south Texas."[93]

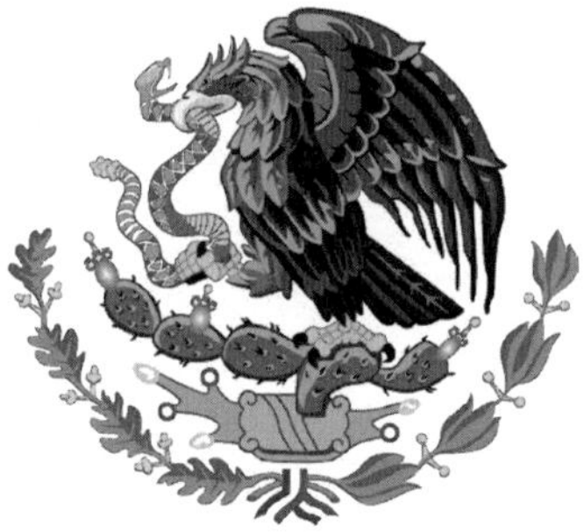

The coat of arms of Mexico with an eagle standing on a prickly pear cactus, a favorite food of the Hape and other Coahuiltecan Indians. *From http://en.wikipedia.org/wiki/File:Coat_of_arms_of_Mexico.svg (accessed November 15, 2013).*

In 1675, an expedition led by Bosque-Larios contacted fifty-four Hape and Yorica Indians near Eagle Pass. They carried large loads of dried buffalo meat and were en route to their settlements south of the Rio Grande. They related that their enemies, the Ocana, Pataguo and Yurbipame, moved nomadically to the east and north toward the Nueces River and the Frio River. There were about five hundred Hape Indians in 1688, but their numbers fell off drastically due to a smallpox epidemic. The survivors of the epidemic died by the next year at the hands of some enemies from the east.[94]

FRANCES COX HENDERSON

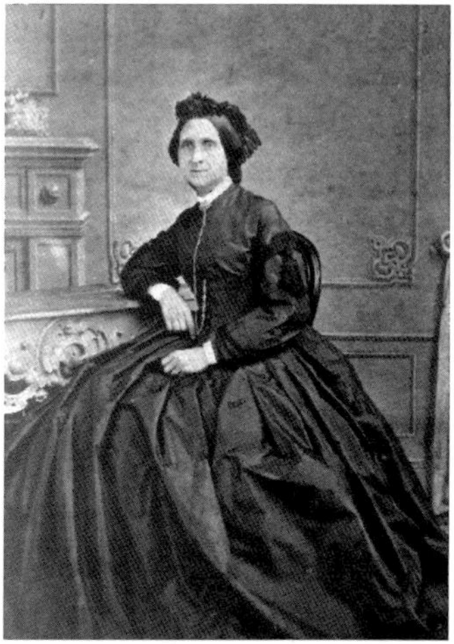

Frances Cox Henderson. *Courtesy Texas State Library and Archives Commission, Prints and Photographs Collection, #1/102-223.*

Frances Cox Henderson was an uncommonly talented and influential woman in early Texas. She was born into a prominent family in Philadelphia, studied in Paris and married in London. She married a diplomat for the Republic of Texas, translated short stories into English from many languages and was the first "first lady" of the state of Texas. The young Ms. Cox met J. Pinckney Henderson in Paris, France, when he was posted there as a diplomat representing the Republic of Texas. They were mutually drawn to each other and married at St. George's Chapel in London. Afterward, they moved to Texas, where they settled in San Augustine.

Frances Cox Henderson was a noted mathematician and linguist. She spoke twenty-five languages, eighteen of them fluently! She was one of the first people to advocate extending the right to vote to women, decades before women's suffrage took hold in American politics and seventy-five years before an amendment to the U.S.

Constitution established this as a right.

Henderson and her husband practiced a more thorough partnership in their marriage than did most married couples in the early 1800s. For example, her husband trusted her judgment and skill so much that she ran his law office when he was away on business.[95]

J. Pinckney Henderson was often in Washington, D.C., on diplomatic business for Texas. For example, on April 12, 1844, he and Isaac Van Zandt signed a treaty with John C. Calhoun, U.S. secretary of state for President John Tyler. This treaty called for the Republic of Texas to be annexed by the United States to change its name to the state of Texas and become the twenty-eighth state in the Union.[96] The U.S. Senate never ratified the treaty. Texas would wait nearly two more years to change its name.

One of the most remarkable examples of Frances Cox Henderson's leadership was her direct involvement in the expansion of the Episcopal Church in Texas. The Episcopal Committee on Domestic Missions acted slowly to send ministers to Texas. The lay governing body of her San Augustine parish, the vestry, "conferred their authority on her to call a minister." She journeyed to Philadelphia and met with the Episcopal hierarchy. They were likely surprised to have a woman produce her credentials. Only males held ordained office in the Episcopal Church until the 1970s. Her presentation proved successful, and she "got her minister, a shocking

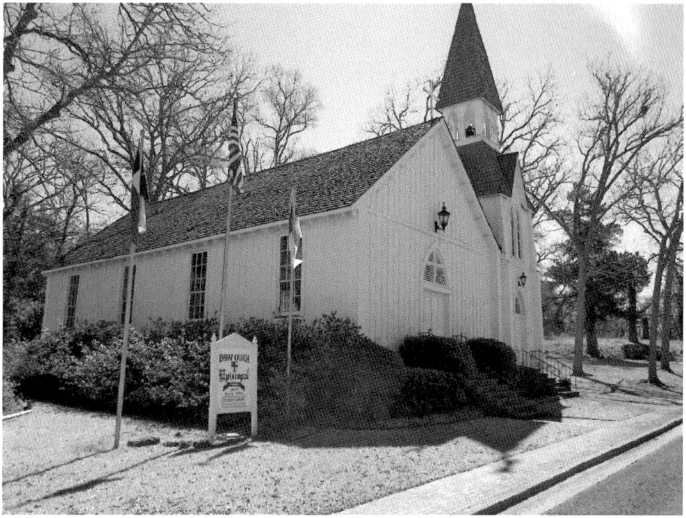

Christ Church Episcopal in San Augustine, Texas. *Photograph by the author.*

piece of behavior from the first lady of Texas."[97] The Reverend Henry Samson arrived in April 1848 "to do missionary work in San Augustine and Nacogdoches" at Christ Church Episcopal in San Augustine.[98]

Frances Cox Henderson is an example of the talent, strength and leadership that women demonstrated in early Texas. One of the most interesting tidbits about her life was her preference to remain in San Augustine rather than move to Austin after her husband was elected the first governor of the state of Texas. She did not want to spend her time as the official hostess in the governor's residence.

FRANCISCO HIDALGO

Francisco Hidalgo spent most of his sixty-seven years trying to secure missions in east Texas to serve the Native Americans there, primarily Caddo Indians. He was born in Spain in 1659 and was probably orphaned at a young age. He joined the Franciscans at age fifteen. After his ordination, he joined others in 1683 to go to New Spain. He was a twenty-four-year-old priest when he arrived to establish the first seminary in New Spain devoted to enlarging the number of clergy to serve as missionaries to the Native Americans. The Colegio of Santa Cruz de Querétaro (see page 71) grew to supply many priests and friars to Texas during the next several decades.

Hidalgo began his missionary work near Saltillo and Monclova. He was aware of Alonso de León's discovery of the ruined French Fort St. Louis in 1689, but he did not accompany this expedition. He joined the journey in 1691 led by Domingo Terán de los Ríos, and he stayed in east Texas with the new mission San Francisco de los Tejas (see page 185). He remained there until it was abandoned in 1693. Five years later, the Colegio sent Hidalgo to help found new missions. He assisted in establishing San Juan Bautista on St. John's Day, June 24, 1699, on the Río Sabinas, twenty-five miles north of present-day Lampazos, Nuevo León, Mexico. A few months later, it moved to its present location just south of the Rio Grande in the present-day city of Guerrero, Coahuila, Mexico. Many Franciscans used this mission as a place to resupply and gather strength before moving north into Texas to start new missions.

After waiting more than a decade to begin anew in eastern Texas, Hidalgo remained determined to serve the people he had left in 1693. He took the unusual step to write the French governor of Louisiana seeking help in starting missions again in eastern Texas. Antoine de la Mothe, Sieur de Cadillac, responded by sending Louis Juchereau de St. Denis to Texas. St. Denis traveled to Natchitoches, Louisiana, and then to San Juan Bautista in July 1714. The unusual letter from Hidalgo and St. Denis's presence in Texas spurred both the French and Spanish to recommit to the borderlands separating them from each other along the course of the Sabine and Red Rivers that lay in disputed boundary lands between Spanish New Spain and French Louisiana.[99] The area in contention is shown on Guillaume de l'Isle's 1718 map, just west of Natchitoches.

Spain claimed the eastern border was the Red River. The French claimed the Sabine River as their western boundary. Into this forty-five-mile disputed territory, both kingdoms built anew. The French built a fort in Natchitoches. The Spanish countered with two new missions; one was San Miguel de Linares de Los Adaes, just west of Natchitoches. A

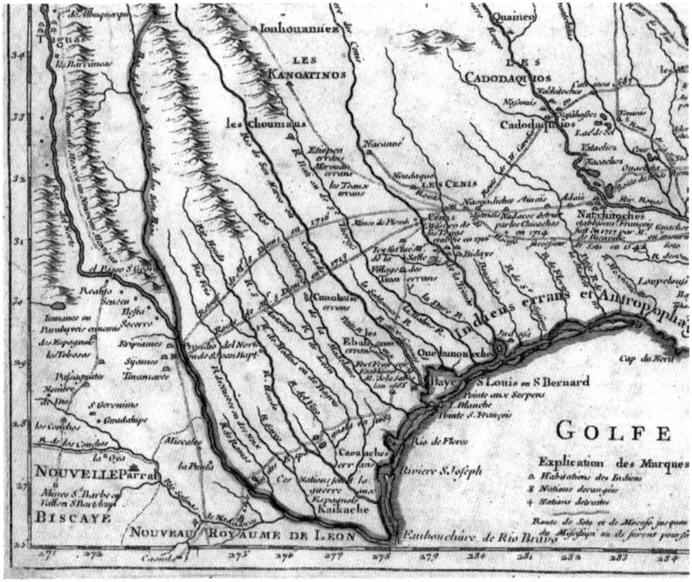

Detail of *Carte de la Louisiane et du Cours du Mississipi: Dressée Sur un Grand Nombre de Memoirs Entrautres Sur Ceux de Mr. le Marie*, a 1718 map by Guillaume De L'isle featuring the location of Los Adaes (Les Adaie in French), west of Natchitoches, the land of Antonio Gil Ibarvo's birth. *Courtesy Library of Congress, item 46 in LC Kohl exhibition, March to June 1993, public domain.*

few years later, in 1721, the Spanish built a fort, Nuestra Señora del Pilar de Los Adaes, near present-day Robeline, Louisiana. The territorial dispute was not settled until the Treaty of Fontainebleu in 1762, when France ceded the land west of the Mississippi River to Spain.[100]

Francisco Hidalgo finally saw a new mission near the

Caddo Indians, Nuestro Padre San Francisco de los Tejas. He was appointed to be the priest to lead this mission. He stayed there until the Spanish misperceived that warfare had erupted with the French in 1719. A French officer, Lieutenant Philippe Blondel had come from Natchitoches to attack the closest Spanish target, San Miguel de Linares de los Adaes Mission. He only found one lay brother and one soldier and some chickens. Lieutenant Blondel gathered the chickens, and when he began to ride with them tied to his pommel, his horse threw him off to the dirt. The lay brother ran and told other Spaniards at Nuestra Señora de los Dolores de los Ais at present-day San Augustine that the French had begun a war. This "Chicken War" report scared the Spaniards, who fled westward toward San Antonio.[101]

Father Hidalgo returned to live at San Antonio de Valero Mission in San Antonio until 1725. He resigned and asked permission to work with the Apaches. His request was denied. He then left to retire at the San Juan Bautista Mission, where he lived until he died the next year.[102]

I

ANTONIO GIL IBARVO

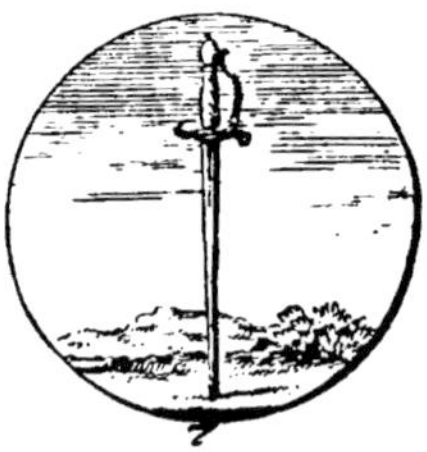

Antonio Gil Ibarvo lived a long life in the borderlands claimed by Spain and France. He was born of Spanish parents in 1729 at the presidio at Los Adaes, which was the most eastern fort of Spanish Texas, near present-day Natchitoches, Louisiana.

He grew up living with the Spanish trade system that required all goods be sent to Vera Cruz and then Mexico City in New Spain. Trade goods coming into the Natchitoches settlements had to come from Spanish sources, and the nearest one was at present-day San Antonio. As with many others, living such far distances from their required trading partners, it was tempting to trade more closely with the French, who were only a few miles away. Consequently much of the trade that occurred was likely illegal, a violation of the Spanish mercantile trade policy that was established to assure that all goods entered and left only Spanish hands so that any profits would go ultimately to the Spanish crown. This mercantile policy was also practiced by other powers in North America.[103]

Ibarvo married María Padilla and built a cattle ranch called Rancho Lobanillo in present-day Sabine County, Texas. They prospered but grew concerned as the Seven Years' War wound down with the secret Treaty of Fontainebleu in 1762, which called for France to cede Louisiana west of the Mississippi River to Spain. The treaty became publicly known in 1764. This new status took away Spain's need to have defensive positions with forts and missions in the Natchitoches area. Spain's King Carlos III ordered a thorough review of the northern reaches of New Spain and recommend how Spain should now plan its defenses. The king commissioned the Marqués de Rubí, Cayetano María Pignatelli Corbera y Saint Climent and Barón de Llinas, to perform this inspection of current facilities and recommend future needs.[104]

Marqués de Rubí traveled for twenty-three months a distance of an estimated 7,600 miles from the Gulf of

California to Louisiana. On April 10, 1768, the marquis submitted his report in Mexico City. The report called for a reduction in the number of presidios to fifteen, spread west to east along what is now the border between Mexico and the United States. Only Santa Fe in present-day New Mexico and San Antonio were recommended to stay north of that line of forts. In effect, the report called for an abandonment of eastern Texas, particularly the area where Ibarvo lived. The marquis also called for "a war of extermination against the Lipan Apaches."

In 1772, the Spanish king proclaimed the New Regulations for Presidios, adopting many of Rubí's recommendations. The proclamation called for the abandonment of all presidios and missions in Texas except one at La Bahía and San Antonio. San Antonio was designated to be the new capital of Texas. All settlers were to be moved out of east Texas. Instead of a war of extermination, the proclamation called for a renewed effort to improve relations with the Apaches.[105]

The proclamation called for immediate action. The entire population of settlers, missionaries and military officers and men, about five hundred people, were ordered to leave and go to San Antonio. This proved particularly difficult for people like Ibarvo, who was born there and knew only the ways of eastern Texas. The mission at Los Adaes had been there for more than fifty years, and the settlers felt a deep connection to the area. Some hid away quietly with friendly Native Americans while most went west 360 miles to San Antonio.

Once in San Antonio, Ibarvo met with officials and tried to find a way to return to his homeland. The Inspector-in-Chief Hugh O'Conor was concerned that an illegal trade with the new owners of lands east of the Mississippi, the English, would bring contraband into New Spain. He was especially worried about Native Americans getting access to rifles and ammunition. Ibarvo did not give up and decided to go to Mexico City to appeal directly to the viceroy. He, Gil Flores and the chief of the Tejas Caddo Indians petitioned the viceroy, who agreed to allow the return to the Nuestra Señora de Los Dolores de los Ais Mission at present-day San Augustine, Texas. O'Conor protested and the viceroy issued a compromise that allowed the establishment of a new settlement on the Trinity River. Ibarvo was named captain of the new post named Nuestra Señora del Pilar de Bucareli, in honor of Viceroy Antonio María Bucareli y Ursúa.

Ibarvo and a band of followers founded the new town at Paso Tomás on the Trinity River (see page 77). It prospered for several years until it became a favorite destination of marauding Comanches who stole horses and cattle, injured and killed settlers and raised general alarm. The town was also vulnerable to flooding and had a significant flood in December 1778. Heeding a warning from Padre Garza (see page 81) and following the leadership of Ibarvo, the settlers left Bucareli and headed east in January 1779. The colonists gathered at the abandoned Nuestra Señora de Guadalupe de los Nacogdoches Mission.

Spanish authorities sanctioned this move, termed it a permanent pueblo and even promoted Ibarvo from captain to lieutenant governor of Nacogdoches. This settlement still exists as the city of Nacogdoches, Texas.

One of Ibarvo's lasting accomplishments is the building of *La Casa Piedra*, the Stone House, later called Stone Fort, in 1779. This was a two-story building on a corner of the central plaza. When it was built, it was the largest building in Texas. The Stone Fort served as a trading post. In later years, it was occasionally used as a jail. It was dismantled in 1902 but reconstructed in 1936 using the original stones. It stands today on the campus of Stephen F. Austin State University.[106]

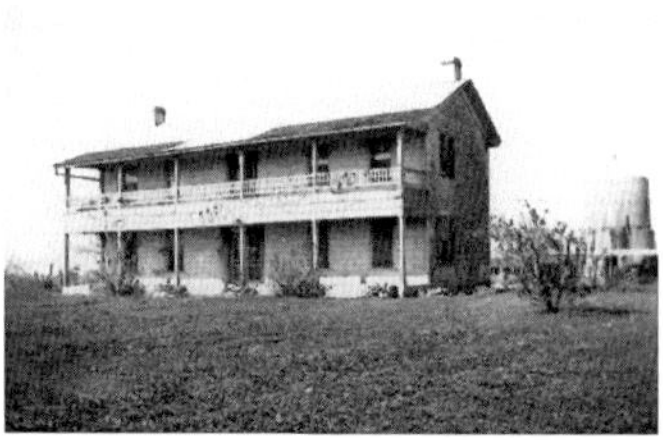

La Casa Piedra (Stone House) later known as the Old Stone Fort, built by Antonio Gil Ibarvo in 1779 in Nacogdoches, Texas. *Courtesy Texas State Library and Archives Commission, Prints and Photographs Collection, #1970/101-1008.*

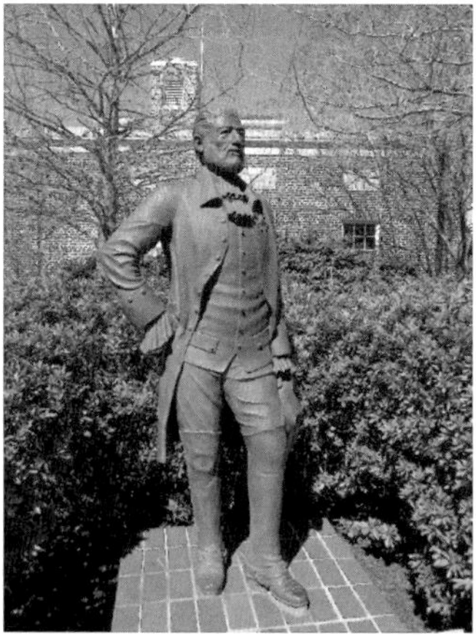

A statue of Antonio Gil Ibarvo at the Plaza Principal in Nacogdoches, Texas. *Photograph by the author.*

Ibarvo is honored with a large statue on the Nacogdoches Plaza Principal. Many of his descendants lived in the Nacogdoches area and Louisiana as late as the 1990s.[107]

INDEPENDENCE

Independence is a small town in Washington County, once part of the Austin Colony. Independence is near Washington-on-the-Brazos, where men declared Texas an independent nation, separate from Mexico, on March 2, 1836. Although less consequential than hosting a Constitutional Convention, Independence was the site of other noteworthy events in Texas history.

Early settlers founded a Baptist church in Independence in 1839 that Sam Houston attended. He was baptized in nearby Rocky Creek on November 19, 1854. When he heard that his sins would be washed away, he uttered one of his characteristically wry comments: "Pity the fish downstream."[108] Sam and Margaret Houston worshipped there for several years. The church has been at its current location, at the intersection of Texas Highway 50 and Texas Highway 390, since 1853. The current building was erected in 1872.

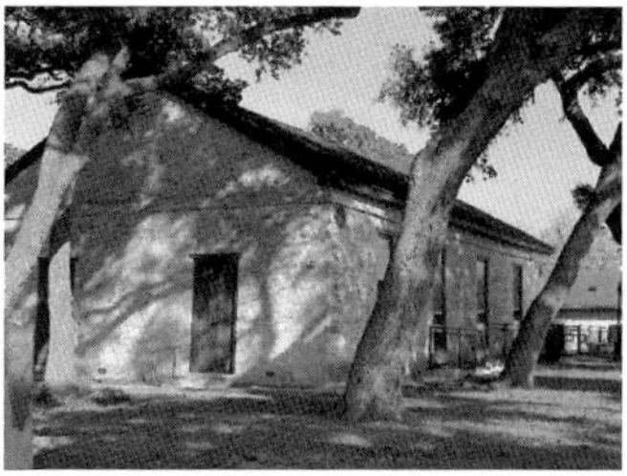

Independence Baptist Church in Independence, Texas. *Photograph by the author.*

Soon after its founding, a school opened in Independence that evolved into two universities. Beginning in May 1846, both boys and girls attended classes at Academy Hill on the west end of town. Five years later, in 1851, the second head of the school, Rufus Burleson, separated the men and women into two colleges. Males attended Baylor College and females attended the Female Department of Baylor College, later called Baylor Female College. Between the two colleges lay Rocky Creek, known as the "River Jordan."

In 1886, both colleges moved from Independence. Baylor College merged with Waco University in Waco, Texas. The new school was named Baylor University. Baylor Female College moved to Belton, Texas, and is now known as the University of Mary Hardin Baylor.

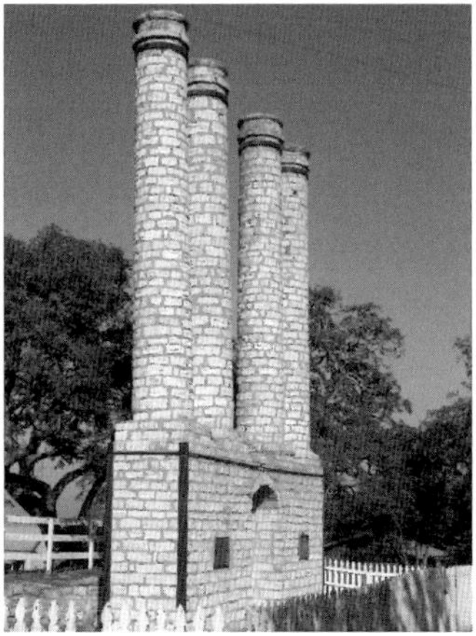

The ruins of Baylor Female College in Independence, Texas. *Photograph by the author.*

The first permanent building in Independence, called the Adobe House, dates from 1835. Sam Houston appointed James P. Coles the first chief justice of Washington County. He used the house as a courtroom and jail from 1836 until 1844 before the county seat moved to Brenham. For many years

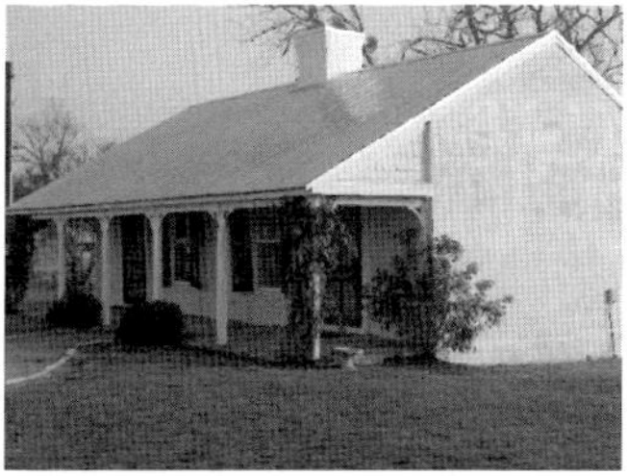

Left: The Adobe House in Independence, Texas. *Photograph by the author.*

Below: Margaret Lea Houston's home in Independence, Texas. *Photograph by the author.*

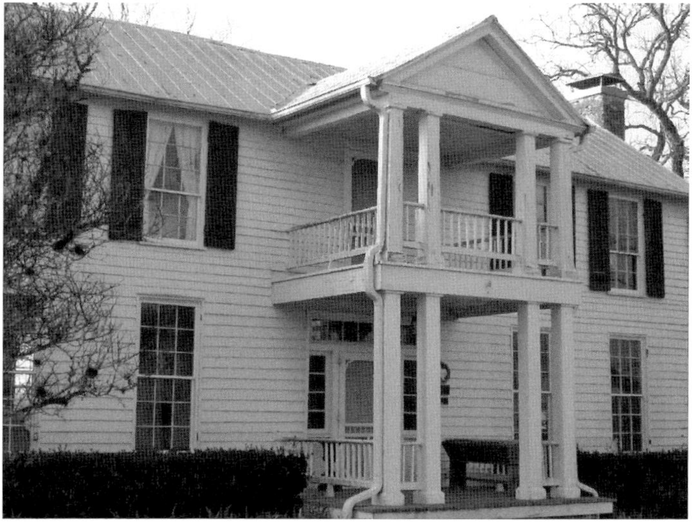

afterward, the house served as offices for attorneys.

Another significant building in early day Independence was one of the earliest Masonic lodges in Texas. Sam Houston and many other Texas leaders were Masons.

In addition to large, public buildings, Independence had

several well-built homes that still stand. The home that Sam Houston rented from 1853 to 1859 for his family still fronts onto the town's square. Between 1859 and 1863, the Houstons lived in Austin and then Huntsville, Texas. Upon her husband's death in 1863, Margaret Lea Houston returned to Independence. She bought the house in 1866, one year before she died.

Mrs. Houston's life in Independence was not easy. She was nearly penniless and lived a harsh existence, even at times unable to pay for basic items, such as food. On December 3, 1867, she died from yellow fever during an epidemic.[109] Due to the fear of contagion, she was not taken to Huntsville to be buried next to her husband. She is buried in the Houston-Lea Family Cemetery in Independence next to her mother, Nancy Moffette Lea, some of her children and other family members.[110]

Although Independence now has a less central role in the life of most Texans than it did in the 1800s, present-day visitors may still feel a sense of the past and see some interesting ruins as well as restored buildings.

J

ANSON JONES

The Republic of Texas lasted for nearly a decade after Texans declared their independence on March 2, 1836. The nation dissolved and joined the United States of America on February 19, 1846. During this time, four men served as president of Texas: David G. Burnet, Sam Houston (twice), Mirabeau B. Lamar and Anson Jones. The last president held office from December 1844 until February 1846.

Anson Jones was born in Massachusetts in 1798. He lived in many places before settling in Texas. He migrated to New York as a young man and studied medicine. He was licensed to practice medicine when he was twenty-two years old in New York. He later operated a drugstore and lived for a while in Harpers Ferry, Virginia (now West Virginia), and then moved to Philadelphia. In 1827, Jones earned an MD degree. He found medicine did not earn as much as he had expected, so he stopped his medical practice after five years. His creditors demanded payment, and he moved again. This time, he went to Venezuela for two years. Jones moved then to New Orleans, where he tried his hand as a commission merchant. He did not fare well financially there, so he looked to Texas as the next location that might improve his fortune. He moved to Brazoria along the Texas coast in 1833.

Jones prospered as a physician in Brazoria. He also found time to become involved in political groups and worked for a more self-governing Texas by promoting dialogue with Mexico's authorities. Although Jones was active and vocal, he did not seek any office or become an official delegate in these efforts to work with Mexico. When talk failed and war erupted, Jones joined the fighting forces at San Jacinto. He sought no high rank and humbly remained a private.

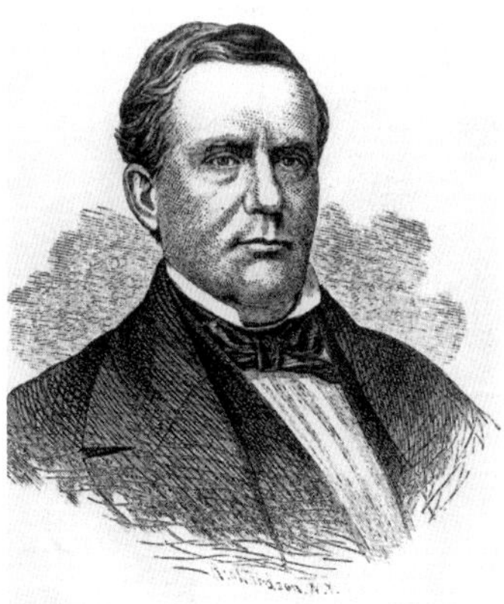

Anson Jones. Illustration in D.W.C. Baker's *Texas Scrapbook. Courtesy Texas State Library and Archives Commission, Prints and Photographs Collection, #1/102-331-A.*

Upon independence, Jones was elected to the new republic's congress. He took a direct role in shaping foreign policy as the chairman of the Committee on Foreign Relations. President Sam Houston appointed Anson Jones minister to the United States in 1838. The next year, Texas's incoming president, Mirabeau B. Lamar, recalled him to Texas. When he arrived, he learned he had been elected to complete a term in the Texas Senate that had become vacant when William H. Wharton passed away.

Jones married in 1841 and returned to Brazoria to resume his medical practice. This did not last very long as Sam Houston tapped Jones once again to serve as secretary of state. The pull to serve in Texas government proved strong for Jones. He was elected president in 1844. He favored annexation yet did not openly campaign for it. Indeed, Jones had worked to have a treaty for Mexico to recognize Texas's independence. During this time, many members of the Texas Congress favored annexation. Anson Jones encountered a political storm by his delays and unclear messages. He was burned in effigy. Some rumors even circulated calling for a coup d'état to remove him from the presidency. The Texas Congress rejected the proposed treaty with Mexico and disapproved of Jones's actions so much that the Congress censured Jones.

Anson Jones lowered the Lone Star flag the final time. He presided over a ceremony to raise the new standard, the flag of the United States. As the

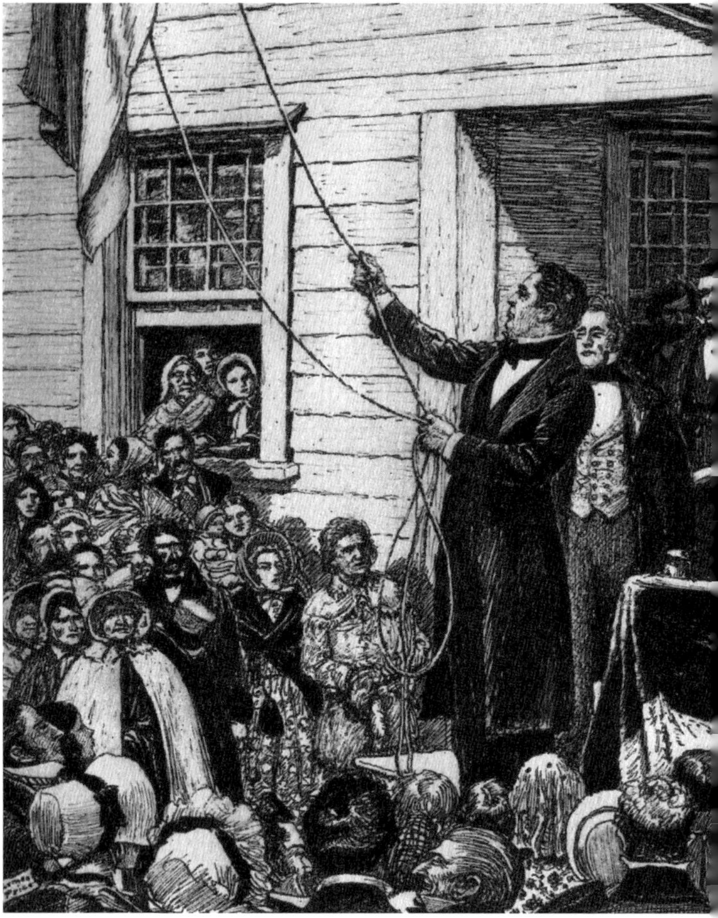

Anson Jones Lowers the Flag of the Republic of Texas. Illustration by Norman Price published by General Foods. *Courtesy Texas State Library and Archives Commission. Prints and Photographs Collection, #1977/62-8.*

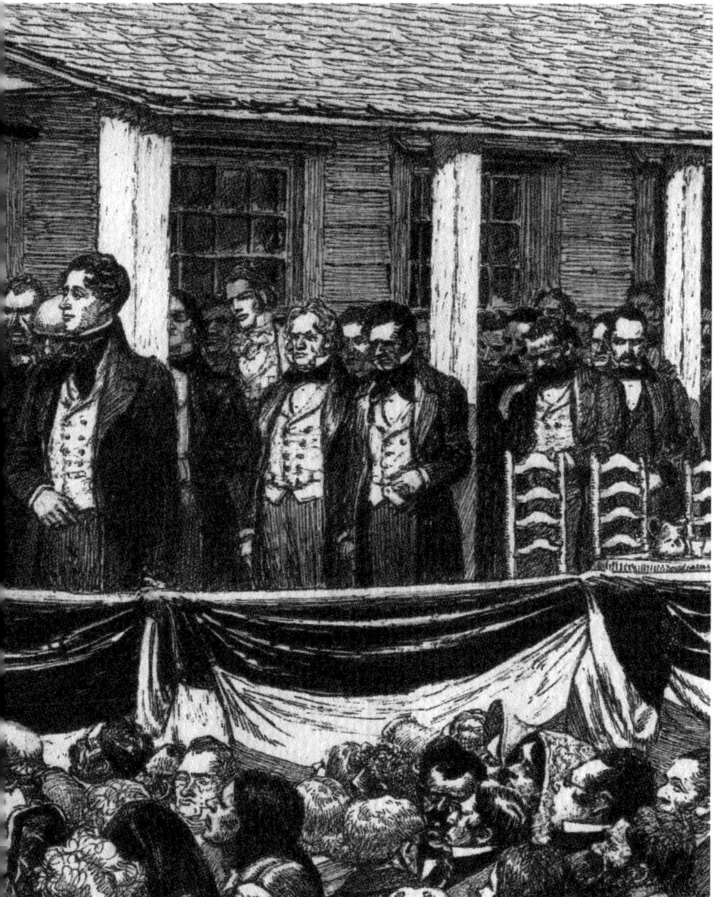

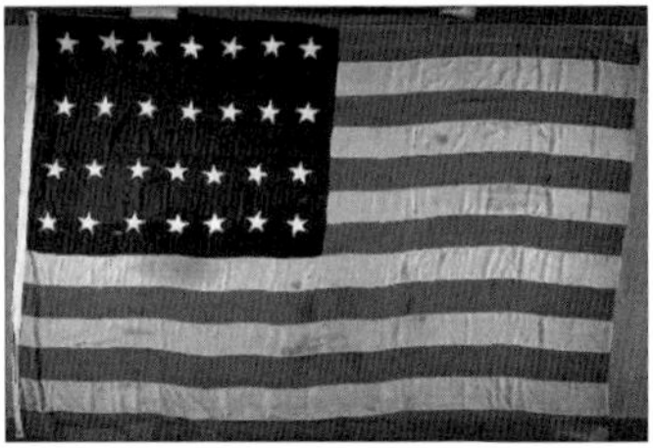

The U.S. flag with Texas as the twenty-eighth star. This flag was used only from July 4, 1846, to July 4, 1847, when Iowa became the twenty-ninth state to join the Union. *Courtesy Texas State Library and Archives Commission, Historic Flags Collection, 306-4064.*

Republic of Texas flag came down the mast on February 19, 1846, Dr. Jones said, "The final act in this great drama is now performed; the Republic of Texas is no more."[111] Texas became the U.S. flag's newest star on its twenty-eight-star flag.

After Texas became a state, Anson Jones had no governmental duties. He prospered as a planter with large estates. He organized the Masons and helped found the Texas Medical Association. Out of the political game, watching from the sidelines held little appeal for Jones. He grew despondent and depressed. He committed suicide in 1858 and is buried in Houston.

Jones is well remembered by many. His house has been moved and is open for visitors at a state museum in Washington-on-the-Brazos, Texas. Anson is the county seat of Jones County in north central Texas.[112] A large statue of Anson Jones dressed as the grand master of the Grand Lodge of the Republic of Texas stands at the main entrance to the Lorenzo de Zavala Texas State Archives and Library Building in Austin, Texas.

JUMANO INDIANS

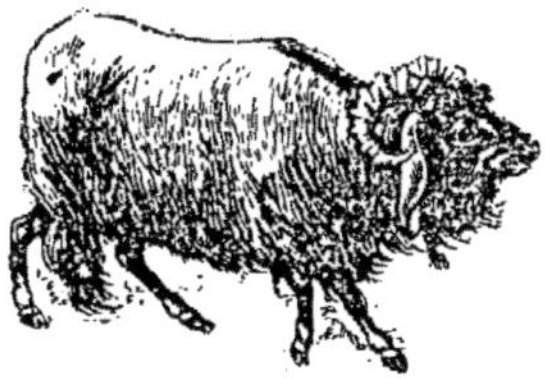

The Jumano Indians lived across a wide expanse of territory before the Spanish came to Texas. The Spanish reported encounters with them between 1500 and 1700. The name was applied to three peoples including (1) the Tompiro speakers, who were Pueblo Indians in Salinas in present-day New Mexico; (2) a group of nomads who traded primarily in the Rio Grande and Rio Conchos area of present-day Texas and Mexico; and (3) the Wichitas, who spoke a Caddoan language and lived along the basins of the Red and Arkansas Rivers (see page 207). The longest lasting presence of the Jumanos was in the plains lands between the Pecos and Colorado Rivers in Texas.

Jumanos wore little clothing and often had tattoos or scarifying marks on their bodies. Spanish explorers often referred to them as *desnudo*, "naked," and *los rayados*, "the striped ones." They hunted buffalo and were traders over much of Texas, often serving "as middlemen between Spanish colonies and various Indian tribes." In this movement and interaction, the Jumanos took on attributes of other peoples. The Spanish no longer counted the Jumanos as a separate people after about 1700.

Various Spanish explorers saw and reported on Jumanos during their journeys. In 1535, Álvar Núñez Cabeza de Vaca met some "People of the Cows" in the La Junta area along the Rio Grande as it is met by the Río Conchos at present-day Presidio, Texas, and Ojinaga, Chihuahua, Mexico. They were probably a group of Jumanos. Cabeza de Vaca reported they lived by farming, fishing and trading among the many groups who met at this juncture of the two rivers. Francisco Vásquez de Coronado may have encountered Jumanos in the 1540s. They were possibly the people he identified as the Teyas, who were fighting with the Quecheros (Apaches). In 1598, Vicente de Zaldívar reported a long-standing war between the Jumanos and Apaches in the region of the Pecos Pueblo in present-day New Mexico. In 1602, Juan de Oñate (see page 148) mentioned seeing Jumanos near the Arkansas River. Likely these were Wichitas. In 1634, Friar Alonso de Benavides said the Apaches dominated the plains area east of New Mexico for one hundred leagues. By the mid-1600s, refugees from the Apaches fled east and south toward the Rio Grande and Nueces Rivers. Some Jumanos tried to form an alliance with the Spanish to stem the advance of the Apaches. Juan Domingo de Mendoza, the lead Spanish soldier at this time, did not favor making an alliance. By the late 1600s, Jumanos were observed along the Rio Grande, especially in the Eagle Pass region, and farther south in the province of Coahuila, Mexico. In the late 1680s, members of LaSalle's colony encountered some Jumanos.

After 1700, the historical record has no more Jumano sightings or interactions.

Historians puzzle over what happened and where they went. This is sometimes called the "Jumano problem." The Jumanos lost their territory in repeated advances by the Apaches, who came to dominate the South Plains by the end of the seventeenth century: "The Jumanos had lost their entire territorial base, their trade routes were broken, and they ceased to exist as an identifiably distinct people." Many died of European diseases for which they had no resistance. Some remaining Jumanos in the west incorporated into Apache bands; some may have gone to live among their eastern trading partners, the Caddos and Wichitas. It is possible that some of the horse herders of the Río Nueces region "survived to become the nucleus of the Kiowa Indians, who appeared in the central plains toward the end of the eighteenth century."[113]

As of 2008, a people has emerged calling itself Apache-Jumano (*Jumano-Ndé*, "Red Mud Painted People") in southwest Texas. The group comprises members who are Jumano, Comanche and Apache. This group aspires to be named a separate and official tribe recognized by the United States government. As of 2013, the group registered three hundred people. Gabriel Carrasco, the tribal chieftain, believes there are another three thousand people who would qualify as members of the Apache-Jumano tribe.[114]

K

KADOHADACHO CONFEDERACY

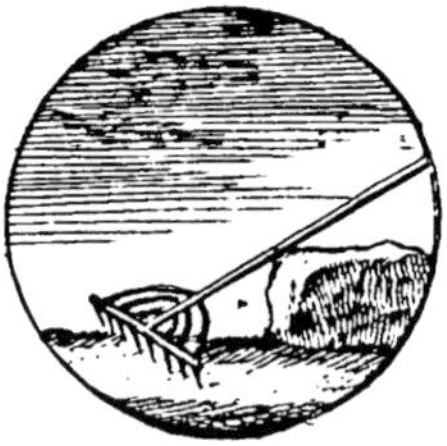

The Spanish were the first Europeans visitors to Texas. They first came in the early 1500s searching for gold. In the next century, they began to come again to plant missions, intending to convert the Native Americans to Christianity. These missions did not last. They had a few priests, a few workers and no military defense. In 1715, the Spanish decided to try again to stabilize their claim to eastern Texas. This time, the Indians, "with proper instruction," could "serve as a barrier against the further advance of the French. Watchfulness and constant activity alone could save Texas to be the crown of Spain."[115]

The people of the borderlands of what would become Arkansas, Louisiana, Texas and Oklahoma were primarily Caddos. The Caddos lived in "three loose confederacies: the Kadohadachos, the Natchitoches, and the Hasinais."[116] These Indians were more agricultural, less dependent on hunting than the Plains Indians in the central and western parts of Texas. The Kadohadacho culturally were similar to other Native Americans to the east. Anthropologists classify the Caddo culture as Mississippian since the Caddos shared a heritage with the Choctaw, Cherokee and Creek tribes found in the southeastern region of what became the United States.

Their economy focused on farms worked by both men and women. They hunted game to supplement their crops of corn, squash, pole beans and other vegetables. Their domestic life centered on small villages of round houses furnished with many woven baskets, rugs and pottery. Politically, they relied on a hierarchy of blood-related leaders served by a large bureaucracy of civil religious leaders. The great chief of all tribes was the Grand Caddi.[117]

Europeans "found their culture more related to theirs than that of any other" Indians in Texas "and destroyed them most easily."[118] The Caddoan Indians never took well to the life offered by European missionaries. Generally, they refused to become Christians and did not want to become serfs who labored for the benefit of others. The Caddo people already had strong religious beliefs and customs.[119] The Caddo people also had a political and social system that they had found useful for centuries and saw little benefit in becoming subservient to the Spanish missionaries.[120] At the same time, these Indians were trading with the French, who had settlements to the east. Significantly, the Spanish had a disadvantage with the Indians because they would not offer guns or ammunition in trade while the French traders did.

An insight into Caddo culture can be seen at two locations on each side of Texas Highway 21, six miles west of Alto, Texas. On the south side of the highway, a Texas State Historical Survey Committee marker notes the site of a Caddo village inhabited from 500 to 1100. Two mounds were ceremonial and were surrounded by many round houses.

Across the highway is the Caddo Mounds State Historic Site. One of the reasons the Caddos lived here was likely the presence of a natural spring flowing from here to the nearby Angelina River. Archaeologists believe the mounds were built between 800 and 1300. One of the mounds is a burial site.

Captain Zebulon Montgomery Pike explored much of the middle of North America from the Mississippi to the Rocky Mountains. On his way back to the United States, he strayed south into Spanish lands. On this journey, he mentioned the mounds that he saw in 1807. When he camped at this site, Pike was a captive of Spanish authorities being forcibly returned to United States territory. (Pike's

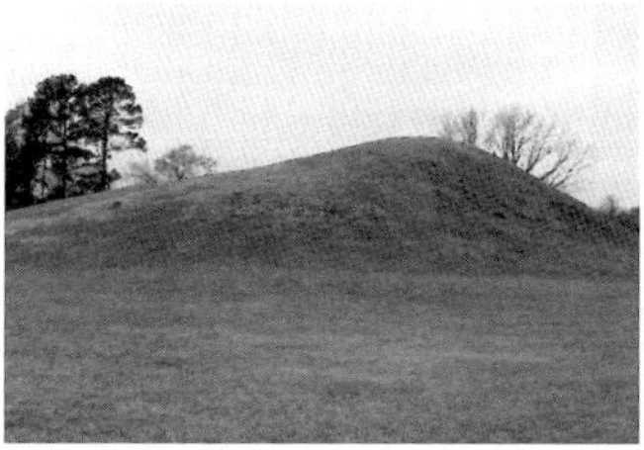

The Caddo Burial Mound at Caddo Mounds state historic site. *Photograph by the author.*

travels are further discussed on page 161.)

In 1874, the Kadohadacho and the Nadacos merged together and considered themselves a united tribe of the Caddos.[121] As with most Native Americans, the Caddo "still exist…[and] most, while adapting to the new order, have proudly retained their Native American identity."[122] In the early twenty-first century, the descendants of the Kadohadacho live primarily near the Caddo Nation location in Binger, Oklahoma.[123]

Contemporary visitors can see what Pike saw and walk the grounds surrounding the mounds. Visitors may also learn from a museum administered by the Texas Historical Commission. The museum offers exhibits of pottery, tools, weapons and other instructive materials.

KARANKAWA INDIANS

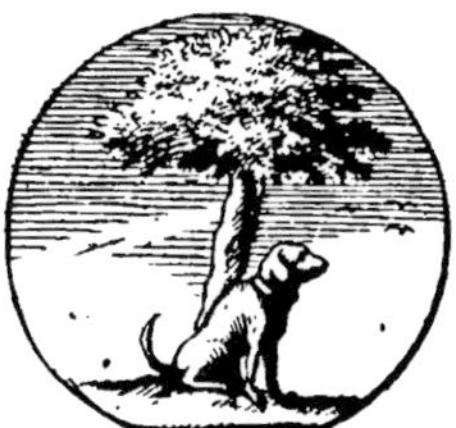

Karankawa is a collective name used by the Spaniards to refer to various similar peoples along the Texas coast from present-day Galveston and Corpus Christi. Tribes in this group included the Capoques (Coaques, Cocos), Kohanis, Kopanes (Copanes) and Karankawas. The word likely means "dog-lovers" or "dog-raisers," which seems appropriate because they were reputed to raise and use fox- and coyote-like dogs.

Karankawas based their livelihood on hunting, fishing and gathering as they migrated in their region following the food supplies and responding to climate changes. As migratory people, they often moved in small groups of thirty to forty people and stayed in one place for several weeks, setting up a camp living in a portable structure, a *ba-ak*, which could house seven to eight people. They often traveled in dugout canoes. Their primary weapons were bows and arrows. Like the Jumanos (see page 107), they often tattooed their bodies.

The Karankawas held large gatherings, *mitotes*, which included dancing and the consumption of an intoxicating drink by the men.[124] Karankawas had an unusual concept and practice of gender identification. In addition to males and females, they had a third gender, called *berdache*, who were males who generally took female roles and activities, had designated roles in religious ceremonies and acted as "passive sexual partners for other males."[125] Perhaps the most noteworthy attribute about the Karankawas was the practice of ritual cannibalism, which was also practiced by other coastal tribes of Texas and Louisiana. A 1768 account by a Spanish priest noted they ate their captive's flesh during a ceremony while the captive was staked to the ground and watched as the Karankawas roasted and ate his flesh. The priest thought the Karankawas believed this practice would give the Karankawas the power that their captive had. More than two hundred years before this account, in 1528, Álvar Núñez Cabeza de Vaca lived among the Karankawas for several years and did not report any cannibalism. It is possible that the Karankawas were mistaken for another tribe, the Atakapans, who live eastward from Galveston Bay to Louisiana.[126] The Karankawas, as the Jumanos (see page 107), are no longer a recognizable tribe. Several problems overwhelmed them as they fell victim to European diseases, merged with other groups like the Apaches and died during various battles over hundreds of years. Stephen F. Austin planned a war of extermination against the Karankawas. In 1824, he led a force that drove ninety men to the mission at La Bahía. A priest negotiated a peace whereby Chief Antonio of the Karankawas agreed to live west of the Lavaca River. This was renewed in 1827 by Green DeWitt and Chiefs Antonio and Delgado. Despite the agreement, the Karankawas still roamed east of the Lavaca River, just as they had done for centuries. By the time Texas became a republic in 1836, the Karankawas were such a small number they offered little threat to the Texans.

By the mid-1840s, the remaining small band of Karankawas moved south and lived along both sides of the Rio Grande. Sometimes they lived near Reynosa,

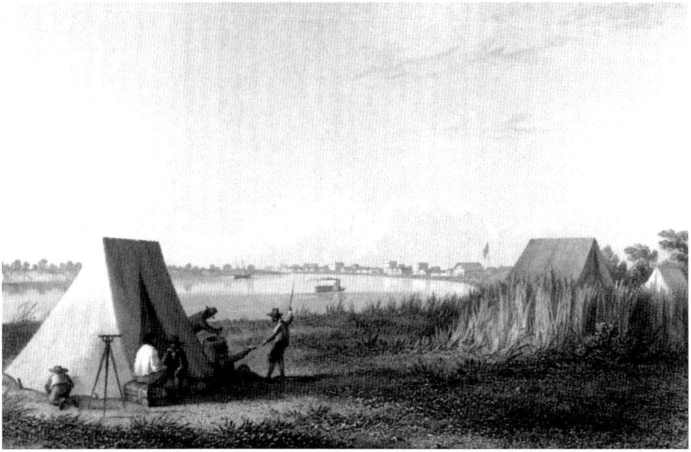

An 1857 scene of the Rio Grande at Brownsville, the area where the Karankawas lived in the 1850s. Photograph by Sean Linehan, in William H. Emory, *United States and Mexican Boundary Survey, Report of William H. Emory*, Washington, D.C.: U.S. Government Printing Office, 1857. *Photograph uploaded to Wikipedia by Arnoname.*

Tamaulipas, Mexico. About ten years later, some moved back north of the Rio Grande near Rio Grande City.

In 1858, the three-hundred-year-long struggle to survive after Europeans entered Texas ended. A force of Texans, led by Juan Nepomuceno Cortina, killed the remaining Karankawas.[127] Cortina had a long life as a military officer; outlaw; governor of Tamaulipas, Mexico; and revolutionary leader.[128]

JANE HERBERT WILKINSON LONG

The United States and Spain signed the Adams-Onís Treaty in 1819, ending years of conflicting claims over lands in the southeastern region of the United States. The United States gained sovereignty over Gulf of Mexico coastlands stretching from the Sabine River on the western border of Louisiana to the Atlantic Ocean. The United States purchased Florida and moved quickly to establish direct control there.

Soon after the Florida purchase, warfare erupted as various Native American tribes sought to maintain their lands and their way of life, most notably the Creeks, Choctaws and Seminoles.

Some Americans were disappointed that the treaty

did not also include Texas. Some of them organized forces to fight to gain Texas. Dr. James Long led one of these forces to "filibuster" in an attempt "invade Texas and establish a Republic."[129] Long's group marched westward from Natchez, Mississippi, toward Nacogdoches in June 1819.

Jane Herbert Wilkinson Long, his wife, and their infant accompanied this expedition. Nacogdoches fell easily and declared its independence with Dr. Long elected president. He went to seek assistance from the famed pirate Jean Lafitte. Lafitte refused to join the effort, saying that a well-disciplined professional army from New Spain would certainly prevail. In the meantime, Spanish forces had, indeed, recaptured Nacogdoches. Fortunately, Jane and their baby had fled to Louisiana. Dr. Long joined them and then soon went to New Orleans to raise more funds and ally himself with an exile from New Spain, José Félix Trespalacios.

In 1820, Dr. Long and Trespalacios's army returned to Texas. Jane had another child. She and the two children went along with the army to build a fort at Point Bolivar, across from Galveston Island. The army was surrounded by Spanish forces and surrendered. Dr. Long was taken as a prisoner to Mexico City, where he died. His death may have actually been an accident, as he was reportedly shot by Don Trespalacios.

Dr. Long's widow, Jane Herbert Wilkinson Long; their two children; and one female slave stayed at Point Bolivar, barely surviving on what they could catch from Galveston Bay. Jane traveled for a while to

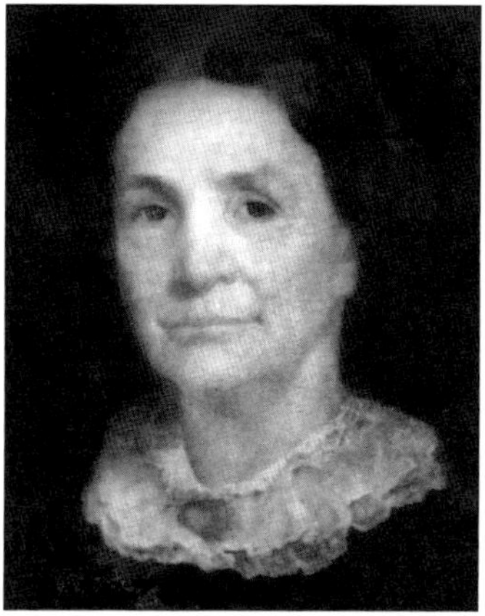

The "Mother of Texas...Jane Long." *Courtesy Texas State Library and Archives Commission, Prints and Photographs Collection, #1/98-1.*

San Antonio and Monterrey, Mexico, hoping for justice.

Eventually, Mrs. Long stopped this fruitless quest and returned to her Mississippi home. Later on, she and the children came back and lived near Richmond, Texas, where she prospered in many ways. It is often told that she was courted by several of the most prominent bachelors in Texas, including Ben Milam, William Travis, Stephen Austin, Sam Houston and Mirabeau Lamar.[130] She refused all entreaties and chose to remain a widow.

Mrs. Long had great strength and stamina. She was orphaned at age fourteen and widowed ten years later at age twenty-four. She worked tirelessly and prospered financially in an era when few women directed their own financial affairs. Jane Long operated two boardinghouses, bought and sold land and, with the work of slaves, raised cattle and cotton.[131]

Jane Long claimed to be the first English-speaking woman to bear a child in Texas. Her affectionate nickname was "Mother of Texas." Indeed, according to an interpretation of census records from 1807 through 1826, the Texana Living History Association concludes that she was not the first English-speaking woman to give birth in Texas.[132] In any case, Jane Long is revered by many Texans as one of the inspiring women of early Texas. She is known for her strength, determination and successful grasp on life in early Texas, where she prospered and reared her children. Jane Herbert Wilkinson Long died at age eighty-two in 1880, after fifty-eight years of widowhood. She is buried in Richmond, Texas, where her gravestone says, "Mrs. Jane H. Long, the Mother of Texas."[133]

M

SAMUEL McCULLOCH JR.

African Americans contributed to early Texas history in many ways. As with other groups, they brought their cultural ways and shared their beliefs and skills, ranging from architecture to cattle raising to quilting. Many historians believe the first black person in Texas was Estevan—or Estevanico, as his nickname is frequently used. Estevanico translates from the Spanish to mean "little, or young, Stephen" in English.[134] Estevan was born in the early 1500s in Azemmour, Morocco. He was enslaved and owned by Andrés Dorantes de Carranca.[135] Spaniards and Portuguese both enslaved Moors from northern Africa at that time. Estevanico and Carranca both accompanied Álvar Núñez Cabeza de Vaca on a journey across Texas in 1528.

Over time, small numbers of African Americans participated in Spanish exploration and settlement. The population of Spaniards and their slaves remained small and widespread from the early 1500s through the late 1700s. By 1792, Texas had only thirty-four blacks who composed 15 percent of the population.[136]

In the 1820s, the newly independent Republic of Mexico abolished slavery in its constitution and offered equality for all citizens, including blacks.[137] At the same time, conversely, Mexico granted large parcels of land to Americans who brought slaves with them to Texas. By 1835, Texas had an estimated population of forty-one thousand people. Anglo Americans from the United States composed 85 percent, or thirty-five thousand, of that number. The remaining six thousand were estimated to be divided evenly between Mexican Texans, Tejanos and blacks.[138] Most African Americans in early Texas "were brought as slaves; others came as free people, indentured servants, or escaped slaves."[139] Most lived in the southeastern part of Texas, which became an extension of the agricultural economy of the southern United States that relied extensively on slave labor to raise cash crops like cotton.

Sometimes it proves insightful to look at the life of one person to understand the society he or she lived in. Samuel McCulloch Jr.'s life illustrates how free blacks fared in early Texas when few African Americans in Texas were free. McCulloch was one of the first to be injured in the Texas Revolution. His participation in Texas's fight for independence gave him a clearly exceptional status. He was often allowed privileges and rights that other African Americans did not have.

Samuel McCulloch Jr. was born in South Carolina on October 11, 1810. He moved to Texas in 1815, when he was five years old. Samuel's father, Samuel McCulloch Sr., brought him and his three sisters—Jane, Harriet and Mahaly—to settle on the Lavaca River in present-day Jackson County, Texas. The family members were considered free blacks with rights to independence and property.

On October 5, 1835, just prior to his twenty-fifth birthday, Samuel McCulloch Jr. joined the Matagorda Volunteer Company, led by George M. Collinsworth. McCulloch was injured when the volunteers routed the Mexican soldiers in their quarters at the Presidio of Nuestra Señora de Loreto de La Bahía in Goliad. This fort's façade embodies the two motives of Spanish colonizers, defense and conversion of the Native Americans. On one side is a powerful cannon aimed outward toward anyone who tries to breach the strong stone wall. Just behind the outer wall is a church with a statue of the Virgin Mary dressed in blue standing above the door.

Despite such formidable defenses, the Texas volunteers waged battle here as the first battle of the Texas Revolution. Samuel McCulloch Jr. is a central figure in a painting by Kermit Oliver titled *The Battle of Goliad*, which is located at the University of Texas at

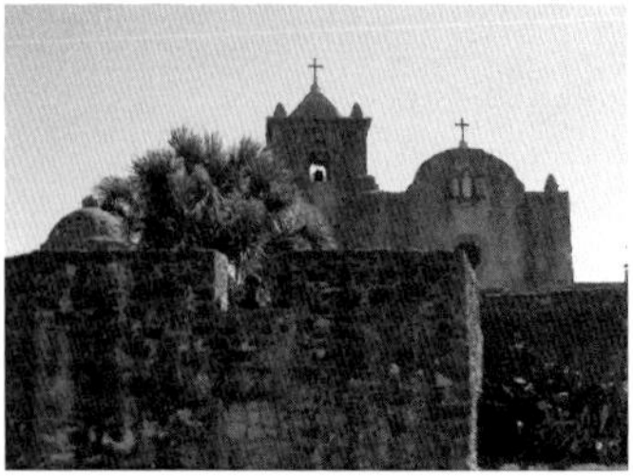

Presidio Nuestra Señora de Loreto de La Bahía, known commonly as Presidio La Bahía in Goliad, Texas. *Photograph by the author.*

San Antonio's Institute of Texan Cultures. McCulloch is featured prominently in a heroic pose at the front of a crowd of soldiers, riding a white horse, grasping a rifle and urging the soldiers forward to do battle. McCulloch was shot in his right shoulder and so severely injured that he stayed in Goliad for three weeks until going to Victoria. After enduring pain for nine months, a surgeon removed the musket ball from McCulloch's shoulder on July 8, 1836.[140]

Texas declared its independence on March 2, 1836. Two months later, Texas's congress passed a law granting permanent residence rights to all free blacks who lived in Texas at the time of the declaration. Just a few months later, the Texas Constitution of September 1836 barred "Africans [and] descendants of Africans and Indians" from citizenship. Free blacks were required to apply to the congress for citizenship in the Texas Republic. McCulloch's petition was set aside, and he remained in Texas living under the protection of the June 5, 1836 law.[141]

McCulloch married Mary Vess, an Anglo American, on August 11, 1837. They were never prosecuted for violating the Texas law prohibiting interracial marriage. The McCullochs had four children

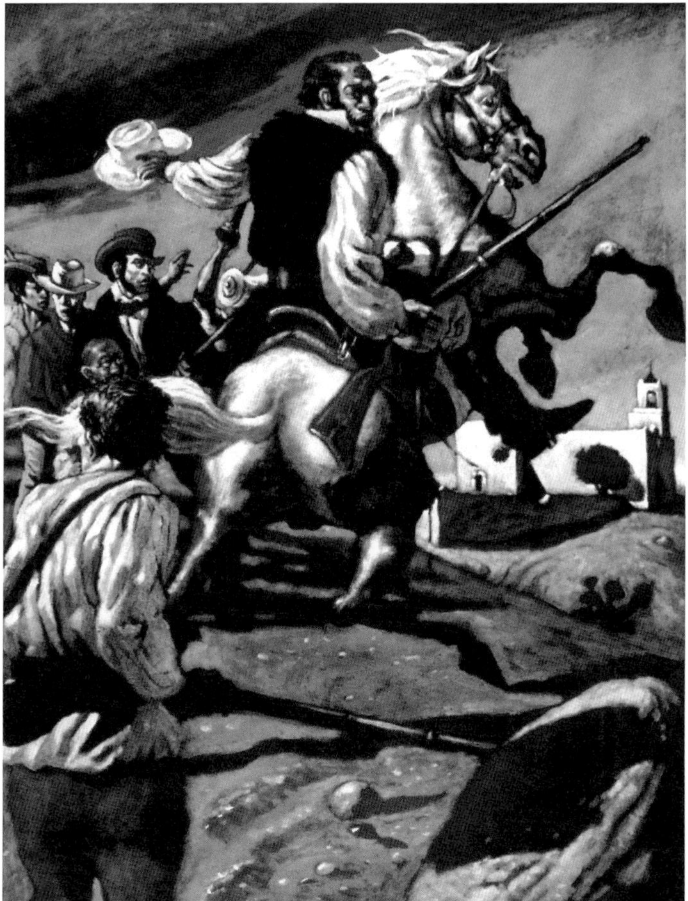

The Battle of Goliad. A painting by Kermit Oliver. *Courtesy University of Texas at San Antonio Special Collections.*

before Mrs. McCulloch died in 1847. One son, Lewis Clark McCulloch, fought in the Confederate army.[142]

An 1840 law, the Ashworth Act, sought to expel free blacks from the republic by 1842 or have them sold into slavery. McCulloch and his family were exempted. He continued to serve by fighting in the 1840 battle at Plum Creek against the Comanches.

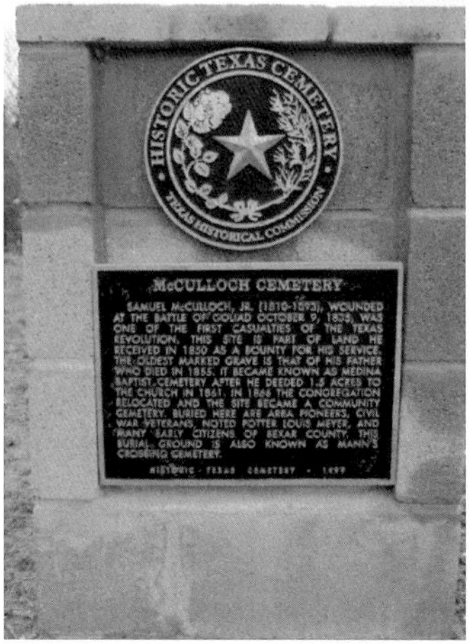

McCulloch Cemetery, a historic Texas cemetery. *Photograph by the author.*

Samuel McCulloch Jr. was granted land in 1850 near San Antonio in southwestern Bexar County for his distinguished service during the Texas Revolution. He lived as a farmer and cattle rancher on this land next to the Medina River near present-day Van Ormy. He deeded one and a half acres to found a cemetery that now bears his name. His father, Samuel McCullogh Sr. was the first person buried there in 1855. Upon his death on November 2, 1893, McCulloch joined his father and was buried there. His headstone bears the initials "T.W.V.," honoring him as a Texas War Veteran.[143]

ATHANASE DE MÉZIÈRES

During the late 1770s, the Spanish renewed their efforts to plant permanent missions and presidios in Texas. They reasoned that the best way to do so would be to gain a lasting peace with the Native Americans. Their goal was to convert the four to five thousand Indians and rule them in a disciplined manner "so that they might be employed in the event of a conflict with their rivals."[144]

Barón de Ripperdá arrived in San Antonio in 1770 as the new Spanish governor of Texas in San Antonio. He looked for the best way to maintain and strengthen Spain's sovereignty in Texas. In an uncharacteristic departure for the usual way of Spanish governance, the baron relied on the expertise of a Frenchman who lived now under Spanish control in Louisiana, Athanase de Mézières.

Athanase de Mézières was from a family of explorers and colonizers. He was born in Paris and came to Louisiana as a young man. He served in the French army in Natchitoches, the area adjacent to Spanish lands along the unclear border between Louisiana and Texas. Mézières was the son-in-law of Louis Juchereau de St. Denis who had explored the Mississippi region and Texas and assisted the Spanish in founding missions and a fort in Texas in the early 1700s.

Mézières had lived in Louisiana for thirty years when the Spanish appointed him lieutenant governor of the Natchitoches region in 1769. His knowledge of languages was an asset. He knew French, Spanish, Latin and some

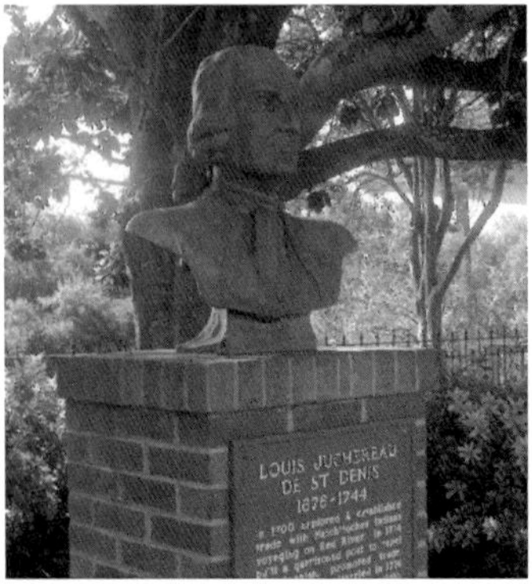

A bust of Louis Juchereau de St. Denis in Natchitoches, Louisiana. *Photograph Billy Hathorn.*

Native American languages. He was very familiar with Texas Indians. As the Spanish agent to the Indians, he traveled extensively, especially in the northern parts of Texas. He negotiated a peace in northern Texas in 1771 with three groups of the Wichitas: the Taovayas, Wacos and Tawakonis. This was especially significant since the Wichitas had once warred alongside the Comanches. Mézières also concluded a peace agreement with a band of the Comanches in 1774.

Barón de Ripperdá considered how he could use some of the Indians as allies to fight the constant menace coming from the Apaches. He asked Athanase de Mézières for his insight. Mézières reported to the Spanish officials that the Texas Indians could be classified into three categories: coastal tribes, eastern inland nations and those on the western and northern frontiers. The coastal tribes, such as the Karankawas, could be ignored and considered a low threat to the Spaniards.

Many of the tribes in the eastern regions, especially the Caddos, had been severely affected by diseases brought by the Europeans. One of the remaining groups, the Tejas, was friendly and not very warlike.

The frontier Indians, including the Tonkawas, Wichitas and Comanches, could be very aggressive warriors. They might fight the eastward-moving Apaches encroaching into Comanche territory. Mezieres thought it would be possible to make an alliance between the Spanish and Comanches to make war on the Apaches.[145]

Athanase de Mézières was transferred to Texas and appointed to become the next governor, replacing Barón de Ripperdá. Even though Louisiana passed from French to Spanish control in 1763, the appointment of a Frenchman to hold a governorship in a Spanish land was unprecedented.

It is unknown whether Mézières' plan to ally Spain and the Comanches against the Apaches would have worked. On his way to San Antonio, he was thrown off his horse and seriously injured his head. He learned of his appointment when he arrived in September 1779, but he was not well enough to take office. Mézières never regained his strength and was unable to begin his work as governor. He died on November 2, 1779.[146]

N

FELIPE ENRIQUE NERI

Felipe Enrique Neri was a singularly fascinating person who lived in various places assuming differing names and ranks in society before coming to Texas. He made some important contributions to the early history of Texas, especially as an intermediary for Moses and Stephen Austin and as a legislator for Coahuila y Tejas.

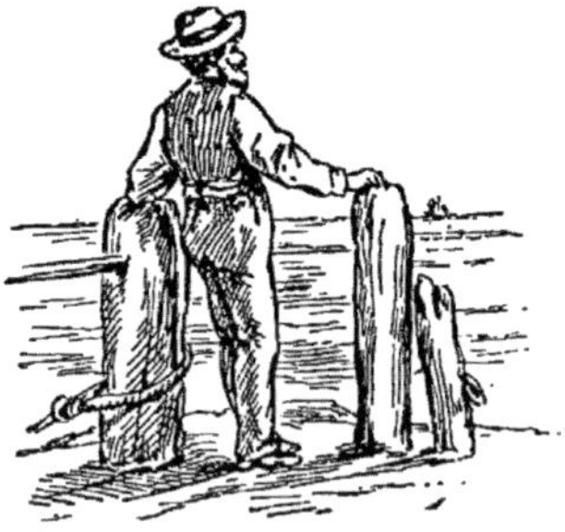

Felipe Enrique Neri is the Spanish name used by Philip Hendrik Nering Bögel. He was born in Paramaribo, Surinam (Dutch Guyana), in South America on November 23, 1759. He and his Dutch parents moved to the Netherlands when he was five years old. In 1779, Bögel joined the cavalry of Holland and Upper Issel. He married and settled in Leeuwarden in Friesland province, where he worked as a tax collector. He and his wife had five children. His cavalry service and position as a tax collector implied that he supported the established hierarchy at a time of upheaval and revolution following the French Revolution that began in 1792. Bögel later said he left the Netherlands when the French invaded his country. Actually, he fled in 1793 before he could be tried for embezzling tax revenues. He left his wife and five children but took the money that he had embezzled. The Leeuwarden Court of Justice offered a one-thousand-gold-ducat reward for his return. At this point, Bögel took on the identity of Baron de Bastrop and fled.

The newly created Baron de Bastrop arrived in Louisiana in 1795 in the guise of a member of the Dutch nobility. The Spanish authorities who governed Louisiana at the time allowed him to set up a colony in the Ouachita River Valley and to trade in Louisiana and Kentucky:[147] "Fewer than 100 colonists actually settled in the area. The baron lost his fortune."[148]

After the United States purchased Louisiana in 1803, Bastrop moved to Texas, where he lived in San Fernando de Béxar, present-day San Antonio. He started a freight-hauling business and took part in the villa's administration. By 1810, Bastrop had become the second *alcalde*, "deputy mayor," in the *ayuntamiento*, "local government."

One day in 1820, while walking in the plaza, Bastrop saw an old friend, Moses Austin, whom he had known twenty years before while traveling and staying in a roadhouse in Missouri.[149] Antonio María Martínez, the last Spanish governor of Texas,[150] had just denied Moses Austin's petition to serve as an *empresario*, "entrepreneur," to bring in three hundred settlers. Bastrop met with the governor and persuaded him to reconsider Austin's request. In response to the intercession by the trusted deputy mayor, Martínez reversed his decision. Moses Austin was granted his request. Unfortunately, Moses Austin died before he could complete his role. Again, with Bastrop's endorsement, the governor allowed Moses's son, Stephen, to take over as empresario.[151]

Stephen F. Austin took over his father's grant and brought in the "Old Three Hundred" families to settle lands in south-central Texas. In July 1823, Luciano García, interim governor for several months in 1823, appointed Bastrop a commissioner to issue land titles to try to keep order among the many grants of Texas lands given to various empresarios.[152] García favored the empresario process and was receptive to Bastrop's pleas on Stephen Austin's behalf.

In 1824, the deputy mayor was elected to represent Béxar in Mexico's newly established state of Coahuila y Tejas. In the legislature, he promoted the immigration of more settlers from the United States and the establishment of a port in Galveston.

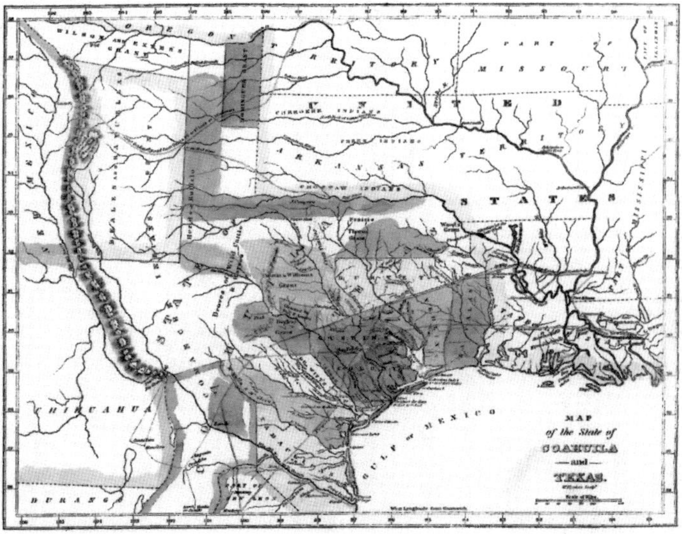

An 1833 map of Coahuila and Texas from 1833 by Mary Austin Holley, Armstrong & Plaskitt. The map features the land grants made to empresarios who brought immigrants from the United States into Texas. *Courtesy Texas State Library and Archives Commission, Map Collection, No. 1607b.*

When Bastrop died on February 23, 1827, at age sixty-seven, he was a pauper. His income from two sources for the last several years was very meager. As a legislator he was supposed to be paid by his constituents, but they contributed very little. As a land commissioner issuing land titles for the Austin colony, Bastrop earned only a small fee with each grant.[153] The penniless baron's estate did not even have enough to pay for his burial. Juan Antonio Padilla, a fellow legislator, paid the baron's final expenses and was later reimbursed by some other legislators. The man of many names—Philip Hendrik Nering Bögel, Felipe Enrique Neri, Baron de Bastrop—was buried in Saltillo, the capital of Coahuila y Tejas.[154]

Although Bastrop led an ignoble life at times and pretended to be nobility when he was not, he is generally remembered favorably. There are many schools and streets in Texas and Louisiana named in his honor. Texas and Louisiana have a city named for him. Texas also has a county and state park named in his honor. The Daughters of the Texas Revolution have a chapter named in his honor.

PHILIP NOLAN

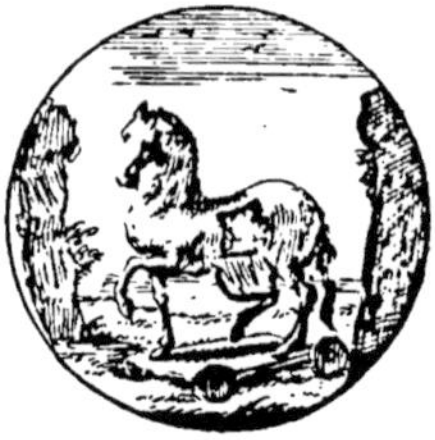

Philip Nolan was born in Belfast. He left Ireland in the late 1700s for the western edges of the European settlements in America. He lived for a while with the highest-ranking general in the U.S. Army, General James Wilkinson (see page 211). He served Wilkinson as a bookkeeper and an agent in his dealings in New Orleans. He also lived along the borders of French Louisiana and Spanish Texas. By 1785, he was known as a trader of mustangs, wild horses that he caught and sold.

While scouting for horses, he drafted detailed maps.

In 1797, he gave a Texas map to the French governor of Louisiana, Baron de Carondelet. The baron contracted with Nolan to secure horses to sell to a French regiment. Unfortunately, the map was lost and has never been found. At the same time, Nolan secretly worked with General Wilkinson on plans to undermine Spanish control over Texas, a part of New Spain.

Philip Nolan was also sought after to share his firsthand authoritative knowledge of wild horses. Thomas Jefferson wrote to Nolan in 1798 asking him to report on the natural life of the wild horses of Texas. Jefferson was interested to learn how horses lived in nature to "enable our Philosophical society to add so interesting a chapter to the history of this animal." He asked Nolan to relate particularly about the horse's "manners, habits, and laws of his existence, which are peculiar to his wild state."[155]

In the fall of 1800, Nolan took about twenty free and enslaved Americans into Texas to gather more horses for his trading operation. Texas governor Juan Bautista de Elguézabal feared the growing presence of Americans on the eastern frontier of Texas. He ordered the arrest of anyone whose actions were suspect. Nolan was on this list because the Spanish governor believed he planned to encourage a revolution to overthrow Spanish rule and make himself the king of Texas.

Nolan defeated the Spanish troops in eastern Texas. Then he fled with three hundred horses and went as far west as the Brazos River to get away from the Spanish. A company of soldiers led by Lieutenant Músquiz followed Nolan's trail, surrounded the Americans and attacked at dawn on March 21, 1801. Nolan was shot and killed. César and Robert, Nolan's slaves, buried him at the battle site on Texas State Highway 174, near the Nolan River, between present-day Rio Vista in Johnson County and Blum in Hill County, Texas.[156]

After the battle, some Americans surrendered, were taken prisoner and went south, deeper into New Spain. Most died in captivity from illness and neglect. One lost a lottery and was hanged.

One of Philip Nolan's lieutenants, Peter Ellis Bean, escaped and later fought in both the American and Mexican armies. Bean eventually became a colonel in the Mexican army and died a wealthy man in

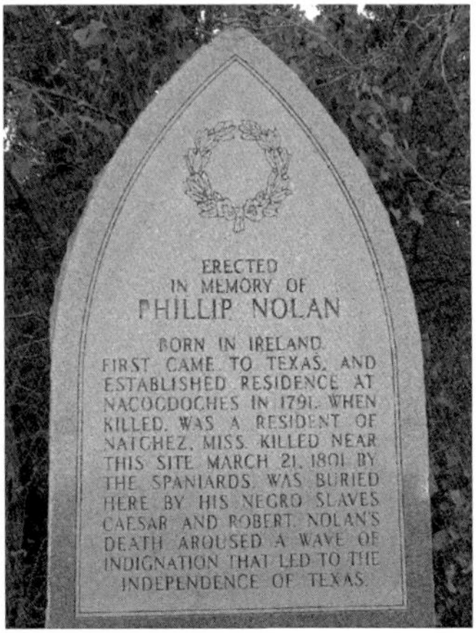

A marker "Erected in memory of Phillip Nolan" on Texas State Highway 174, near the Nolan River, between present-day Rio Vista in Johnson County and Blum in Hill County, Texas. *Photograph by the author.*

Mexico City.[157] Philip Nolan's legacy was noted in official U.S. government maps. Captain Zebulon Montgomery Pike explored and mapped much of the western United States soon after Nolan's death (see page 161). Pike's map of the *Internal Provinces of New Spain* was published in 1807. In the area marked "Province of Texas," there were hundreds of miles left without any specific features north of San Antonio to the Red River. These open ranges were marked as having "Immense Herds of Wild Horses."[158]

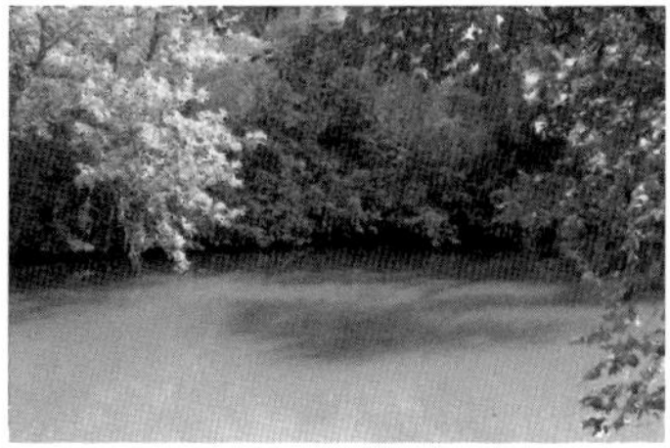

A view of the Nolan River at Texas State Highway 174. *Photograph by the author.*

A namesake of Philip Nolan was Colonel Philip Noland Luckett who was quartermaster and commissary general of the state of Texas in early 1861. When the Civil War began, he served as aide-de-camp to Colonel Earl van Dorn.[159] Eventually, Luckett was promoted to colonel and commander of the land forces of the eastern subdistrict of Texas in 1863.[160]

Philip Nolan's memory was also honored in three place names. In addition to the Nolan River in central Texas and Nolan County in west Texas, he is remembered in the naming of the town Nolanville, which was the original name of the present-day city of Belton, the county seat of Bell County.[161]

NUESTRA SEÑORA DEL ESPÍRITU SANTO DE ZÚÑIGA MISSION

As with other missions, Nuestra Señora del Espíritu Santo de Zúñiga Mission was established to convert the Native Americans to Christianity, foster an agricultural economy and represent Spain's determination to retain its

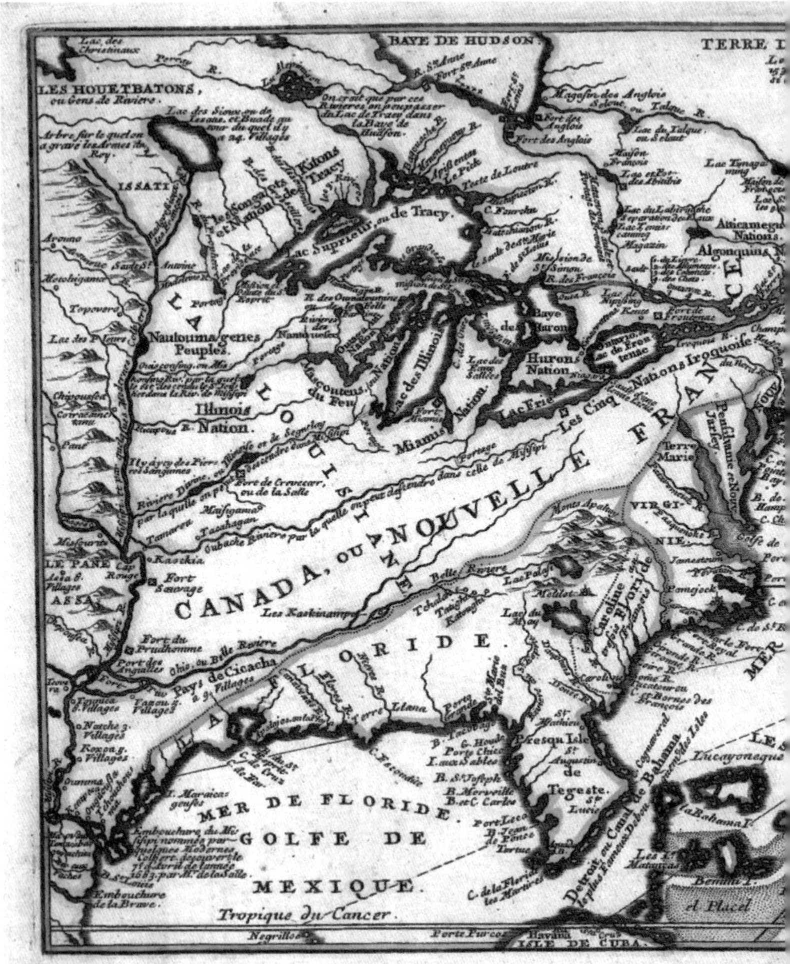
BAYE DE HUDSON
TERRE
LES HOUETBATONS, ou Gens de Riviere
Lac Suprieur, ou de Tracy
Lac des Illinois
Lac Erie
Ontario, ou Lac de Frontenac
Hurons Nation
Les Cinq Nations Iroquoise
Algonquins
Illinois Nation
Nadouessis
Mascoutens, ou Nation du Feu
Miamis Nation
Fort de Crevecoeur, ou de la Salle
Kaskekia
Fort Sauvage
Fort du Prudhomme
Ohio, ou Belle Riviere
Pays de Cicacha
Les Kaskinampo
LA LOUISIANE
CANADA, ou NOUVELLE FRANCE
LA FLORIDE
VIRGINIE
Caroline
Floride Françoise
Pensilvanie
Terre Marie
Jamestown
Monts Apalaches
Tegeste
MER DE FLORIDE
GOLFE DE MEXIQUE
Embouchure du Misisipi nommée par quelques Modernes Colbert, decouverte le 7 d'Avril de l'année 1683 par Mr. de la Salle
Embouchure de la Brave
Tropique du Cancer
ISLE DE CUBA
Havana
Negrillo
Porte Purcos
Detroit, ou Canal de Bahama
La Bahama I.
Les Matancas
el Placel
Bemini I.
Lucayoneque
MER

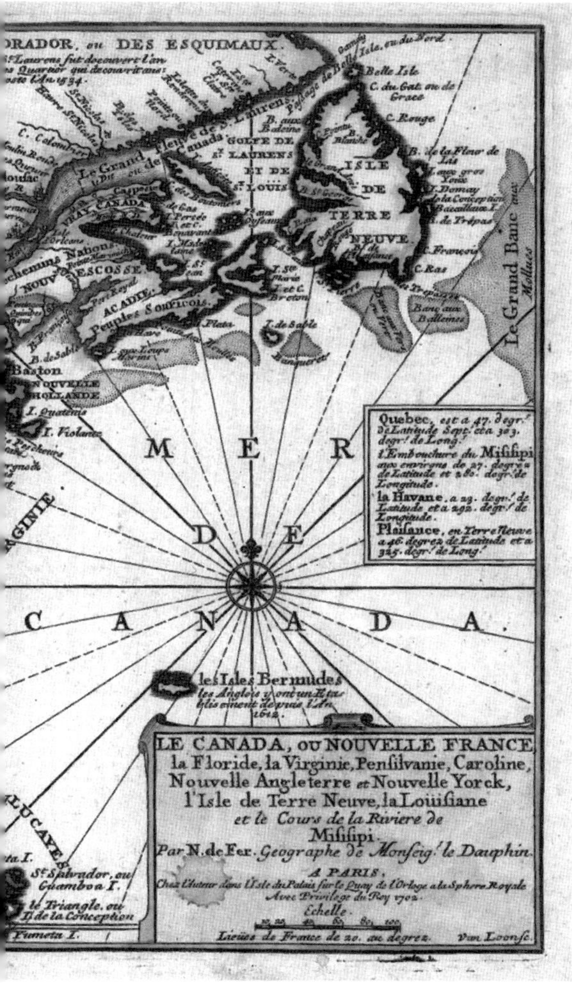

Nicolas de Fer's 1702 map of Canada, New France and North America. http://en.wikipedia.org/wiki/File:Fer_-_Le_Canada_ou_Nouvelle_France,_la_Floride,_la_Virginie,_Pensilvanie,_Caroline.png. *Photograph by Frank Schulenburg.*

lands in the northern reaches of New Spain. The mission honored the Virgin Mary at the Holy Spirit Bay (now known as Matagorda and Lavaca Bay) and Báthasar de Zúñiga, a viceroy of New Spain.[162]

The original 1721 location was very near the site of Fort St. Louis, La Salle's failed attempt to defend France's claim to this region of North America (see page 31). Just as La Salle's settlers fell to the raids of the nearby Karankawas (see page 34), so did the people of Espíritu Santo. In 1775, the mission and the protecting soldiers moved away from the coast, thirty miles inland. In the next year, another mission was established nearby along the Guadalupe River. This mission struggled to thrive. One of the problems surfaced quickly when the Karankawas, who were the intended recipients of the missionaries' work, fell ill and died from epidemics of diseases that the Spaniards brought with them. The Karankawas, as often happened, faced possible extinction. They fled to their coastal marshes and "killed any Spaniards who came after them. The Karankawas ever afterward avoided all contact with Europeans, but they had already received a fatal blow."[163]

Eventually, in 1749, Espíritu Santo was relocated to its fourth and final site on the lower San Antonio River near the current city of Goliad.

The mission had a difficult time defending itself from Apache raids and experienced great trouble economically. By 1780, the cattle herd had declined by 80 percent. By 1786, only 116 people still lived at the mission. It fell

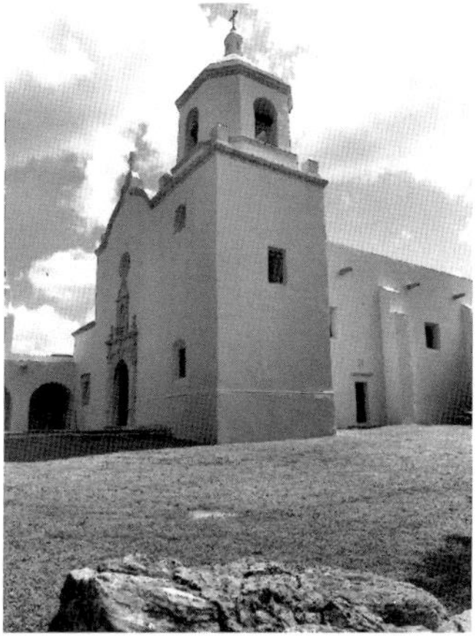

Mission Nuestra Señora de Espíritu Santo de Zúñiga (Espíritu Santo Mission). *Photograph by Larry D. Moore.*

on more hard times, and by 1830, no Native Americans lived at the mission: "Although the mission had lasted 109 years—longer than most other missions—the charge to Christianize the native peoples had not succeeded."[164]

Despite the noted difficulties, the mission did succeed in planting successfully the seeds of a cattle-raising economy: "Espíritu Santo is traditionally recognized as the first great cattle ranch in Texas." The herd was estimated to have forty thousand heads of cattle in 1778. Native American cowhands drove the cattle to eastern Texas and Louisiana, where they "exchanged [them] for corn and other supplies."[165]

Nuestra Señora del Espíritu Santo de Zúñiga Mission fell into disrepair over time from lack of maintenance and abuse. The mission has been beautifully restored by the Civilian Conservation Corps and the Works Progress Administration with supervision by the National Park Service and the University of Texas during the New Deal era from 1933 to 1941. The mission is now part of the Goliad State Historical Park administered by the Texas Parks and Wildlife Department.[166]

OLD SAN ANTONIO ROAD

A developing society seeking to thrive and maintain its dominance in its territory needs practical and reliable transportation for hunters, explorers, immigrants, soldiers, missionaries and traders. In the United States for hundreds of years, Native Americans made trails that European immigrants turned into roads suitable for wagon travel. These roads evolved into highways and, in some cases, controlled access and egress to interstate highways serving thousands of cars and trucks every day. In 1751, a private land company, the Ohio Company, created Braddock Trail connecting the Potomac River population with the site where the Monongahela and Allegheny Rivers meet to form the Ohio River, the future site of Pittsburgh, Pennsylvania. One of the first federal expenses to foster transportation and trade followed the Braddock Trail. It was called the Cumberland Road, authorized by President Thomas Jefferson in 1806. It went west from Cumberland, Maryland, toward the newly settled state of Ohio. In 1811, the road was extended and reached the Ohio River in 1818, when it was renamed the National Road. Today, much of that road is U.S. Highway 40 and, in some places, Interstate 70.[167]

In Texas, a similar development pattern occurred with the evolution of an east–west road that began in several places as Native American trails. The Old San Antonio Road is the name currently used for the eighteenth-century road known historically as *El Camino Real*, the King's Highway. This Spanish term is also found in California along the south–north route connecting the Spanish missions from San Diego de Alcalá to San Francisco de Solano, north of the San Francisco Bay. It is also the name of a highway in western Texas and New Mexico as the south–north road between El Paso, Texas, to Santa Fe and Taos, New Mexico.

The Spanish explorers, soldiers and missionaries developed the King's Highway during the course of three expeditions. Alonso de León led his fourth expedition in 1690 to eastern Texas to establish a mission, San Francisco de los Tejas (see page 88). His route often followed some trails used by the Caddos for hundreds of years. In the next year, Domingo Terán de los Ríos,

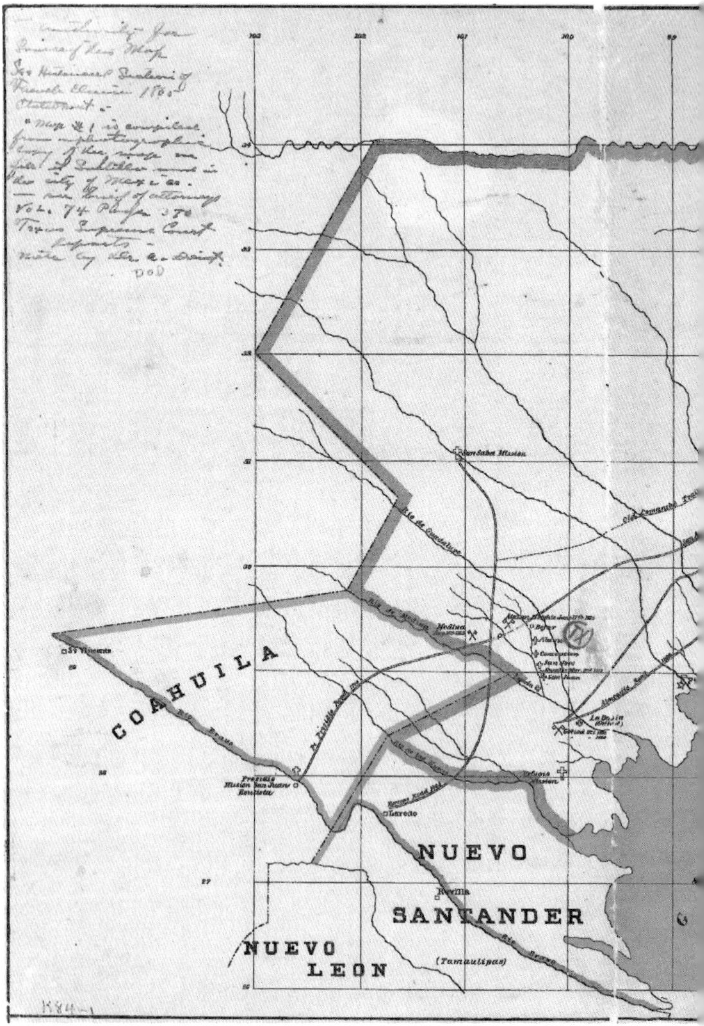
COAHUILA
NUEVO
SANTANDER
(Tamaulipas)
NUEVO
LEON
Laredo
Revilla
Rio Bravo
San Saba Mission
Presidio Mision San Juan Bautista
La Bahia
Bejar
Medina
Rio de Guadalupe

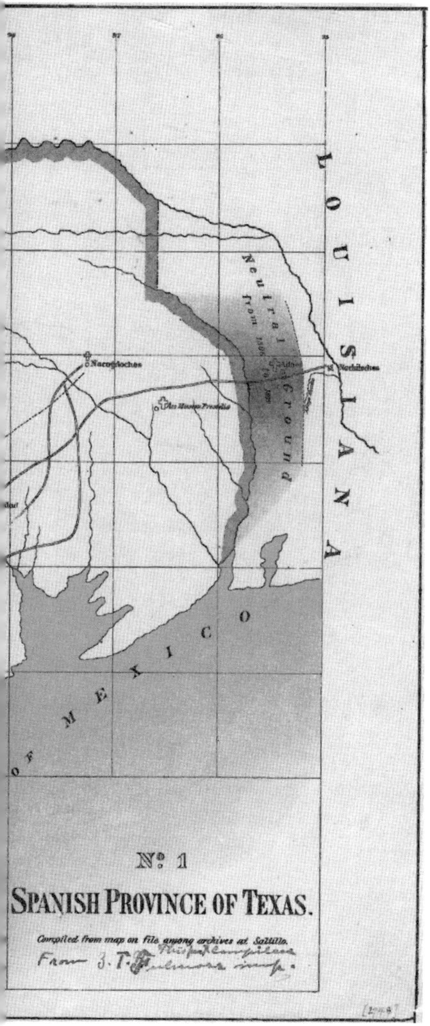

the first governor of Coahuila y Tejas, forded the Rio Grande as he escorted missionaries to the new mission that León had just helped establish. In 1693, Gregorio de Salinas Varona (see page 171) left Monclova, a major city in Coahuila y Tejas, to bring supplies to the same new mission. In 1714, Louis Juchereau de St. Denis, a Frenchman, journeyed west from Natchitoches in present-day Louisiana to the San Juan Bautista Mission on the south bank of the Rio Grande, near present-day Guerrero, Coahuila.

A map of *Spanish Province of Texas*, circa 1700–1821. The Old San Antonio Road is shown from its southwestern beginning at the Presidio and Mission San Juan Bautista in Coahuila, Mexico, as it crosses the Rio Grande and then goes northeasterly to Natchitoches, Louisiana. *Courtesy State and Library and Archives Commission, Maps Collection, Map Number 2748.*

Over time, the road encompassed several related routes that generally followed an east–west direction on a south–north axis, from Saltillo, Coahuila, to Natchitoches, Louisiana: "The Old San Antonio Road [was] a network of trails with different routes used at different times. Feeder roads branched off the main course." The road took on three major directions: the lower, middle and upper road. Stephen F. Austin called the route he used to bring immigrants to his colony in Texas the *Camino Arriba*, the Upper Road.[168]

The Old San Antonio Road, with all its many variations, traversed 2,500 miles as it "linked a variety of cultural and linguistic groups and served as an agent for cultural diffusion, biological exchange, and communication."[169] An example of the cultural interaction is described in the diary of Pierre Marie François de Pagés, who made several journeys on the road in eastern Texas. In 1768, he wrote about a chance encounter with some Ais Indians. He was welcomed by women "with cakes made of wild fruit" and men who "were at great pains to put me in the best path, and to instruct me what stages were most convenient for feeding my mule."[170] The road was used as an early cattle trail to drive cattle from the coastal savannah lands of Texas to the more arid city of Saltillo, Coahuila.

In 1915, the Texas legislature employed V.N. Zively, a professional engineer, to study and determine the actual route of the Old San Antonio Road. After studying historic records and physical features, he laid out a 540-mile-long route from the Rio Grande at Paso de Francia north to Cotulla, Poteet and San Antonio and then northeast to cross the Sabine River at Gaines Ferry into Louisiana.[171] In 1918, the Daughters of the American Revolution paid for 123 roadside markers to be placed along the route that Zively had set. In 1929, the Texas legislature officially designated Zively's route as the Old San Antonio Road.

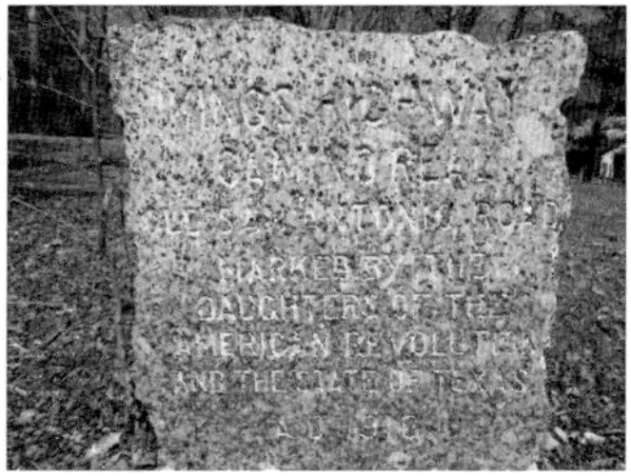

A marker of the "King's Highway, El Camino Real, Old San Antonio Road. Marker placed by the Daughters of the American Revolution and the State of Texas, A.D. 1918." Located at the Nuestra Señora de los Dolores de los Aies Mission in San Augustine, Texas. *Photograph by the author.*

In 2004, President George W. Bush "signed a bill designating The El Camino Real de los Tejas, of which the Old San Antonio Road is part, a National Historic Trail."[172] The U.S. National Park Service operates the National Historic Trail with visitor centers, interpretive information and educational presentations.

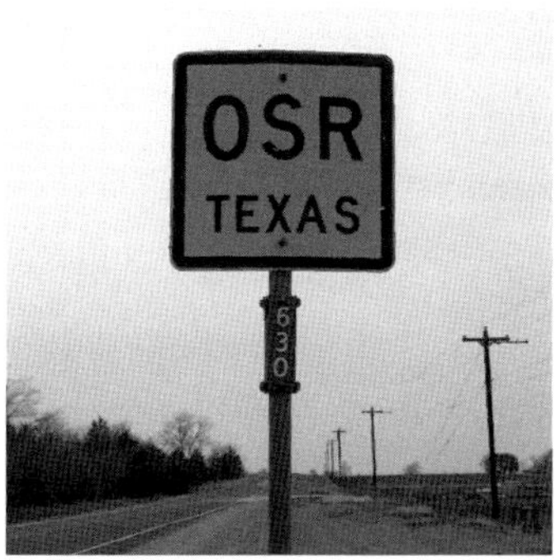

A highway sign on Texas State Highway 21 located 15.4 miles west of Crockett, Texas, marking "OSR Texas," the Old San Antonio Road. *Photograph by the author.*

JUAN DE OÑATE

Francisco Vásquez de Coronado led a Spanish exploration in the 1540s north from New Spain into what would become the southwestern United States. Coronado so thoroughly squandered opportunity, gambled and fiercely treated Pueblo Indians that he was tried by Spanish authorities. Juan de Oñate followed up Coronado's explorations.

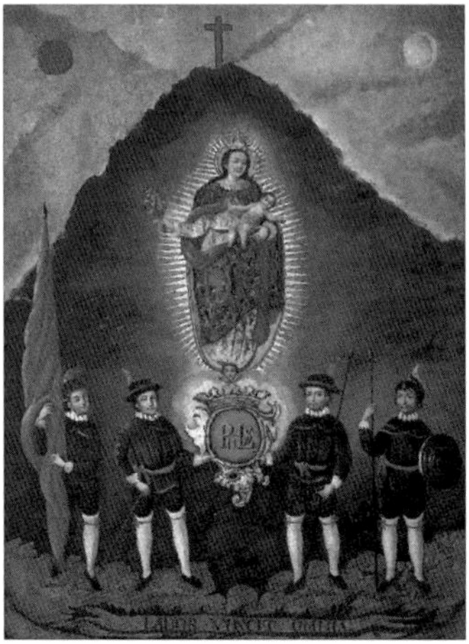

Image of the original banner as a coat of arms granted to the city of Zacatecas, Juan de Oñate's birthplace. *Photograph by anonimo.*

Oñate was well born in Zacatecas, New Spain; related to powerful leaders; and a descendant of Hernán Cortés. Zacatecas was an important city in central Mexico as shown in its coat of arms on the banner commemorating King Philip II's royal grant in 1584. The motto reads *Labor Vincit Omni*, "labor conquers all." The Spaniards who claimed and settled New Spain followed this creed attributed to Virgil in *Georgic, Book I.* Virgil was promoting "Augustus Caesar's 'Back to the land' policy encouraging more Romans to become farmers."[173] The state of Zacatecas still embraces this motto.

This call to industry and labor was heard by Juan de Oñate. He lived his life in

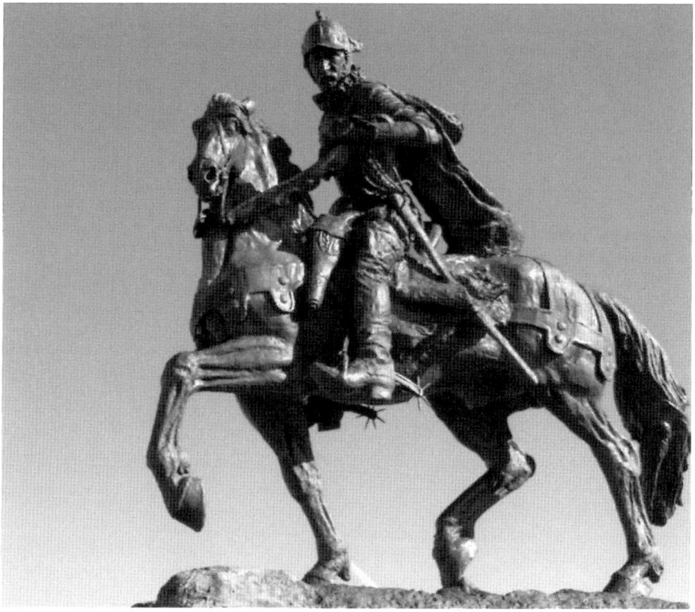

Equestrian statue of Juan de Oñate at the San Juan Pueblo, Oñate Monument Center, Alcalde, New Mexico. *Photograph by Mario1952.*

service to his king and his causes, laboring hard for many years. Oñate answered the call to work when he came north nearly sixty years after Coronado to make a more permanent claim on the new lands, its people and its resources. Oñate also dealt brutal punishment to the people of Acoma Pueblo tribe; he treated them so severely that he was also tried and convicted

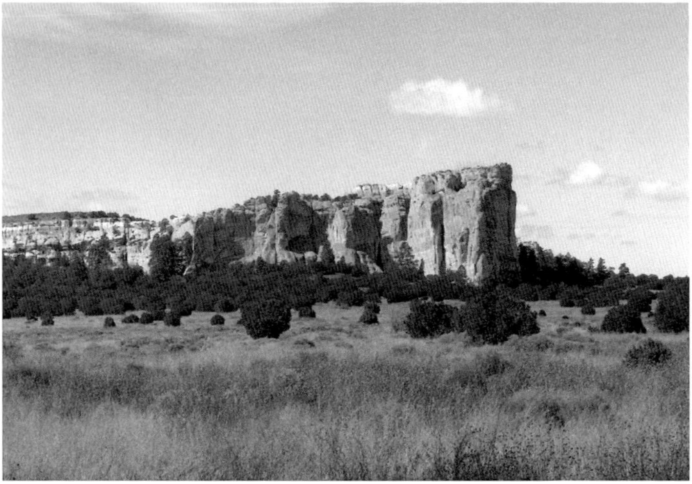

El Morro (the Headland), site of Inscription Rock, where Juan de Oñate carved his message in 1605. *Photograph by Joel Mills.*

of his cruel amputations, murders and enslavement of more than one thousand people. Oñate's guilty verdict was overturned, and he regained the favor of Spanish royalty so much that he was named governor and captain general of the province of New Mexico.

On May 8, 1598, he crossed the Rio Grande and named the crossing at this northern pass in the mountains "El Paso del Río del Norte."[174] Americans know this river as the Rio Grande and the site as El Paso.

Juan de Oñate's entourage included three types of people specialized to do different tasks all working together to solidify Spanish dominance in the new lands. First, soldiers came to round up and take control of the Native American populations. Second, priests worked to convert and baptize the Indians and lead them to support the economy of the Spanish missions and settlements. Third, 130 families accompanied the soldiers and were there to set roots in the new lands and bring a permanent colonial society "to set a Spanish peasantry in North American soil."[175] In addition to these significant Spanish people accompanying him, Oñate brought along seven thousand domestic animals, including horses and cattle. Introducing these animals forever changed the society, economy and warfare practiced in Texas and the American southwest.

In 1601, Oñate went farther north and east into present-day Oklahoma. He was searching for a fabled city of great wealth, Quivira. There he fought with the Wichita Indians, who killed or wounded most of his men. Oñate retreated westward toward present-day New Mexico, where he founded Santa Fe, the capital of New Mexico. Oñate's journey north to Oklahoma marked the end of Spain's quests to find Quivira, a place of golden wealth.[176]

While on one of his journeys through the area, he stopped at a large mountain outcropping and carved his name into what is now called "Inscription Rock" at El Morro National Monument in New Mexico. On April 16, 1605, he left this message: "*Paso por aqui*" (Passed by here).[177]

P

PENATEKA COMANCHE INDIANS

The early Spanish explorers of the southwestern United States saw so many buffaloes they could not count them. There were millions upon millions of them. The economy of the Plains Indians was based on the hunting of the buffalo for food and other uses, such as hides for shelter and fur for winter robes.

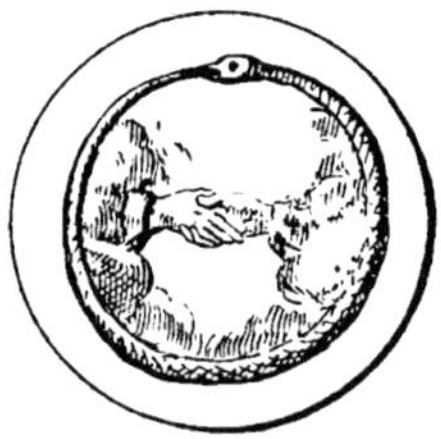

One of the largest groups of Plains Indians was the Comanches, who divided themselves into several territories. The Penateka Comanches lived in south-central Texas, along the

Balcones Escarpment, the area many Texans now call the Hill Country.

In the early 1840s, one of Queen Victoria's cousins, Prince Carl of Solms-Braunfels, came to Texas to select locations for future German settlers. Thousands of Germans, primarily from Hesses, Hannover and Brunswick, answered the call to *Geh mit ins Texas*, meaning "Go with us to Texas." The prince's deputy, Baron Otfried Hans, Freiherr von Meusebach, led the immigrants from the Texas coastal towns of Galveston and Indianola inland and helped establish New Braunfels. Later on, he was known as John O. Meusebach.

Baron Meusebach, accompanied by Major Robert S. Neighbors, met with several Penateka chiefs near present-day Mason. He proposed a treaty to mark the cooperation he envisioned between the Native Americans and the German immigrants. The baron said he recognized that the Penatekas owned this area and stressed that he and his people were different from others whom they had come to distrust. He said his people were neither Mexicans nor Texans. They were *alemanes*, Germans.

The Penateka leaders agreed to share their hunting territory with the Germans, as they thought of them as a separate tribe. Meusebach offered $1,000 cash and other gifts. Two Delaware war chiefs, Jim Shaw and John Conner, participated in the negotiations in early March 1847.

The German immigrants and the Comanche Indians concluded their negotiations and signed the "Treaty Between

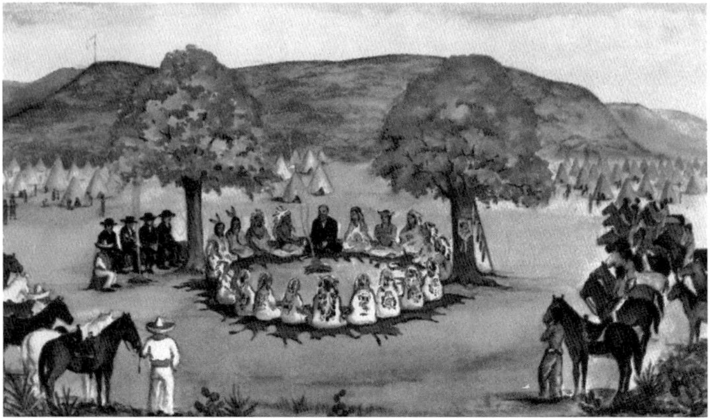

Treaty of Peace by John O. Meusebach and Colonists with the Comanches, March 2, 1847. A painting by Mrs. Ernest Marshall, daughter of John O. Meusebach. *Courtesy Texas State Library and Archives Commission, Prints and Photographs Collection, No. 1/104-196.*

the Commissary General of the German Immigration Company and the Comanche Nation" on May 9, 1847.[178]

Both sides found a reliable guarantee of an essential need. The Germans could build their farms and towns while respecting the rights of the Penatekas to continue hunting in the surrounding lands.

Major Neighbors was impressed with the success of this treaty and worked to adapt it in a wider scale. In 1851, as a member of the Texas House of Representatives, Neighbors was appointed chairman of the Committee on Indian Affairs (see page 210). He and his friend Captain John S. Ford, a member of the Texas Senate,

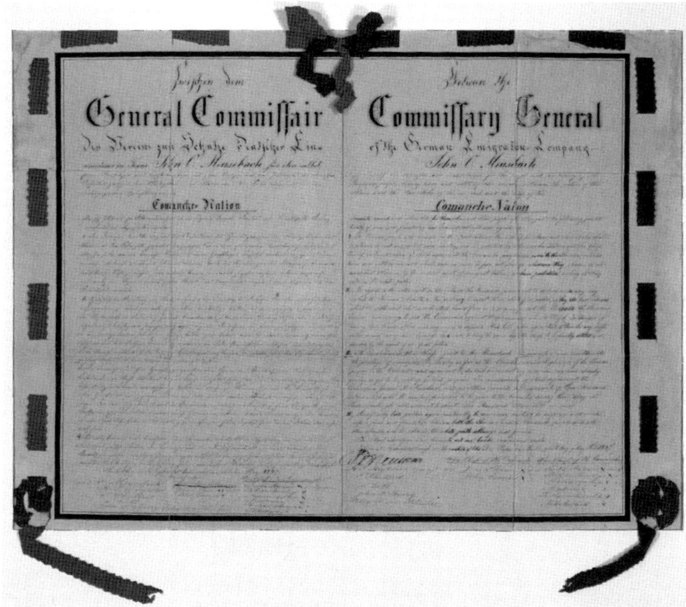

The treaty document "Between the General Commissary of the German Immigration Company John O. Meusebach and the Comanche Nation," May 9, 1847. *Courtesy Texas State Library and Archives Commission, Prints and Photographs Collection, #1973/3-1-B.*

"introduced a joint resolution authorizing the [Texas] governor to negotiate with the president of the United States for the establishment of an Indian territory in the northern part of the state."[179] Neither the territory nor its peaceful motives ever became a reality.

Although the Penateka Comanches had often fought previously and would do so in the future with other Texans, their friendly relations with the German settlers remain intact to the present day. The treaty is written in both German and English. It was a rarity in American history, a treaty between Native Americans and Euro-Americans that "was never broken."[180]

The treaty document was taken to Germany. In 1970, Mrs. Irene Marschall King and Dr. Cornelia Marschall Smith, granddaughters of John O. Meusebach, returned the document to Texas.[181] They presented it to the Texas State Archives in Austin, Texas. The treaty is occasionally featured in an exhibit at the archives' lobby.

After extensive public service, including service as member of the Texas Senate, John O. Meusebach lived the rest of his life as a merchant, farmer and rancher. His last home was in Loyal Valley, Texas. He lived eighty-two years, dying in 1897. He is buried in the Marschall-Meusebach Cemetery along with his extended family in the Cherry Spring community north of Fredericksburg, Texas. His motto, "Texas Forever," is carved into his tombstone providing information on two sides, one in German and one in English.

PETROGLYPHS AND PICTOGRAPHS

Early Texas history derived and understood from documentary evidence begins with the arrival of Europeans in the 1500s.

However, there exists an earlier record of human life and distinct culture from at least ten thousand years before the Europeans arrived. Thousands of years ago, people lived in Texas. They led a full life using stone tools as they hunted and gathered their food, built shelters and lived connected directly to their location's terrain and its mineral resources, water, plants and animals. Their lives involved work and an appreciation of spirituality, and they were recorded and shared in art. Petroglyphs are rock carvings and pictographs are rock paintings; they have been found at many Texas archaeological sites.

The size of petroglyphs and pictographs vary greatly. Some are only one or two inches tall while others are as high as eighteen feet. Some are high above ground level, and others are hidden deeply inside caves. Most commonly, the colors used are earth tones created from powdered minerals mixed with animal fats. Black and red are most frequently seen, as well as white, yellow, brown and orange.

Styles and subjects include human figures, hand and foot outlines and animals, such as deer, mountain lions, buffalo, snakes and birds. One may infer from the stylistic differences between such locations as Hueco Tanks and the Pecos River Valley styles that the cultures differed significantly.

Symbols are employed of various natural elements such as the sun, trees and various shapes. Sometimes a group is depicted in communal or spiritual activity. Images suggest shamanic and ceremonial action. The art relates work, hunting, warfare, dancing and likely stories or myths. Some sites show what appear to be tallies. Some even appear humorous.

This amazing trove of beautiful art was made at different times in different places. Archaeologists believe the dates range from about ten thousand years ago to historic times as late as the 1700s showing European influences.[182]

Early Texans lived in places dispersed around the state, including the following partial list. Each site records related but different cultures living in different millennia.

- Alibates Flint Quarries National Monument in Moore and Potter Counties, near Amarillo, Texas
- Amistad National Recreation Area near Del Rio, Texas
- Big Bend Ranch State Natural Area
- Burro Mesa Archeological District in Big Bend National Park
- Devil's River State Park in rough terrain many miles from Del Rio, Texas
- Hueco Tanks State Historic Site, thirty-two miles northeast of El Paso, Texas
- Landergin Mesa near Adrian, Texas
- Levi Rock Shelter, a National Historic Place, along Lick Creek, west of Austin, Texas
- Lobo Valley Petroglyph Site in southern Culberson County, Texas
- Lubbock Lake Site in Lubbock, Texas

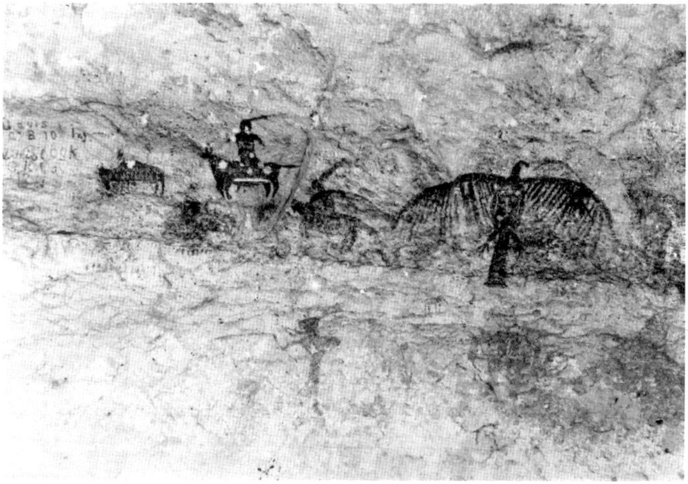

A rock painting found in Brewster County, Texas, photographed in 1936 by Everett Ewing Townsend (1871–1948). He worked for decades to create Big Bend National Park and is known as the park's father. The images suggest hunters and a large bird. *Courtesy Texas State Library and Archives Commission, Prints & Photographs Collection # 1936-009-11.*

- M.D. Harrell Site near South Bend, Texas, in Young County
- Paint Rock, sixteen miles south of Ballinger, Texas
- Panther Cave Site, near Seminole Canyon State Park
- Rattlesnake Canyon, west of Langtry, Texas, in Val Verde County.
- Running Water Draw, near Plainview, Texas
- Seminole Canyon State Historical Park, nine miles west of Comstock, Texas

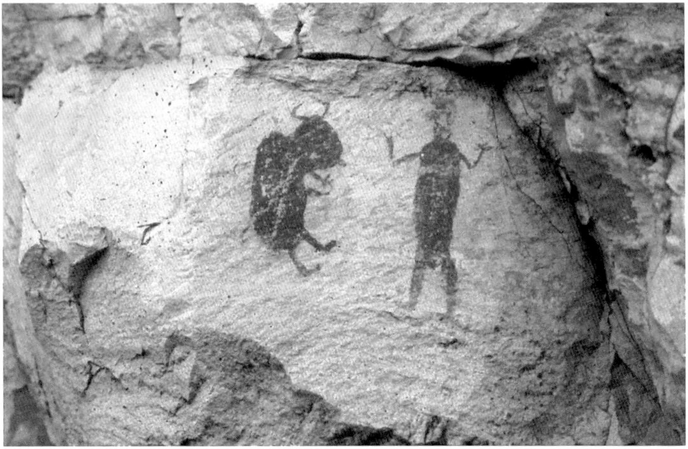

A rock painting found at the RNK Ranch near Del Rio, Texas. The two figures appear to be a hunter and a bison. The Texas Tourist Development Agency took this photograph in the 1970s to use in promoting tourism in Texas. *Courtesy Texas State Library and Archives Commission, Prints & Photographs Collection # 1991-007-413-10.*

Individuals, faculty and students of several Texas universities; curators and staff of Texas museums; members of private organizations such as the Rock Art Foundation and the Texas Archeological Society; and staff of governmental agencies, such as the Texas Parks and Wildlife Department and the United States National Park Service have worked for decades to study, preserve, curate and record the incomparable art in the petroglyphs and pictographs.

ZEBULON MONTGOMERY PIKE

Zebulon Montgomery Pike had a brief life of only thirty-four years, but he had a long-lasting impact as a military officer, explorer and cartographer. He was born in New Jersey in 1779 during the American Revolutionary War and died in Canada at the Battle of York at present-day Toronto, Ontario, in 1813 during the War of 1812.[183]

Pike was instrumental in exploring, mapping and reporting on the people, topography, vegetation, animals, waters and other geographic details about the places he explored. His reports spurred interest among Americans leading to their continued emigration from the eastern United States into Spanish territory, particularly to Texas.

Pike's family moved westward to frontier outposts as the nation grew. He joined his father's regiment as a cadet at age fifteen and was commissioned at age twenty. He married Clarissa Harlow Brown in 1801, and they had one daughter, Clarissa Brown Pike. She married John Cleves Symmes Harrison, a son of President William Henry Harrison.

While working in logistics and doing administrative tasks at Fort Bellefontaine near St. Louis, Missouri, he was noticed by General James Wilkinson (see page 211), who became Pike's mentor. While Lewis and Clark trekked west to follow the Missouri River and seek for a route to the Pacific Ocean, Pike went north in 1805 to find the source of the Mississippi River. Pike reported the

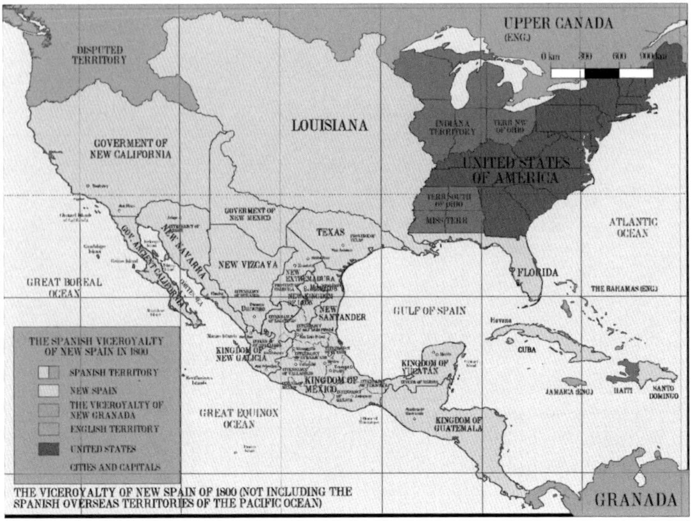

A map of the viceroyalty of New Spain in 1800. *From http://en.wikipedia.org/wiki/File:Viceroyalty_of_New_Spain_1800_(without_Philippines).png (accessed March 14, 2014).*

details of his exploration in *An Account of a Voyage*.

Upon his return, the general ordered Pike in 1806 to locate the source of the Arkansas and Red Rivers. President Thomas Jefferson wanted to know more details and have a map of Louisiana that included "its contour and main waters, giving them a 'skeleton to be filled up with details hereafter.'"[184] The known areas of North America show Spain dominating much of western North America at this time.

During this expedition into Spanish territory, present-day New Mexico, Captain Pike was apprehended by

Spanish authorities and taken first to Santa Fe and then to Chihuahua. He was treated well and enjoyed the good wines and food the Spanish served him. At the same time, he felt great empathy for another American held captive there, David Ferro. Ferro had served as Pike's father's aide-de-camp when he was younger. Ferro was captured in 1801 when he was with Philip Nolan and others on a horse-gathering trip. They planned to gather horses and take them to Louisiana to sell them. Nolan and some others were killed in a skirmish near present-day Blum and Rio Vista, Texas (see page 136). Pike said, "Our meeting was affecting, tears standing in his eyes."[185] Pike kept extensive notes, which the Spanish read and translated for their use.[186] The Spanish alleged Pike was a spy. President Jefferson denied this in a letter of August 10, 1807, to Secretary of War James Madison "by saying that this government has never employed a spy in any case & that Pike's mission was to ascend the Arkansas & descend the Red River for the purpose of ascertaining their geography."[187]

The Spanish escorted Pike and most of his men back to the United States through Texas. Pike's journey began on June 1, 1807, going from Chihuahua northeast to the Rio Grande, which he crossed and went through what is now Carrizo Springs, across the Nueces, Frio and Medina Rivers to San Antonio. The men continued northeast across the San Antonio, Comal, Guadalupe and Colorado Rivers through what is now Bastrop and then across the Brazos River near Bryan. They then jogged north across the Trinity River through Crockett and turned east to cross the Angelina River to Nacogdoches, where they continued east across the Sabine River to arrive in Natchitoches, Louisiana, on July 1, 1807.[188] On June 24, 1807, Pike camped at the site of the Caddoan Mounds (see page 112) near present-day Alto, Texas.[189] After Captain Pike returned to the United States, his map of the Spanish lands was of great interest to many Americans. Americans now knew more details of what lay west of Louisiana and what the future may hold for possible expansion westward.

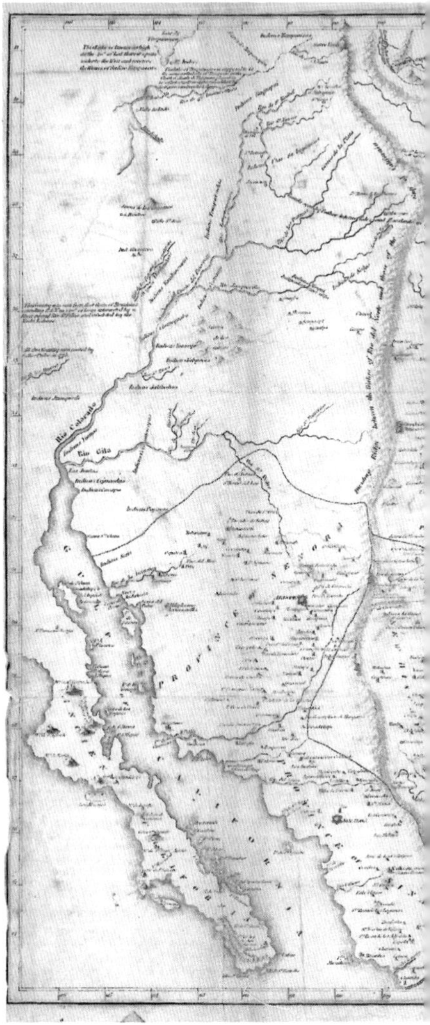

Zebulon Montgomery Pike's journey and reports provided detailed information about new lands to the west of American settlement. Few individuals have had such significant impact on the nation's development in such a short life. The nation mourned as he fell at the Battle of York

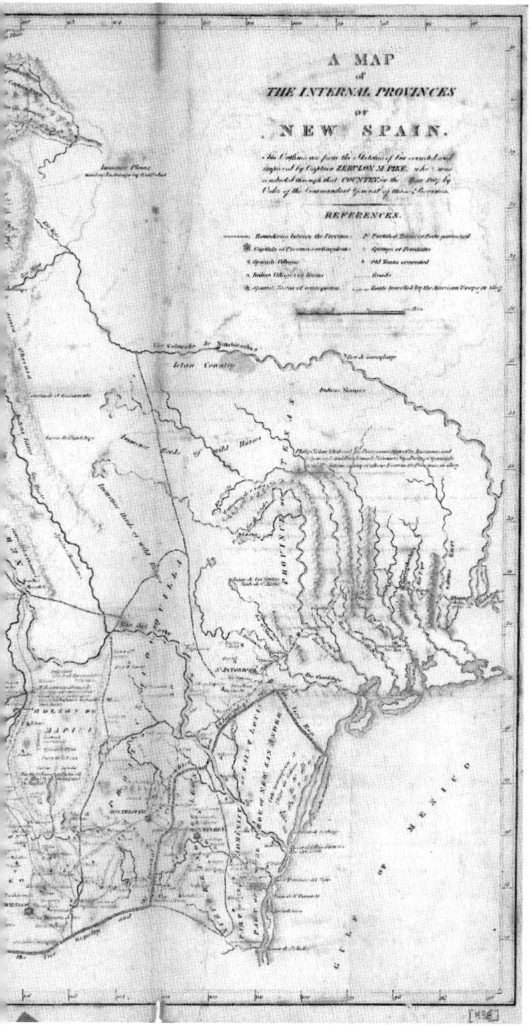

Captain Zebulon Pike's 1807 *Map of the Interior Provinces of New Spain. Courtesy Texas State Library and Archives Commission, Map Collection No. 1438.*

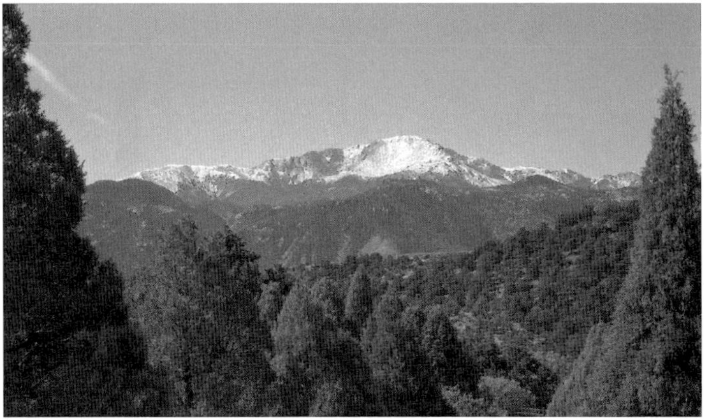

Pike's Peak. *Photograph by Hogs555.*

when the British detonated their powder magazine and killed Pike and 21 others and wounded 222 more soldiers.[190]

Colorado has fifty-four mountains higher than 14,000 feet. The easternmost of these is the Arapaho-named *heey-otoyoo* (long mountain). The Spanish later called it *El Capitán.* This 14,115-foot-high mountain that Zebulon Pike and his men explored in November 1806 is known to most people now as Pike's Peak, named for Zebulon Montgomery Pike Jr.[191]

QUILTING

Few activities were as widespread in Texas history as quilting. Quilting offered many ways to satisfy early Texans. Quilts provided a way for people to stay warm in the depth of a winter fraught with "blue northers" bringing falling temperatures and rain, sleet and even snow in the northern reaches of Texas.

Making quilts also gave women a way to meet one another, share work, socialize with old friends and make new friends at a "quilting bee" that would last from one day to several days. Quilters sometimes sold their quilts to have some extra family income or have a fund for the makers to have for their own use. Sometimes this was called "pin money." Quilts were also used as a trade good for bartering with neighbors. In some cases, quilts were even used to wrap a body for burial.

Women from many cultures quilted and brought their skills and traditions to Texas with them. Many women in eighteenth-century Spanish Texas made beautiful quilts for their family's use as well as a way to express artistic interests. They used embroidery and other fine needlecrafts in their quilts, often featuring bright colors. The *colchas bordadas*, "embroidered quilts," followed styles popular in early Mexico.

When people painted "GTT" on their doors and barns, they were telling neighbors they had "Gone to Texas." Quilts were in those wagons heading west to Texas from the United States. These women built on the European traditions they had known in the design, fabric and quilting methods used.[192] They followed familiar traditions and patterns, including "wedding ring" and "crazy" quilts.

The African American slaves who moved to Texas contributed some styles from Africa, especially found in quilts they made for themselves. For example, they made "string quilts" similar to textiles found in West Africa. Often, these quilts used whatever fabric was available, such as old socks, pants, shirts, coats and flour sacks.[193]

In later years, quilting was found in clothing as well as in bed coverings. Japanese immigrants brought with them the centuries-old use of quilting outerwear to guard against a winter chill and totes and purses to provide strength.

One of the most famous quilts in Texas history was made by

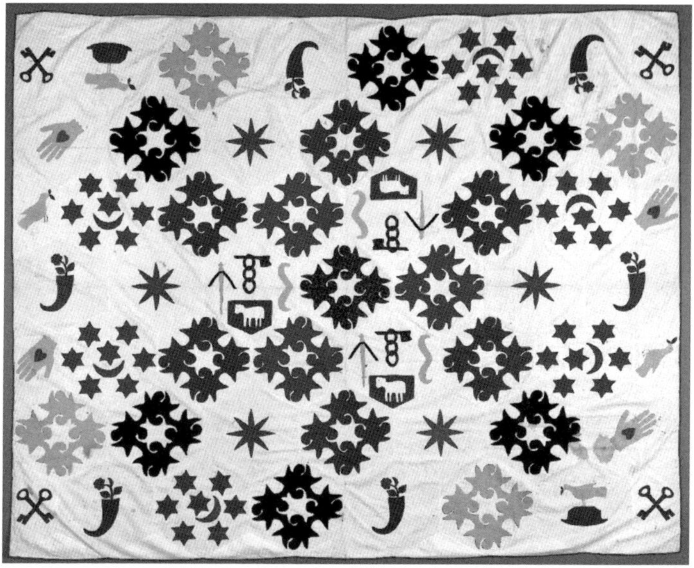

Margaret Lea Houston's summer spread. *Courtesy Texas State Library and Archives Commission, DSC_9260.*

Sam Houston's wife, Margaret Moffette Lea Houston, whom he married in 1840. It is displayed at the Sam Houston Memorial Museum in Huntsville.[194]

Margaret Lea Houston made a "summer spread." It has bright colors of blues, greens and reds on a muslin spread. The imagery intricately uses appliques of varied shapes and images, including some Masonic symbols. This quilt is featured in an award-winning documentary, *Quilts in Women's Lives*, by Pat Ferrero.[195]

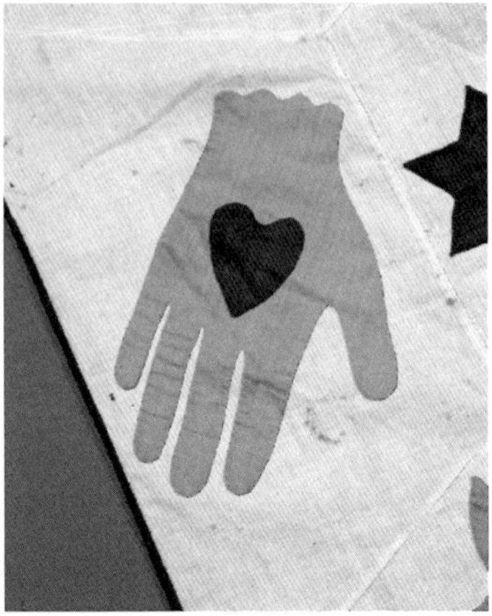

Quilting remains popular and practiced all throughout Texas. Contemporary quilts are just as often made for artistic expression as for practical use. Thousands of quilters meet regularly in more than twenty guilds offering classes, demonstrations, lectures and exhibits. Annual shows draw thousands of visitors each year.[196] Smithville, Texas, still honors the traditional "airing of the quilts" every fall with quilts displayed while airing along the main street of the town.

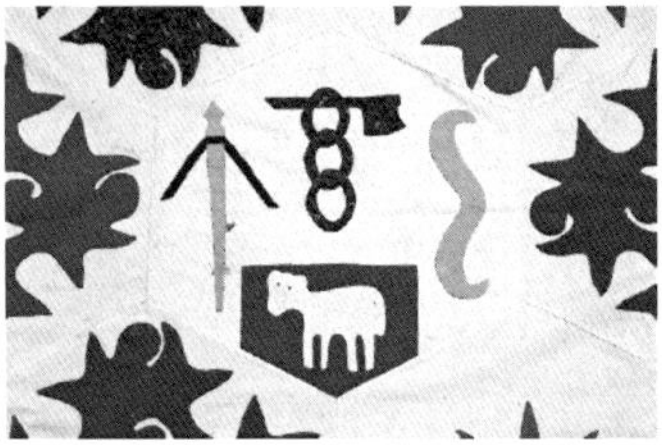

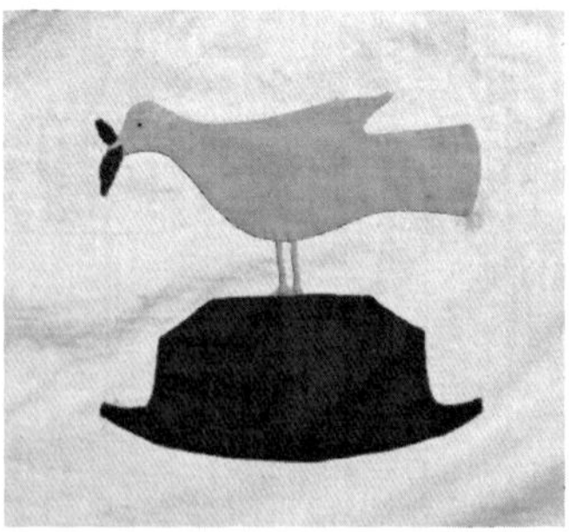

Top: Detail of a heart on a hand in Margaret Lea Houston's summer spread. *Courtesy of Texas State Library and Archives Commission, DSC_9260.*

Middle: Detail of Masonic symbols in Margaret Lea Houston's summer spread. *Courtesy of Texas State Library and Archives Commission, DSC_9260.*

Bottom: Detail of the dove of peace in Margaret Lea Houston's summer spread. *Courtesy of Texas State Library and Archives Commission, DSC_9260.*

R

DIEGO AND DOMINGO RAMÓN

Diego and Domingo Ramón were father and son who served for fifty years in the vanguard of Spanish settlement efforts in northern New Spain.

Diego Ramón was a soldier with the 1674 Bosque-Larios Expedition in Coahuila, New Spain. He crossed the Rio Grande in 1688 into Texas with Governor Alonso de León to capture a Frenchman, Jean Jarry. Upon de León's death in 1691, Diego Ramón was the interim governor of Coahuila y Tejas. He was succeeded by Gregorio de Salinas Varona (see page 45). Diego Ramón assisted in founding a mission, San Francisco Xavier near Monclova, Coahuila. He also aided in the move of the San Juan Bautista Mission (see page 88) to its new site near present-day Guerrero, Coahuila. He continued to serve as a guardian of the mission there until he died in 1724.[197]

One of Diego Ramón's most notable feats was an expedition that he led beginning on Mach 9, 1707, to accomplish three tasks: (1) punish some Native Americans who had raided settlements in Coahuila and Nuevo León, in northern New Spain; (2) recruit some more Native Americans who would be willing to move to the Rio Grande–area missions; and (3) explore the region.[198] The ford he used to cross the Rio Grande is named for him, the *Paso de Diego Ramón*. It is one of five fords across the river near the San Juan Bautista Mission.[199]

On March 22, 1707, Diego Ramón led forty-four soldiers and some Native American allies attacking a camp of Coahuiltecan Indians near present-day Cotulla, Texas. Five Coahuiltecan men died and twenty-five others, mostly women and children, were captured. Similar action took place at another nearby camp. Then Ramón returned an old man to talk with others and bring them gifts. The message he delivered was that the troops represented the Spanish king, who "had come to bring peace among the Indians and to save their souls, if they would gather in pueblos and missions they could enjoy many conveniences, both spiritual and temporal, and would be favored by the king."[200] The Coahuiltecans went with Ramón and reached the San Juan Bautista Mission on April 3, 1707. As Ramón entered the plaza, the soldiers fired celebratory rounds in the air and brought Native Americans to the mission to begin their new lives. The prisoners were put under guard, but eventually, they were freed and released into the care of the missionaries.[201]

The Spanish had not forgotten their claim to Texas, even though they had paid little attention and few people had settled there between 1693 and 1715. In order to counteract the French claims, especially in the area around the Sabine and Red Rivers and the coastal areas of Texas, the Spanish felt compelled to reassert their authority and sovereignty. Domingo Ramón was a significant actor in this effort to resettle Texas.

Domingo Ramón followed his father's profession as a soldier in service to the Spanish king. His most noteworthy action began on September 30, 1715, when he was named commander of a force charged to reestablish Spain's claim to Texas, especially in eastern Texas, where the French vied with Spain for dominance. The Ramón Expedition left on April 27, 1716, from the Rio Grande, guided by a Frenchman, Louis Juchereau de St. Denis (see page 89). The group included soldiers, friars, priests and some of the soldier's family members, totaling seventy-five people. They took livestock, supplies and equipment intended for use in the resettlement of the region. Fortunately, Domingo Ramón kept a diary, and we may learn many details of his travels.

The expedition arrived in late June near the original mission location. On the trail, the Spaniards encountered many Native Americans who were friendly and shared food with them. They also shared *a large pipe which is the one used solely for peace... The captains* [Native Americans leaders] *smoked first, and in this manner, the first puff of smoke towards the heaven, the second puff to the east, the third puff to the west, the fourth puff to the north, the fifth to the south, and the sixth to the earth, these demonstrations are those of true peace.*[202]

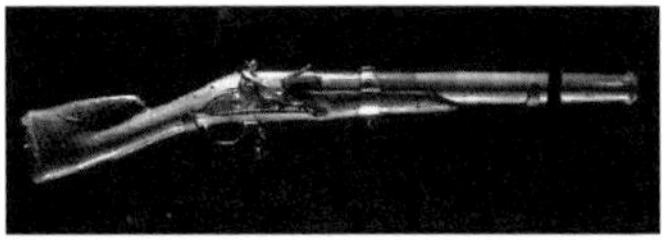

A French blunderbuss, very similar to the harquebus used on the Ramón Expedition of 1716. *Photograph by PHGCOM.*

On June 28, 1716, the expedition met more than 150 Native Americans and had a greeting that lasted more than one hour, including celebratory shots from French-made harquebuses. The exuberance continued in a more somber vein with the singing of a hymn of praise, "Te Deum Laudamus."

By July 3, 1716, the expedition had established Nuestro Padre Francisco de los Tejas Mission "in the town of Neches."[203] This is in the vicinity of the mission that was abandoned on October 25, 1693, when Father Damián Massanet set it afire and retreated to Coahuila, New Spain (see page 88). The Spanish founded three more missions in the area during 1716, including Nuestra Señora de la Purísima Concepción, Nuestra Señora de Guadalupe and San José de los Nazonis. Two more followed in 1717, Nuestra Señora de los Dolores de los Ais in present-day San Augustine. The last one they founded was San Miguel de Linares de los Adaes near

Natchitoches in present-day Louisiana (see page 90).[204]

Domingo Ramón remained in eastern Texas until all the Spanish left once again in 1719, following the "Chicken War" (see page 91) and retreating to San Antonio. He assisted the Marqués de Aguayo (see page 19) when he founded Nuestra Señora de Loreto Presidio at La Bahía, at the site of the ill-fated French Fort St. Louis. Domingo Ramón died on December 23, 1723, from a wound he suffered at a battle with the Karankawa Indians (see page 117).[205]

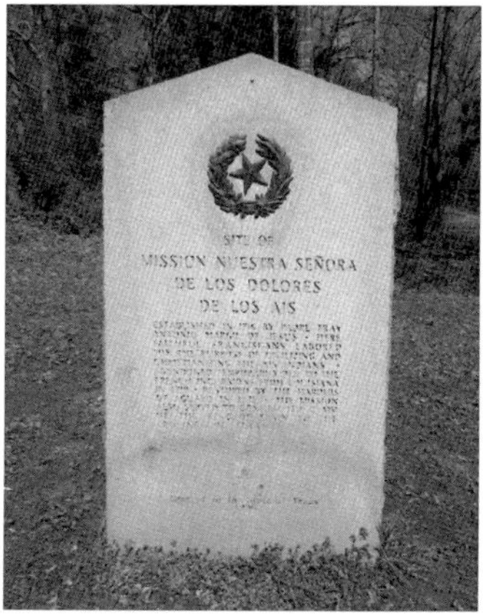

State of Texas centennial marker from 1936, marking the site of the Nuestra Señora de los Dolores de los Ais Mission in San Augustine, Texas. *Photograph by the author.*

Both Diego Ramón and his son Domingo were instrumental in keeping Spain's claim to northern New Spain, especially Texas. The efforts of Domingo Ramón and the others in his expedition "gave Spain a claim to lands north of the Rio Grande did much to determine that Texas would be Spanish, not French, and helped advance the eventual boundary between Texas and the United States to the Sabine River."[206]

REFUGIO MISSION

Spain had several motives for coming to the New World that involved the Native

Americans they met. One of the most powerful motives was to transplant Spanish ideals of civilization. Increasing the realm of Christendom was uppermost in the thoughts of many who came to the New World. Christopher Columbus had a "conviction that God destined him to be an instrument for spreading the faith [that] was far more potent than the desire to win glory, wealth and worldly honors, to which he was certainly far from indifferent."[207]

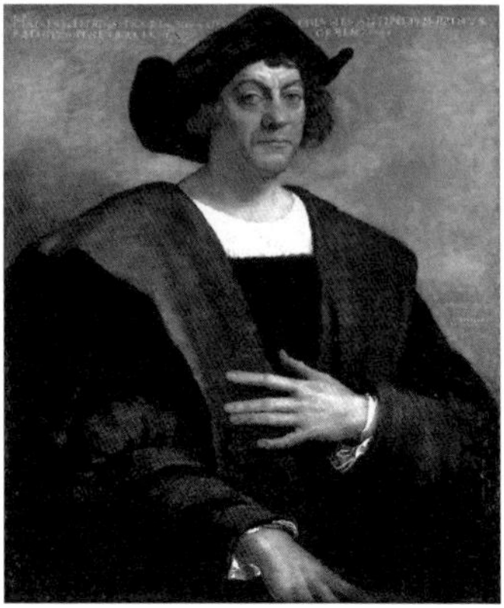

Christopher Columbus. An oil painting by Sebastian de Piombo, 1519. *Photograph by Tn.*

The Spaniards brought with them the *encomienda* system. Beginning in southern Spain in the thirteenth century, this feudal system was built on a relationship based on royal grants to aristocrats and other worthy men. The grant holders were allowed to "collect tribute, labor, and personal services."[208] Juan de Oñate (see page 148) "introduced the *encomienda* [system] to New Mexico around 1600,"[209] and it spread to Texas. This system was led by priests and friars who would operate the encomienda grant by founding missions. In addition to creating an economy, the missionaries would bring Christianity to the people already living in Texas.

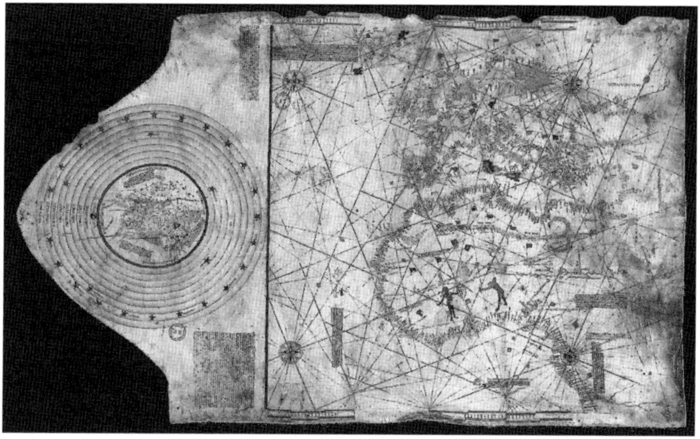

Map of Europe and Africa by Christopher Columbus from the Lisbon, Portugal workshop of his brother Bartolomeo Columbus, 1490. *Photograph by World Imaging.*

With this in mind, the Spanish built more than twenty missions between the East Texas forts and the northernmost towns of Coahuila in Mexico. The missions planned to "reduce" the local people so they would become subject to Spanish power and be baptized as Christians.[210] The planned society envisioned the Native Americans at the bottom to be workers and farmers whose labors would form the foundation on which a Spanish society could flourish.[211] In effect, in this transplanted feudal society, the Native Americans would serve as serfs.

In 1793, the Spanish placed a new mission on the Texas coast near Matagorda Bay. This was the first church in what would become known as the Diocese of Corpus Christi.[212]

The Nuestra Señora del Refugio Mission was the last mission the Spanish built in Texas. The Franciscans founded this mission on January 31, 1793, to serve the Karankawa Indians, the third attempt to work with this tribe. They had deserted the missions at Rosario and Espíritu Santo. The building went slowly and poorly with water seeping into the small wooden structures.

The local Native Americans were not so welcoming. Indeed, the Karankawa chief, Fresada Pinta, was so antagonistic that he even led an attack on the mission in 1794. The site was moved to Mosquitos Creek between the San Antonio and Guadalupe Rivers. Chief Pinta continued his raids, and food supplies were inadequate. Again the mission was moved in 1795 to its current site in present-day Refugio. This location was thought to have better soils for farming.

The venture prospered some for a short while, until Comanches began attacking it at least once a year. Eventually, the mission was abandoned and left to ruin. Although the numbers were never very high, members of seven tribes in addition to the Karankawas were listed as converts, including Copanes, Cocos, Cojanes, Guapites, Malaguitas, Piguiques and Pamiques.[213]

Even though this mission failed, others did prosper and succeed, especially among hunters and gatherers who roamed the countryside, such as some of the Coahuiltecans of northern Mexico and southern Texas. They turned to the missions to find "greater subsistence and security, as well as trying to find allies against the plains bands that raided" them.[214]

In the 1830s, Irish immigrants named their

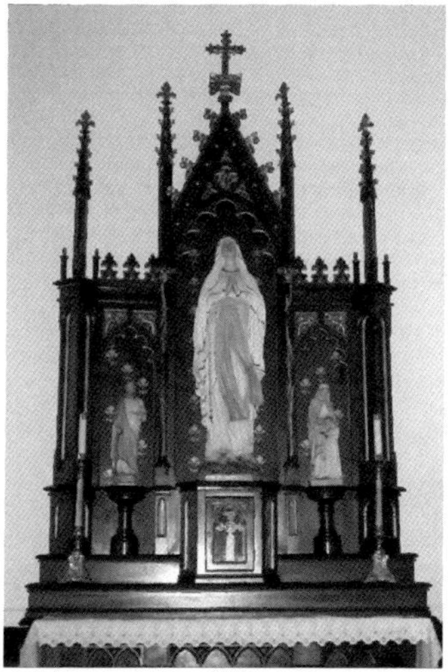

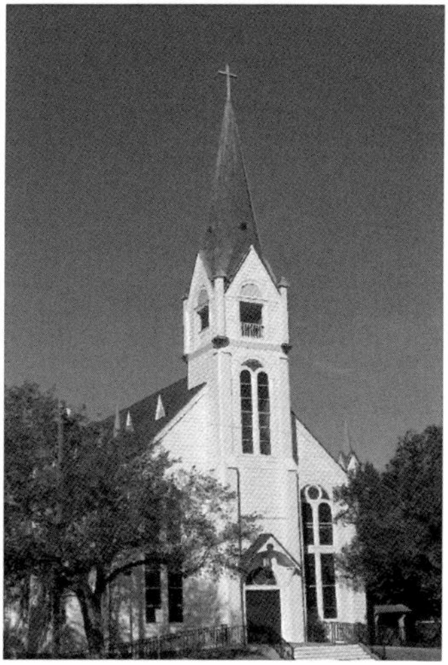

town in the area Refugio, in commemoration of the mission. Although the original attempt failed, a permanent church did grow from the ruins of the mission. Our Lady of Refuge Catholic Church incorporated some of the original mission's stone when the current church was built. The new structure hosted its first Mass on Palm Sunday in 1901.[215]

This newer church building sustains and embodies the hope of the eighteenth-century Spanish mission. *Refugio*, meaning "refuge," continues to be used in the name of the city, which is the county seat of Refugio County.

Top: An altar with the Virgin Mary in Our Lady of Refuge Catholic Church in Refugio, Texas. *Photograph by the author.*

Left: The front elevation of Our Lady of Refuge Catholic Church in Refugio, Texas. *Photograph by the author.*

SAN FERNANDO CATHEDRAL

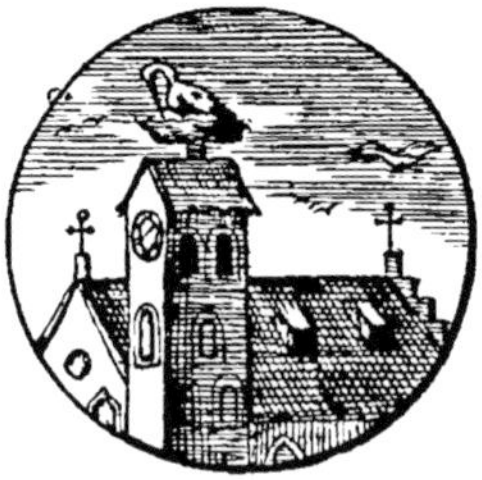

San Fernando Cathedral began as a parish church known as Nuestra Señora de la Candelaria y Guadalupe to serve the people of the Villa San Fernando de Béxar. Juan Antonio Pérez de Almazán, captain of the presidio, marked the location of the central plaza for the new villa in 1731.[216] The church was built between 1728 and 1749.[217] The church was named in honor of both Old World and New World representatives of the faith. One honoree was the thirteenth-century Castilian king Fernando III, who was canonized in 1671.[218] The church was also dedicated to the Virgin of Candelaria, the patron saint of the Canary Islands, the original home of many early settlers in the town. The third honoree was Our Lady of Guadalupe, the patron saint of New Spain. King Charles III of Spain gave the baptismal font in 1759. The Canary islanders (see page 38) who built the church honored their patron saint with a painting of the Virgin of Candelaria, a black Madonna and child, inside the church.[219]

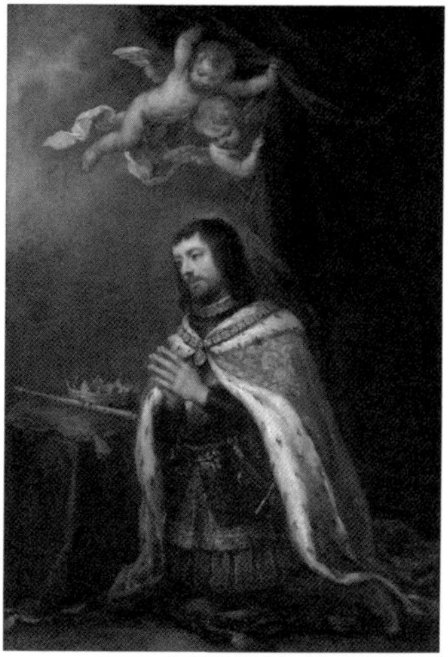

Fernando III, Saint and King of Castille and León. Oil painting by Bartolomé Esteban Murillo (1618–1682). *Photograph by Lancastermerrin88.*

The church grew in size with the villa's population. For many decades, it was the only Christian place of worship in San Antonio, as the Catholic Church was the only one recognized and authorized by the government of Spain and later Mexico.[220]

In 1793, the San Antonio de Valero Mission, known more familiarly as the Alamo, was secularized. The four other missions in the vicinity were secularized in 1824. All of their church vestments, vessels

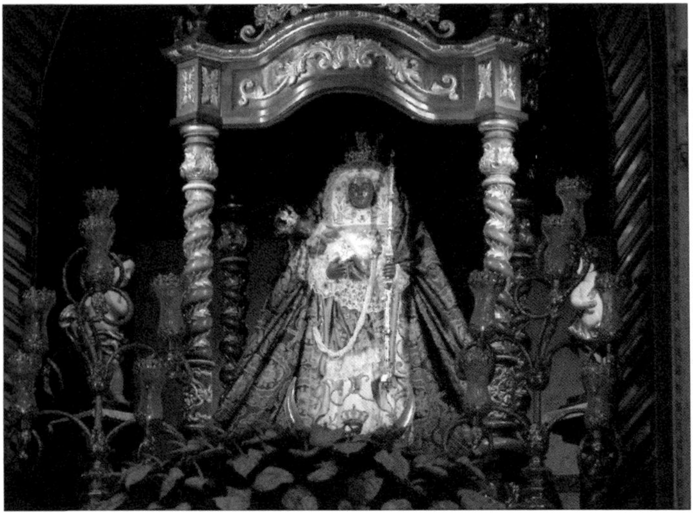

La Virgen de la Candelaria, one of the saints honored at San Fernando Cathedral, in the basilica of Nuestra Señora de la Candelaria in Teneriffa, the Canary Islands. *Photograph by Berthold Werner.*

and records were moved to the Nuestra Señora de la Candelaria y Guadalupe.[221] By the middle of the nineteenth century, the villa had outgrown its single parish.

The church played a significant role in the revolutionary upheavals of the 1820s and 1830s. It was here in 1831 that James Bowie married Ursula de Veramendi, the daughter of the vice-governor of Coahuila y Tejas, Juan Martín de Veramendi (see page 203). In 1832, Veramendi was named governor of the province. Bowie died in the Battle of the Alamo in 1836.

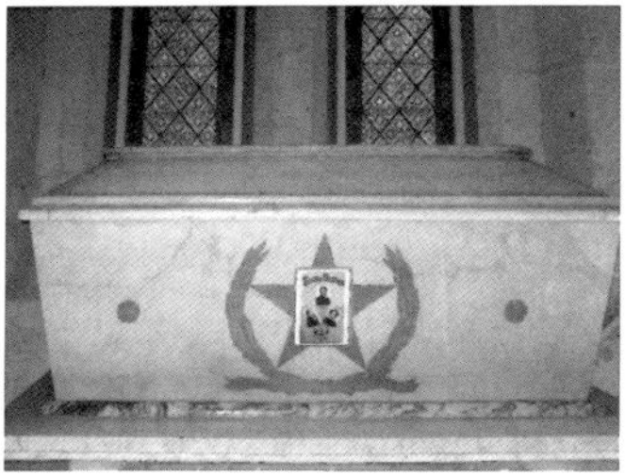

The tomb of David Crockett, William Travis and James Bowie in San Fernando Cathedral. *Photograph bySvs220.*

It was at this church that General Antonio López de Santa Anna ordered a red flag to be raised to signal "no quarter," meaning that no prisoners would be taken; the battle would continue until the last defender of the Alamo had died.

In 1899, Juan de Seguín said the remains of three Alamo heroes were buried in the cathedral. Historians often doubt this assertion. Regardless of the controversy, the cathedral has a tomb inside labeled as the burial location of the remains of David Crockett, William Travis and James Bowie.[222]

Architect François P. Giraud began a thorough renovation in 1868. Much of the original church was razed and a new Gothic-style façade with twin towers was built. The new church was consecrated in 1873. It became a cathedral when the Diocese of San Antonio was created in 1874.

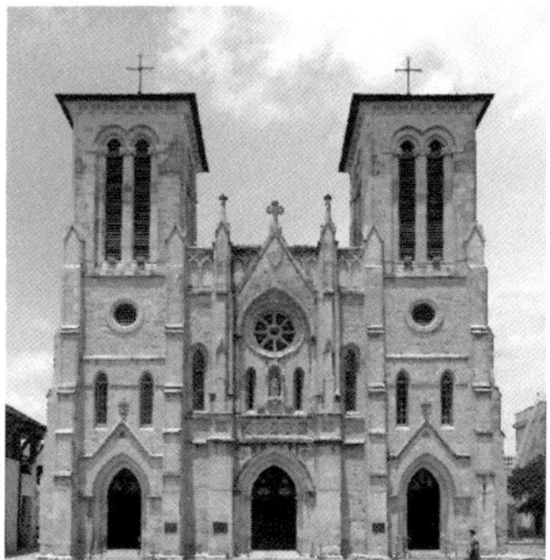

San Fernando Cathedral. *Photograph by I, Daniel Schwen.*

The cathedral continues to serve the people of San Antonio as a parish for local people and as the cathedral for the Diocese of San Antonio. The cathedral hosted Pope John Paul II on September 13, 1987, the only pope to visit Texas. A marble marker commemorates this occasion at the cathedral.[223]

SAN FRANCISCO DE LOS TEJAS MISSION

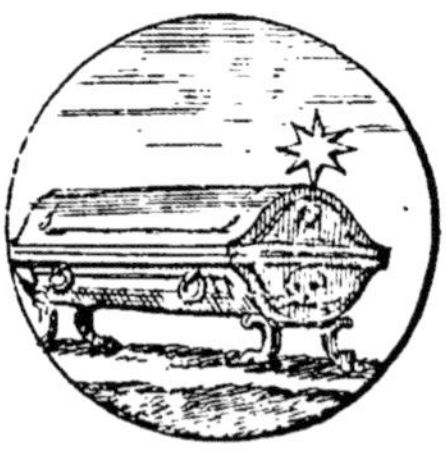

The story of hope, despair, loss, renewal, abandonment and relocation of the San Francisco de los Tejas Mission is the story of how difficult it was for the Spanish to fulfill their two goals of converting the Native Americans and defending their claim to the land we now call Texas. The logistical requirements to staff, supply and protect a mission in eastern Texas from a base in Monclova, Coahuila, were insurmountable. It is 654 miles from Weches, Texas (the site of the mission), to Monclova, Coahuila. Even with twenty-first-century automobiles, it would take an estimated eleven hours and twenty-seven minutes to drive between these two places.[224] In addition to logistical problems, European diseases could kill thousands of Native Americans in epidemics that swept through their lands as a hot wind.

For forty-one years, from 1690 until 1731, the Spanish

tried to establish a missionary presence in eastern Texas. The San Francisco de los Tejas Mission, the first Spanish mission in eastern Texas, began as a small mission near present-day Weches, Texas, and ended with a new name, San Francisco de la Espada, in San Antonio. The mission was built, abandoned, burned, rebuilt, renamed and moved during these forty-one years. The first name was taken from the mission's location among the Tejas Indians, the source of the name Texas. The second name includes *de la Espada*, which translates as "of the sword." The exact origin of the name "is long forgotten."[225]

As in many instances, the Spanish acted to counter French actions. Spanish officials were deeply concerned to learn that a Frenchman, Sieur de La Salle, had led an expedition that landed on the Texas coast, claimed the land and built Fort St. Louis. The Frenchmen were soon killed or captured, and the fort was in ruin (see page 34) when Alonso de León and Damián Massanet saw the site in 1689. While in the area, León's party met with members of the Hasinai (Tejas) Confederacy, one of the tribes of the Caddos who lived in three confederacies: the Hasinai, Kadohadachos and Natchitoches (see page 111). León and Massanet thought these Native Americans were suitable candidates for conversion to Christianity and recommended to the viceroy of New Spain, Conde de Galve, that a mission be built in their lands. León also told the viceroy that he had met Frenchmen living among the Hasinai. Galve ordered a mission be built in the Hasinai domain to anchor the Spanish claim to eastern Texas.

In March 1690, Alonso de León led a force from Monclova, Coahuila, to eastern Texas. The expedition had more than one hundred soldiers and four missionaries, Damián Massanet, Miguel de Fontcuberta, Francisco Casañas de Jesús María and Antonio de Bordoy. On the way to the Hasinai, the troops stopped at Fort St. Louis and burned all that remained, thereby erasing the evidence of La Salle's attempt to settle Frenchmen in Texas. As the march continued, the expedition met two young men who had survived the Karankawa attack on the fort, Peter Meunier and Pierre Talon. Meunier later served as an interpreter for the Spanish when they met with the Hasinais.

The León expedition arrived at the Neches River, its planned destination, on May 22, 1690. The men named the mission location San Francisco de los Tejas and began erecting a chapel that was used on May 24 to celebrate Mass. The Spanish flag was raised, and the local chief of the Hasinai was given a staff with a cross on it. He was named governor of the people there. He agreed to encourage his people to welcome the new religion. A log church and buildings to house the priests were built. On June 1, the mission was ready to operate. The governor led the Tejas in attending Mass, and the church was blessed. The next day, León and Massanet left to return to Monclova, leaving behind three soldiers and three priests.

In 1691, another expedition came from Monclova bringing herds of sheep and cattle and more than one thousand horses to the new mission. Another mission had been established nearby, Santísimo Nombre de María, or the "Most Holy Name of Mary." The leader of this party, Domingo Terán de los Ríos, observed little positive change among the Native Americans. He found them more interested in stealing horses than converting to Christianity. Terán de los Ríos and the clergy agreed that it would be fruitless to build more missions. So many horses were now gone that Terán de los Ríos had to take some from the mission in order to have enough for his return journey. He and six friars left for Monclova on January 9, 1692. That same month, floods destroyed the Santísimo Nombre de María Mission.[226] A relief group led by Gregorio de Salinas Varona (see page 171) arrived from Monclova on June 8, 1693, and discovered a chaotic situation. There was a great amount of illness and death. Smallpox had killed an estimated 3,300 people in the winter of 1690–91.[227] Some of the Hasinai thought the baptismal waters would spread death. Salinas da Varona did not bring enough supplies, and he concluded that not much good would come from any attempt to rescue the mission. He left on June 14, 1693, accompanied by two friars. On October 25, 1693, the remaining friars buried the bell and canon, packed their vestments and vessels and burned the mission's church, their housing and outbuildings. They then left for Monclova and arrived there on February 14, 1694.[228]

Most Spanish soldiers and clergy had no hope in continuing missions in eastern Texas. One exception was Francisco Hidalgo (see page 92), who tried several times to relocate the mission and find some Native Americans more accepting of conversion and accommodating to life in a Spanish mission. On July 5, 1716, a new mission was built in the same area and called Nuestro Padre San Francisco de los Tejas. It was abandoned in 1719 following the "Chicken War" (see page 95). Again on August 5, 1721, the mission was reestablished as San Francisco de los Neches. There was little interest among the Hasinai, and the French had little presence in the region at this time. The mission was then moved to the Colorado River in July 1730.

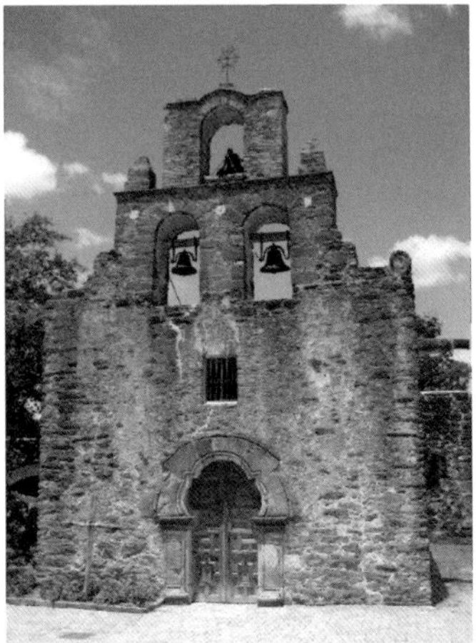

San Francisco de Espada Mission's chapel in San Antonio. *Photograph by Liveon001 ©Travis K. Witt.*

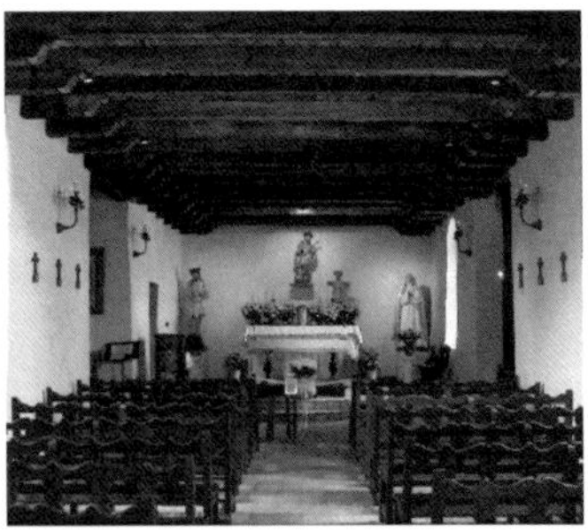

Interior of the San Francisco de Espada Mission in San Antonio. *Photograph by Liveon001 © Travis K. Witt.*

Soon, the mission moved to its final location in present-day San Antonio where it was renamed San Francisco de la Espada. The mission found a permanent home. The chapel is still used to celebrate Mass. The aqueduct that was built to bring water to irrigate the fields still carries water to the mission from the San Antonio River.

SISTERDALE

Europeans moved to Texas in great migrations from every corner of the continent. In addition to the Spanish and French, Texas has communities of Czechs, Poles, Danes, Italians, Greeks, Swedes, Wends, Norwegians, Portuguese and people who represented many of Europe's other cultures. Germans composed one of the larger European groups of immigrants. They planted a ribbon of towns west and north of San Antonio. The towns served as a market for farmers and ranchers as well as centers of German culture. These towns had churches, schools, hospitals, asylums, flour mills and stores modeled on German custom. Generally, German was one of the dominant languages spoken in this part of Texas for one hundred years.

One of the settlements in the area was Sisterdale, a community founded on ideals and principles. Sisterdale began as a place for high morals and progressive ideas, just as the followers of François Marie Charles Fourier sought a utopian society in La Réunion near present-day Dallas (see page 71). In 1847, Nicolaus Zink, a surveyor for Prince Carl of Solms-Braunfels, came to Texas leading some "free thinkers" to start a "Latin Settlement" of scholars and progressive idealists. Many of them were aristocrats, barons and other highly placed people who fled political tumult in Germany after warfare erupted in 1848. One was the brother-in-law of Karl Marx.

The settlers of Sisterdale adopted a plan to work for six goals:

- Equal pay for equal work
- Direct election of the president of the United States
- Abolition of capital punishment
- Abolition of slavery
- Free schools, including universities
- Total separation of church and state[229]

During the Civil War, these "free thinkers" were considered a threat by some Texans, partly because many of the men refused to serve in the Confederate army.

Rather than serve in the Confederate army, sixty-one men fled toward Mexico, but only half of them made it halfway there. On August 10, 1862, on the banks of the Nueces River, a band of Partisan Rangers led by James Duff killed thirty-four of them. Others were executed later.[230]

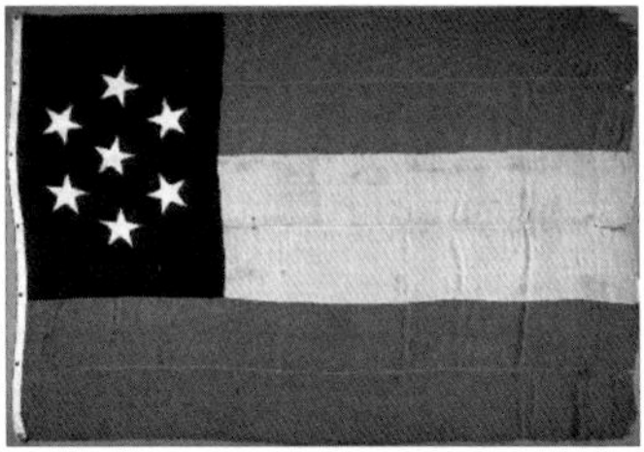

Confederate first national flag in use from 1861 to 1863. *Courtesy Texas State Archives and Library Commission, Historic Flags Collection, #306-4059.*

After the Civil War, a communal funeral was held. The mass funeral of these men on August 20, 1865, was so newsworthy that it was featured in the January 20, 1866 edition of one of the leading journals of the time, ***Harper's Weekly: A Journal of Civilization***.[231]

Kendall County erected a monument in 1866 to remember

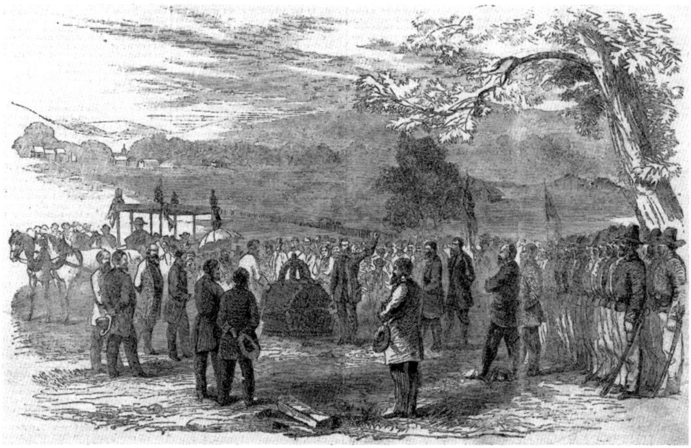

Funeral of German Patriots at Comfort, Texas, August 20, 1865, in *Harper's Weekly, A Journal of Civilization*, New York, January 20, 1866. *Courtesy Texas State Library and Archives Commission, Prints and Photographs Collection, #1992/75-1-1.*

the fallen men of Sisterdale and the surrounding area. It is called the *Treue der Union* Monument, meaning "Loyalty to the Union." The monument is in Comfort, Texas.[232]

In 2010, about twenty-five people lived in Sisterdale. Most of them are affiliated with a well-reputed winery called the Sisterdale Winery.[233]

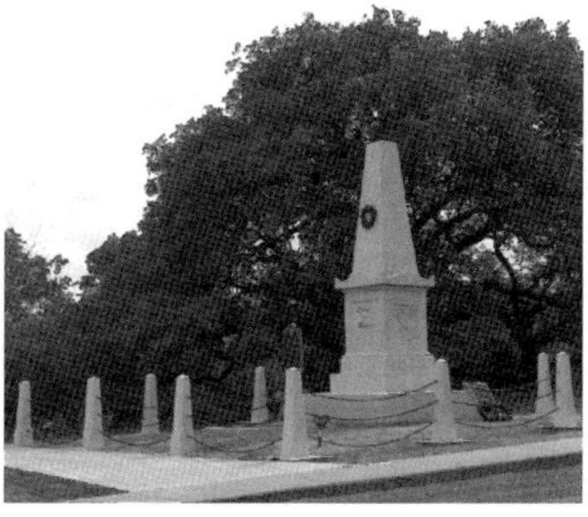

Treue Der Union Monument in Comfort, Texas. *Photograph by Larry D. Moore.*

T

TEXAS NAVY

In the early nineteenth century, travel from Texas towns and forts to the governmental and cultural centers of northern Mexico was difficult. There were no easy routes and few way stations to acquire fresh horses, safe places to rest or food to eat. The terrain was harsh, hot and hard to walk across. Some members of the Mexican army referred to the land along the Rio Grande as the "Desert of Dead Horses."[234] Instead of relying only on land routes, some early Texans thought it would be advantageous to travel to and from Mexico on the Gulf of Mexico. In 1835, one of the first decisions the Texas Council made was to create a navy.

The Texas navy began with four ships. The first one, the *William Robbins*, had operated as a privateer, a privately owned ship authorized to capture and take over enemy vessels. The Texas Council bought it and renamed it the *Liberty*. Three other armed ships were purchased: the *Independence*, *Brutus* and *Invincible*.

These four ships decisively struck at the heart of Mexican commercial shipping. They captured and confiscated Mexican goods and ships. The Mexicans unsuccessfully tried to avoid capture by saying their cargo was bound for New Orleans rather than to Texas. They thought this would stop the Texas navy from attacking them. This attempt to dodge the truth did not usually work. The Texas navy continued to pursue, fire on, board and capture Mexican ships.

The Texas navy played a pivotal role in the success of Texas's war with Mexico. While General López de Santa Anna marched his troops northward from Mexico to fight in San Antonio, General José de Urrea marched northward from Matamoros and stayed near the coastline. On the way to victories in San Patricio and Goliad, General Urrea wanted to remain close to his supply ships. The Texas navy ships raided and defeated Mexico's supply ships and made Urrea's campaigns difficult to sustain. The Mexican army had to have a reliable source of supply to maintain its advance against the Texans. The *Liberty* captured the Mexican schooner *Pelicano* in March 1836, yielding three hundred kegs of gunpowder the Texans could use. On the morning of April 3, 1836, near the mouth of the Rio Grande, the *Invincible* battled the Mexican ship *Montezuma*, which ran aground, causing its sailors

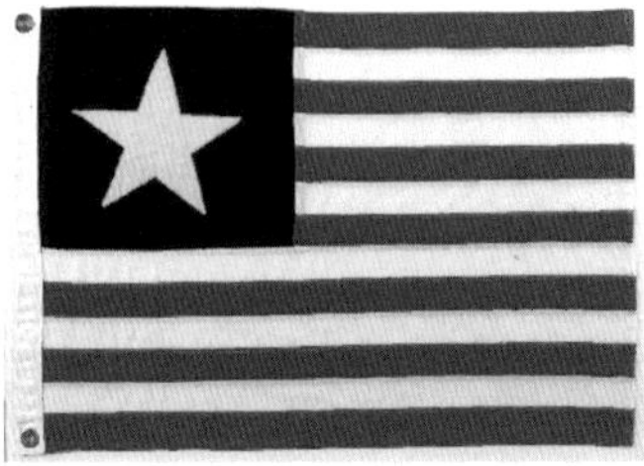

Texas navy flag (reproduction likely from the mid-twentieth century). *Courtesy Texas State Archives and Library Commission, Historic Flags Collection, #306-4053.*

to flee. Later that same day, the *Invincible* captured the *Pocket*, a U.S. civilian vessel carrying war material and Mexican soldiers. The *Invincible* took the *Pocket* as a prize ship and escorted it to Galveston. The *Pocket* became part of the Texas navy.[235]

Perhaps the most fabled and exciting story concerns a privateer, the *Flash*. The citizens of Cincinnati, Ohio, made two six-pound cannons and sent them to Galveston. The Ohioans wanted to assist Texas in its war of independence. The *Flash* put the cannons on board in March 1836, just after the Alamo fell. The *Flash* went to Groce's Retreat (see page 81) on the Brazos River and picked up some refugees from the Alamo battle. Then, on April 11, it delivered the cannons to Morgan's Point and "picked up more refugees, including three Texas cabinet officers, the family of President David Burnet, and Vice-President Lorenzo de Zavala and his family."[236] On April 21, the cannons, dubbed the "Twin Sisters," fired at Mexican troops at the Battle of San Jacinto, the final battle that secured Texas's independence.

The Texas navy continued to threaten Mexican commerce for several more years. This was one reason Mexico hesitated to conclude a peace treaty with Texas, even as late as 1840. On June 2, 1836, the

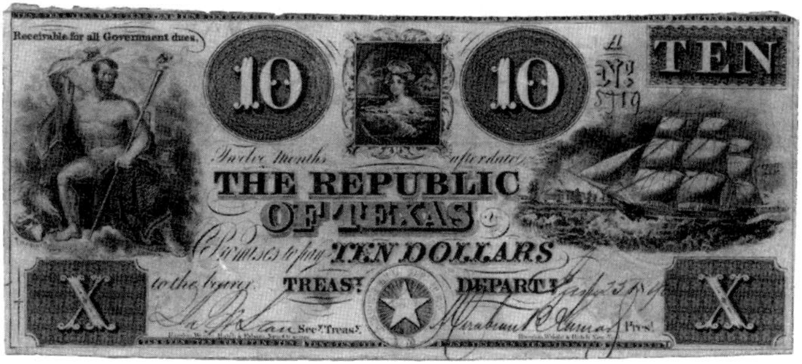

Republic of Texas ten-dollar bill, featuring the brig *Archer*. *Courtesy Texas State Library and Archives Commission, Prints and Photographs Collections, #1989/84-12.*

Texans were so determined to stop the resupply of Mexican forces that some members of the Texas navy, led by Isaac Burton, put their horses on a boat, rowed out to the Mexican ship anchored in the harbor of Copano Bay, boarded the ship and defeated the Mexican navy. In celebration, this event was related for many years in a song titled "The Horse Marines."[237]

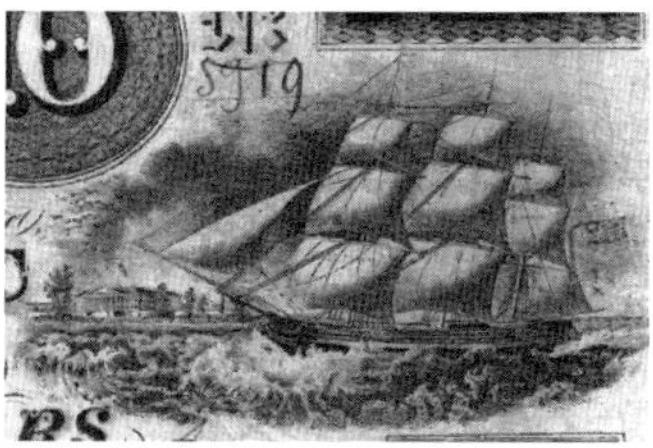

The Texas navy brig *Archer*, a detail of the Republic of Texas ten-dollar bill. *Courtesy Texas State Library and Archives Commission, Prints and Photographs Collections, #1989/84-12.*

The Texas navy was well respected and prized, especially by people in Galveston. Feelings ran so hot that volunteers guarded the ships in Galveston Harbor. This steadfastly popular

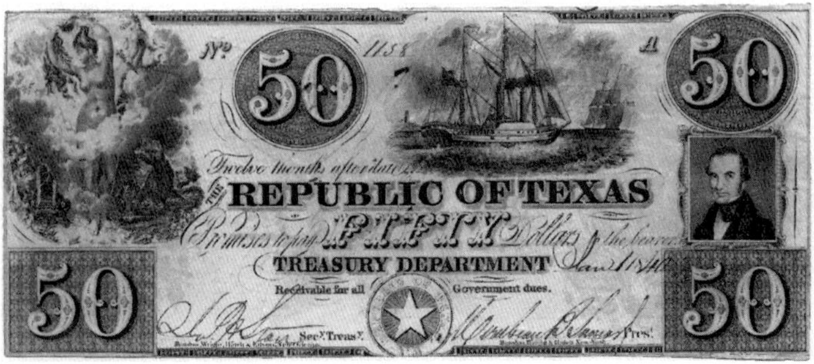

Republic of Texas fifty-dollar bill, featuring the steamship *Zavala*. *Courtesy Texas State Library and Archives Commission, Prints and Photographs Collection, # 1989/84-16.*

support kept Sam Houston, as president of Texas, from selling the four ships and disbanding the Texas navy. When Texas joined the United States, Commodore Edwin Moore's small fleet of ships lowered their Lone Star flag and hoisted the United States flag.

Most nations have images on their currency to honor people they revere and admire. Perhaps one of the most interesting pieces of information about the Texas navy is that its ships are prominently depicted on the currency of the Republic of Texas. Beginning in 1839, the currency had ships in its engravings. The ship on the ten-dollar bill is a brig named *Archer*. The ship on the fifty-dollar bill is the first steamship in the Texas navy, the *Zavala*, named in honor of Lorenzo de Zavala, the Republic's first vice-president (see page 222).

U

JOSÉ DE URRUTIA

José de Urrutia was an exemplary soldier and servant of New Spain in the late 1600s and early 1700s. He participated in significant expeditions, assisted in founding the first mission in eastern Texas, lived with Native Americans and led the garrison as captain of the San Antonio de Béxar Presidio. Urrutia was "probably the best informed of all Spaniards on Indian affairs in Texas."[238]

José de Urrutia was born in the Basque region of northern Spain in 1678 and went to New Spain when he was very young, before 1691. He and his brother Toribio accompanied Domingo de Terán de los Ríos on the trek to the new San Francisco de los Tejas Mission in eastern Texas (see page 185).[239] He stayed there at the garrison. When the missionaries and soldiers left in 1693, he had a serious accident, likely on the Colorado River.

He was unable to travel and stayed with the Kanohatinos, Xarames and Tohos Indians for seven years. While there, he learned their languages and ways. Urrutia rejoined the Spanish in 1700, just after the establishment of the San Juan Bautista Mission (see page 88) near present-day Guerrero, Coahuila. He led a series of forays against the Apaches in 1739 near the same place that Juan Antonio Bustillo y Ceballos had done in 1732 (see page 38).

Urrutia married Antonia Ramón. They had one daughter, Antonia. Later on, his wife died in childbirth. He married again to Rosa Flores y Valdéz. They had four children. One of their sons, Toribio de Urrutia, was named after his uncle. He later served as captain of the San Antonio de Béxar Presidio as his father had done.[240]

UVALDE

The city of Uvalde, Texas, is named for Juan de Ugalde. He was born in 1729 in Cádiz, Spain, to a family of military tradition. Ugalde grew up to become, as did his father, a general in the Spanish army.

Before coming to New Spain, Juan de Ugalde fought in Europe, Africa and South America. In 1777, King Charles III appointed him governor of the province of San Francisco de Coahuila, which included Texas. For the next several years, Ugalde waged campaigns against the Mescalero and Lipan Apaches. While Ugalde was in the field fighting the Indians, he was accused of leaving Coahuila's settlements undefended. In 1783, he was ordered to Mexico City, where he served as commander of a more vast area, including

Coahuila, Nuevo León, Nuevo Santander and Texas.

Ugalde continued to fight the Apaches all across southern Texas from El Paso to San Antonio. A decisive defeat of the Apaches occurred on January 9, 1790, in Sabinal Canyon. This site was renamed in his honor as the Cañón de Ugalde. Juan de Ugalde returned to Spain as a hero and was promoted to general and awarded the Gran Cruz de Hermenegildo, the highest honor awarded by the king. It honors the memory of a sixth-century Visogoth martyr who converted to Catholicism.[241] Juan de Ugalde died at age eighty-seven in Cádiz, his birthplace.[242]

The city and county of Uvalde derive their name from the commemorative naming of the January 1790 battlefield in Sabinal Canyon. The United States Post Office first designated the current city of Uvalde as Encina in 1853. Three years later, the name was changed to Uvalde in remembrance of Juan de Ugalde. Uvalde has become an important regional center of agriculture, education, culture, transportation and politics.

In 2010, the population was 15,751.[243] Few towns of this size have fostered so many notable people whose contributions range from government to the arts to education. Uvalde is the home of many noteworthy people, including the following individuals.

John Nance "Cactus Jack" Garner IV moved to Uvalde as a young man. He served Texas and the United States for nearly forty years. Prior to federal service, he served in the Texas legislature, where he earned the nickname "Cactus

Jack" when he suggested naming the prickly pear the Texas state flower. Garner was a member of the U.S. House of Representatives for thirty years, 1903–33. From 1931 to 1933, Garner led the House of Representatives as its Speaker. Garner was vice president to President Franklin D. Roosevelt for two terms, from 1933 to 1941.[244]

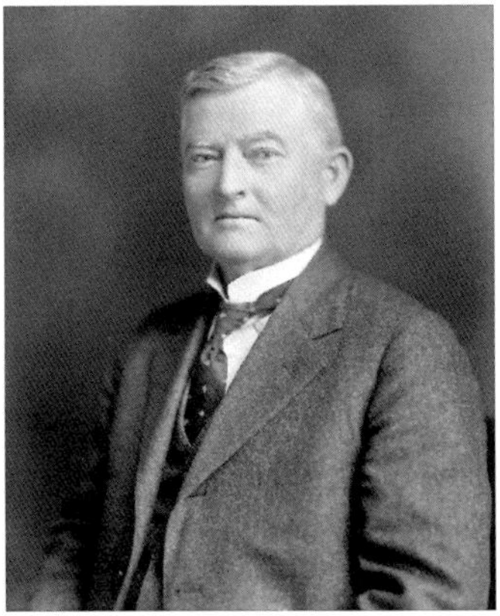

John Nance Garner IV, member of the U.S. House of Representatives, 1903–33, and vice president of the United States, 1933–41. *Photograph by Harris & Ewing. Courtesy Library of Congress, Prints & Photographs Online Catalogue.*

Dolph Briscoe Jr. was a native of Uvalde. He was a noted rancher, banker, state legislator, governor and philanthropist. He spent much of his adult life serving Texans in the state legislature and as governor. In 1949, he sponsored legislation to create a vast expansion of Texas's farm-to-market roads. He was elected to serve as Texas governor in 1972, and in 1976, he was the first governor elected to a four-year term. Briscoe donated $15 million to the University of Texas–Austin's history center that was later named for him as the Dolph Briscoe Center for American History.[245]

Dale Evans, an Uvalde native, was a popular actor in film and television, especially from movies and

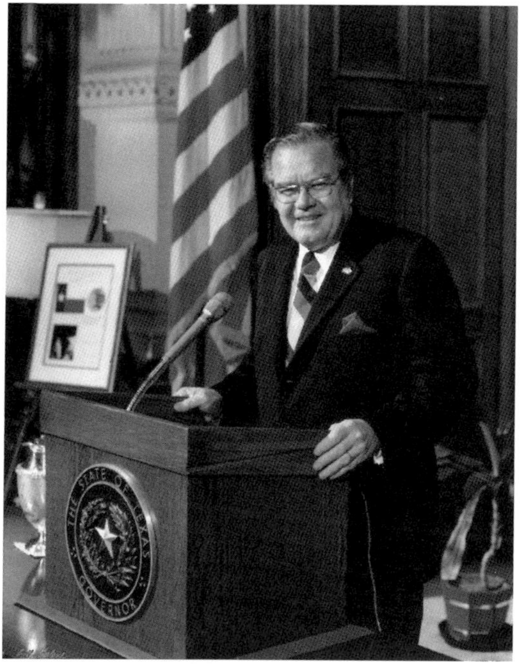

Dolph Briscoe Jr., member of the Texas House of Representatives, 1949–1957, and governor of Texas, 1973–81. *Courtesy Texas State Library and Archives Commission, Prints and Photographs Collection, #1976/46-9.*

shows she made with her husband, Roy Rogers. In addition to acting, Evans was a singer and composer of popular music. Her song "Happy Trails" is a favorite of the mid-twentieth-century American songbook.[246]

Matthew McConaughey[247] was born in Uvalde, lived later in Longview and attended the University of Texas–Austin. He is a popular film actor who has starred in more than fifty movies ranging from comedy, romance, adventure and drama from the 1990s to the present. McConaughey is valued highly by the film industry. In 2014, his performance in *Dallas Buyer's Club* won an Oscar for best actor in a leading role from the Academy of Motion Picture Arts and Sciences as well as the best actor award from the Golden Globes and Screen Actors Guild.

A quartet of brothers, known as Los Palominos, is from Uvalde. This Grammy Award–winning music group is appreciated by its many fans that recognize its contributions to tejano/norteño music. The four brothers won a Grammy twice, in 1999 and 2006.[248]

Lyn McWhirter Fraser of Uvalde is a noted writer of several genres of writing, including contemplative works: *Water from the Rock: Finding Grace in Time of Grief* (1994) and *Prayers From the Darkness: The Difficult Psalms* (2005). Fraser is also coauthor with Aileen M. Ormiston of university-level finance texts: *Understanding the Corporate Annual Report: Nuts, Bolts, and a Few Loose Screws* (2003) and *Understanding Financial Statements* (2012). This last book is an academic bestseller, now in its tenth edition. In 2014, Lyn Fraser published her first mystery novel, *Debits and Credits*, set in Austin, Texas. It features a forensic accountant who doubles as a sleuth.

V

JUAN MARTÍN DE VERAMENDI

Juan Martín de Veramendi was born on December 17, 1778, in San Fernando de Béxar, present-day San Antonio, into a prominent family. His parents were Fernando Veramendi and María Josefa Granados. Fernando had come from Spain around 1770 and married María Josefa, a member of a family from the Canary Islands who settled early Béxar (see page 38). Fernando was "a prominent merchant, landowner and money lender, successful enough to build 'an opulent house on Soledad Street.'"[249] The Veramendi Palace was a large house for the time and resembled the nearby Governor's Palace in design. The word *palace* signified the building had an official

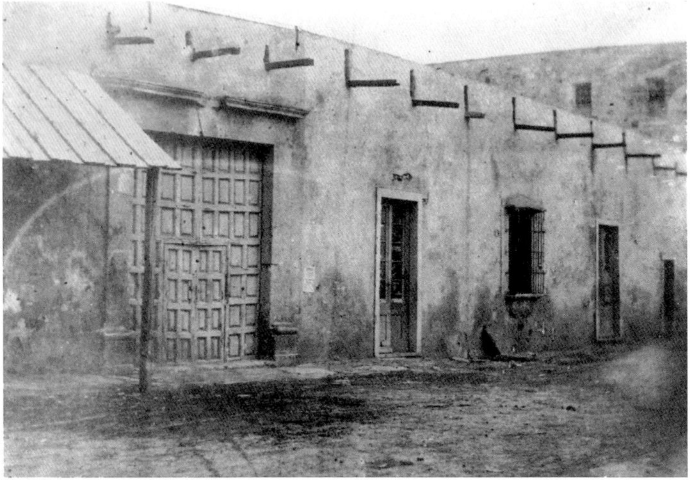

Photograph of the front of the Don Fernando Veramendi Palace in San Antonio. *Photograph by Adolph Phillip for the Historic American Buildings Survey. Courtesy Library of Congress, Prints & Photographs Online Catalogue.*

capacity. This one was the home of a man who was mayor, legislator, then vice-governor and, finally, governor. The palace was destroyed in 1910 in order to widen Soledad Street. The enormous and ornate doors were saved, restored and relocated to the east wall of the Alamo.

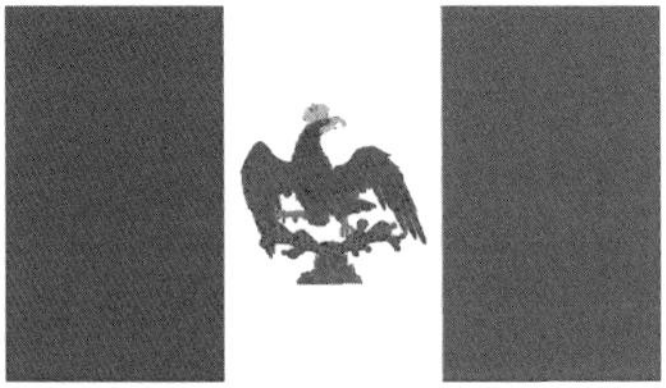

Flag of Mexico used from 1821 to 1823, during the period Juan Martín de Veramendi was active in various government offices. *Photograph by TownDown.*

Like his parents, Juan Martín de Veramendi had a significant role in the civic and economic life of the small city. He "and Juan José Erasmo Seguín met Stephen F. Austin at Natchitoches, Louisiana on June 21, 1821, and accompanied him to Béxar."[250] He was instrumental as an advocate for immigrants coming from the United States to Texas. Veramendi was active politically in various positions. He was a collector of foreign revenue in 1822 and 1823. He was elected to be a deputy of the Texas provincial delegation to the National Constitutional Congress in the newly formed nation of Mexico.

Veramendi was the first *alcalde*, or "mayor," of Béxar in 1824 and 1825. In September 1830, he was elected vice-governor of Coahuila y Tejas. Once the election was confirmed in January 1831, Veramendi moved to Saltillo, the capital city. Upon the death of the governor, José María Letona, in 1832, Veramendi became governor of the state. He favored the new colonists coming from the United States.

In addition to his political life, Veramendi was a landowner. He received five leagues of land—22,140 acres—from the *ayuntamiento*, or "local government," when he was mayor. He learned that the grant came from lands that had been granted to DeWitt, an *empresario*, or "entrepreneur" of land sanctioned by the government of Spain and, subsequently Mexico. Veramendi did not want to be a colonist of any empresario and petitioned the government to have a clear title to a grant of land in his own name. He received

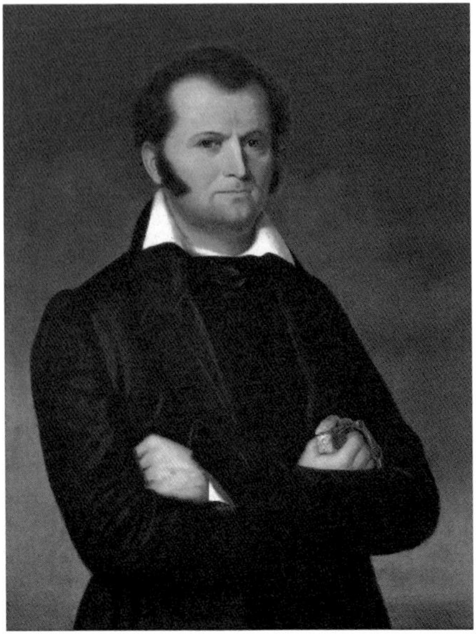

James Bowie, an oil painting. The painting hangs in the Texas Senate Chamber in Austin, Texas. *Courtesy State Preservation Board, Austin, Texas. Accession ID: CHA2001.004; original artist unknown; photographer Eric Beggs, June 25, 2004. Post conservation.*

a grant of eleven leagues of land—48,708 acres—in 1827.

Juan Martín de Veramendi married Josefa Navarro, with whom he had seven children.[251] One daughter, Ursula, was courted by James Bowie. Bowie had come to Béxar in 1830 and became a business partner of Veramendi. He converted to Catholicism and married Ursula on April 25, 1831, at the Church of Nuestra Señora de la Candelaria y Guadalupe (see page 180).[252]

In 1833, a cholera epidemic came to Coahuila y Tejas. Juan Martín, Josefa and their daughter Ursula died at their summer home in Monclova.[253] Ursula's husband, James Bowie, died while defending the Alamo in 1836.

W

WICHITA INDIANS

The Wichita Indians are linguistically and culturally related to the Caddos, who lived east and south of them. The Wichitas lived in a wide region of west-central Texas often called the cross timbers. Their livelihood and culture ranged from farming in the east to hunting in the west. They farmed corn, beans, squash, pumpkins, melons and other vegetables during the spring and summer at fixed villages. In the fall, they moved west to live in camps and hunt buffalo. The Wichitas moved over time until they occupied much of the land from southern Kansas to central Texas. From the mid-1500s until the early 1700s, they lived primarily north of Texas in present-day Oklahoma and southern Kansas. By the end of the 1700s, they lived mainly

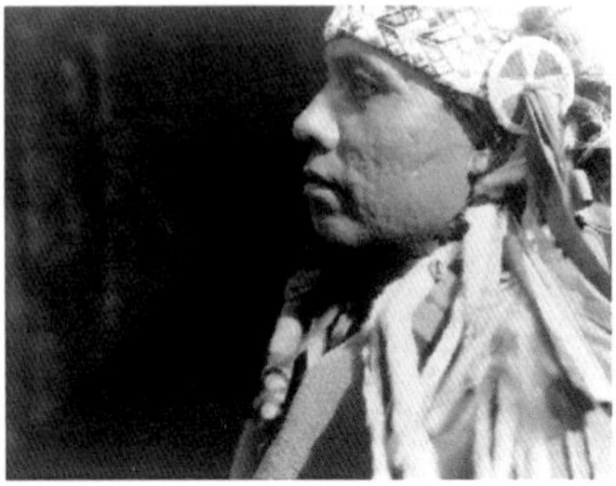

"A Wichita," about 1927.
Photograph by Edward S. Curtis. Courtesy Library of Congress, Prints & Photographs Online Catalogue.

in central Texas as far south as the Pedernales River Valley, as far west as the upper Brazos River Valley and, in the east, as far as the Red River north of Natchitoches, Louisiana.[254]

The Wichitas managed for 250 years to find a balance adapting to the differing policies and practices of first the Spanish, followed by the French and finally the Americans. The Spanish early expeditions, the *entrada*, came looking for gold and converts to Christianity. They never found the falsely imagined city of gold Quivira and gave up trying after Juan de Oñate's final travels and military defeat in 1601 (see page 157).[255] The Spaniards left behind two significant change agents, horses and European diseases. Horses were a boon, bringing mobility and great changes in hunting and raiding parties with neighboring tribes, especially the Osages, Comanches and Apaches. One of the most harmful outcomes was when these tribes captured Wichitas and sold them as slaves to the French in Illinois and to the Spanish in New Mexico.[256]

The Wichitas fared better in some ways with the French *entrée* when they first arrived 117 years after the last Spanish visitors in 1718. The French gave them annual gifts and sought trade more than conquest. The Wichitas

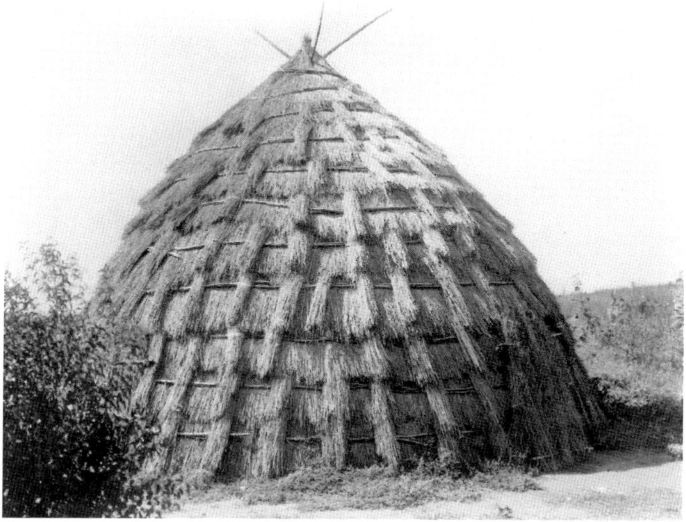

"Wichita Grass-House," about 1927. *Photograph by Edward S. Curtis. Courtesy Library of Congress, Prints & Photographs Online Catalogue.*

prized the French trade goods, especially the guns, powder and ammunition. These new weapons forever changed self-defense, hunting and raiding parties.

By the time the Americans arrived, the Wichitas were greatly "weakened by a century of warfare and disease."[257] Smallpox, measles and cholera also took a great toll. In the late 1770s alone, the Wichitas lost more than one-third of their population.[258]

During the eighteenth and first part of the nineteenth centuries, the Spanish and

French vied for favor and dominance over the Wichitas. At the same time, new tribes moved into the territory, such as the Pawnees, who moved south from the Missouri River area. Faced with all these pressures, the Wichitas' fortunes continued to decline. Eventually, they joined other Texas Indians on the move to reservations in western present-day Oklahoma.

Major Robert S. Neighbors (see page 153) led soldiers who moved the Wichita north to the Indian Territory. Roberts wrote to his wife on August 8, 1859:

> *I have this day crossed all Indians out of the heathen land of "Texas" and am now "out of the land of the Philistines." If you want to hear a full description of our Exodus out of Texas read the Bible where the children of Israel crossed the Red Sea. We have had about the same show, only our enemies did not follow us to the R*[ed] *River. If they had—the Indians would have in all probability sent them back without interposition of Divine Providence.*[259]

Major Neighbors was killed by a fellow Texan and died on September 14, 1859, at Fort Belknap. He is buried in Newcastle, Texas. His wife and two sons survived.

One of the most curious facts about this tribe is that English speakers incorrectly called them Wichitas. Actually, this name derived from a mistake made by a U.S. diplomat when negotiating with the tribe in 1835. For an unknown reason, the entire tribe was named after a small subgroup named the

Guichitas, a Spanish spelling for this small band.[260] The Wichitas were more correctly considered a confederation of many groups and called themselves the Kitikitish. In addition to the Guichitas, the Kitikitish included groups known as the Iscanis, Kichais, Panis Piques, Taovayas, Tawakonis and Wacos.[261]

Several place names commemorate the Wichita Indians in three states: Texas, Oklahoma and Kansas. In Texas, these include the Wichita River, Wichita County and the city of Wichita Falls. In Oklahoma, the Wichita Indians are remembered in the Wichita Mountains, Wichita Mountains State Park and the Wichita Mountains National Wildlife Refuge that preserves a mixed-grass prairie and many animals, "cultural and historical legacy species," of the region, including bison, elk and white-tailed deer.[262] In Kansas, the Wichitas are remembered in the city of Wichita and Wichita State University.

JAMES WILKINSON

James Wilkinson was born on a farm in Maryland on March 24, 1757, and died on December 28, 1825, in Mexico City. During the intervening sixty-eight years, he was a soldier, politician and government official. He served with a great deal of success while he was simultaneously reputed to engage in duplicity, malicious gossip and treasonous behavior. As a politician, he wrangled for Kentucky's separation from Virginia and took part in Pennsylvania's militia to gain political advantage. He was an officer in the American

Revolutionary War who fought in the Massachusetts, Canada, New York and New Jersey campaigns.[263] He served under George Washington's command when he crossed the Delaware River on Christmas night 1776 to stealthily attack Trenton, New Jersey.[264] Later, Wilkinson was a trusted aide to General Horatio Gates, who vied with Washington, even so much as to replace him as the commander of the Continental army. In a March 9, 1792 "Memorandum on General Officers," President George Washington characterized Wilkinson as "lively, sensible, pompous, and ambitious."[265]

After the American Revolution, he served reluctantly under General Anthony Wayne in the newly opening Northwest Territory. Then, from December 15, 1796, until July 13, 1798, Wilkinson "was the senior officer of the United States Army."[266]

Wilkinson conspired with the Spanish governor of Louisiana, Esteban Rodríguez Miró, to gain trade advantages for which Wilkinson swore allegiance to the king of Spain. He even received annual payments from the Spanish.[267] The extent of his involvement with the Spanish was not fully known until Charles Gayarré's 1867 publication of some information found in the Spanish archives. Meanwhile, President James Madison thought there was enough suspicion and evidence to convene a court-martial. Wilkinson was found not guilty in December 1811. This duplicitous conniving with the Spanish and his support to Vice President Aaron Burr's scheme to rule

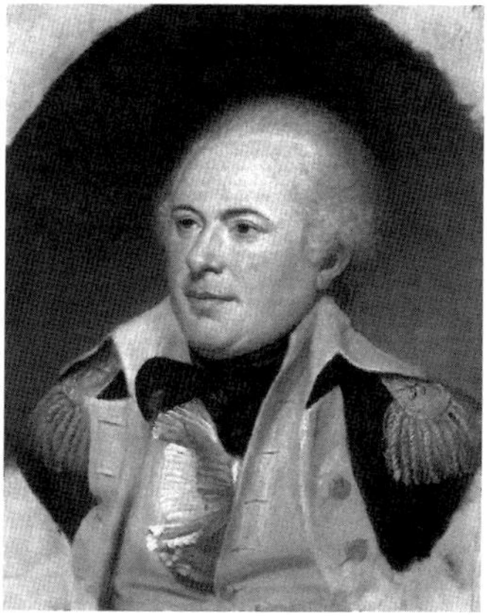

James Wilkinson. An oil painting by Charles Willson Peale, 1797. *Photograph by PhilFree. Courtesy Library of Congress.*

over newly acquired western lands, prompted New York's Governor Theodore Roosevelt to say about Wilkinson: "In all our history there is no more despicable character."[268]

Wilkinson's role in the development of Texas was indirect as someone who influenced and directed the activity of others who were in Texas. Wilkinson's directing actions affecting Texas derived from his appointment as commanding general of the army. Soon afterward, President Thomas Jefferson appointed James Wilkinson to serve as the first governor of Louisiana. His headquarters was in St. Louis, the epicenter of America's expanding horizons to the north, south and west. In this capacity, Wilkinson ordered Philip Nolan and Zebulon Montgomery Pike to undertake missions in dangerous territory. Nolan, a trusted protégé, was sent to Spanish-held Texas to locate and bring back horses to Louisiana. During his 1801 incursion, Nolan and many of his men were killed in a battle with the Spanish army (see page 136). Wilkinson ordered Pike to explore northward to find the source of the

Mississippi River. After this expedition, Wilkinson sent Pike westward to find the sources of the Arkansas and Red Rivers (see page 161). Wilkinson also supported the Long Expedition to take lands and form a republic in Texas. This effort was named for Dr. James Long, the husband of Wilkinson's niece, Jane Long (see page 117).

James Wilkinson's influence in Texas history included his role in meeting with Spain's Lieutenant Colonel Simón de Herrera on November 5, 1806, to find a way "to avert an armed clash" over the border between Louisiana and Texas. Simón de Herrera and Wilkinson established a "neutral ground" between the disputed claims and prohibited settlers from coming in. This was done as a delaying tactic to forswear any serious conflict until a border could be fixed. The neutral ground was about forty miles wide along the east side of the Sabine River, in present-day Louisiana. The agreement, although not a treaty, did hold until the Adams-Onís Treaty was signed on February 22, 1819.[269]

In 1825, James Wilkinson was in Mexico City trying to secure a land grant to settle in Texas. He died there after suffering a long period of poor health on December 28. No land grant was made.[270]

X

FRANCIS XAVIER

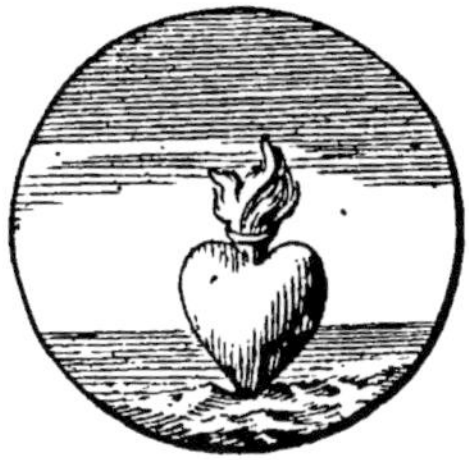

When the Europeans came to America, they carefully decided what name to give to the places they settled. They often chose to honor famous soldiers, nobles, royalty or favorite places they knew in Europe. Sometimes, they named a place for the religious values, individuals in the Bible or people they respected. The Spanish built three missions on the San Xavier River. The river and missions were named to honor a much-loved and respected saint, Francis Xavier.

Francis Xavier was from Navarre in northern Spain. Although he lived for only

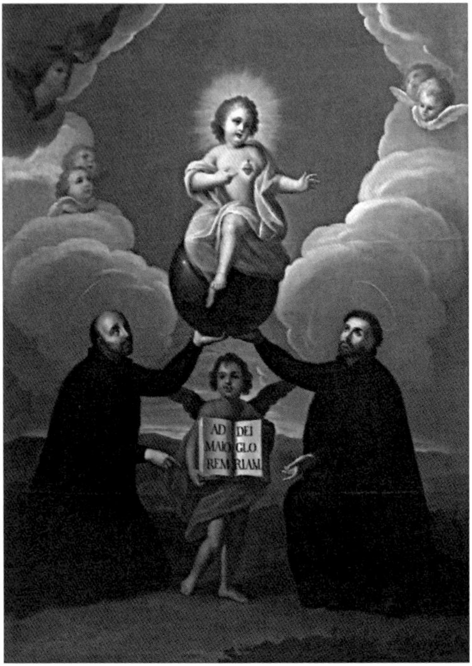

St. Ignatius and St. Francis Xavier. An oil painting in the Cathedral of Córdoba, Spain. The two founders of the Society of Jesus, the Jesuits, are holding the Christ child as he sits on the globe, symbolizing the Jesuits' commitment to global evangelism. *Photograph by Jebulon.*

forty-six years, from 1506 until 1552, he became one of the most far-ranging Christian evangelists since Paul traveled through the Roman Empire in the first century. Xavier studied in Paris alongside Ignatius Loyola, another Spaniard with whom he and five others founded the Society of Jesus, commonly known as the Jesuits. He then worked in Venice and Rome. Soon after his ordination to the priesthood in 1537, King John III of Portugal encouraged him to bring Christianity to the East Indies. Xavier left for India in 1541. He converted many in India, Sri Lanka and Japan. He is believed to have also worked in the Philippines. However, historians are unable to verify this claim. While planning to evangelize in China, he fell ill and died on Sancian, an island near China's coast.

Francis Xavier was named a saint in 1622, at the same time as Ignatius Loyola. After his death, Saint Xavier's remains were taken from China to Goa, a Portuguese colony for more than four hundred years on India's western coast. The remains are enshrined in a Goan church. One of his arms was removed in 1614 and is in a church in Rome.[271] Franciscan friars at the College of Santa Cruz Querétaro in New Spain (see page 71) sponsored the establishment of three San Xavier Missions in the 1740s and 1750s. They were on the San Xavier River. This river is now named the San Gabriel River and runs through the middle of Texas from Georgetown to north of College Station, Texas, where it empties into the Brazos River. These missions were north of present-day Rockdale and were named San Francisco Xavier de Horcasitas, San Ildefonso and Nuestra Señora de los Dolores y Viana.

The three missions had some early success in converting 308 local Native Americans by 1750. However, this success was short-lived. The missions lacked reliable access to water and adequate defenses. Irrigation canals were begun but never finished. The royal support needed to station troops and build forts was slow in approval and not well organized. Indeed,

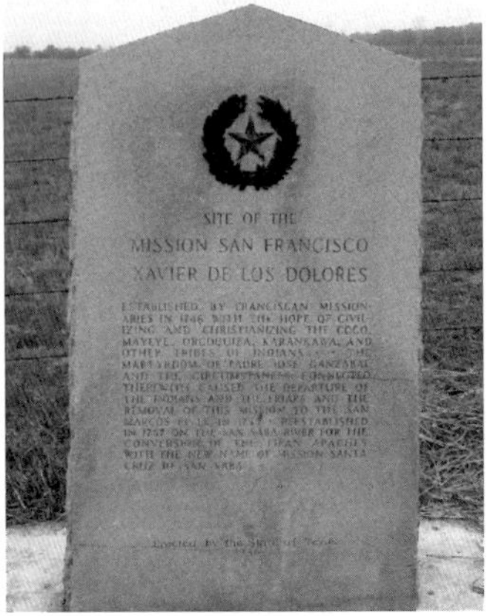

State of Texas marker "Site of the Mission San Francisco Xavier de los Dolores," erected 1936. *Photograph by the author.*

in December 1751, the behavior of the troops was so immoral and harmful toward the Native Americans that the priest excommunicated the soldiers. Diseases also killed many Native Americans and missionaries in the three missions. Finally, unknown individuals killed a priest and a soldier.

In 1755, the military commander of the area, Pedro de Rábago y Terán, ordered the three missions to cease operations and moved to a mission on the San Marcos River. About one thousand Apaches moved to the new mission at San Marcos. Soon some of the newly converted moved to missions in San Antonio and San Sabá.[272]

The San Francisco Xavier Mission on the Guadalupe River, near present-day San Marcos, only lasted a few more years. It was discontinued in 1758.[273]

Y

YSLETA DEL SUR PUEBLO

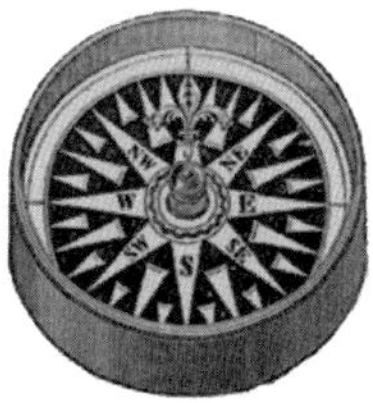

The Ysleta del Sur Pueblo has an unusual history. It is the only pueblo in Texas. When Juan de Oñate (see page 148) traveled north from New Spain in 1598, he crossed the Rio Grande and named this crossing "El Paso del Río de Norte." No one anticipated then that nearly one hundred years later a tribal community known as Ysletans, who spoke a language called Tigua, would move south from northern New Mexico to reestablish itself near El Paso.

In 1680, the Pueblo Indians of present-day New Mexico

revolted against the Spanish colonial priests and soldiers. Many died, and some decided to move. In 1682, the members of the Ysleta Pueblo moved to the El Paso area to establish the Ysleta del Sur Pueblo. *Del sur* means "of the south" or "southern."[274] After the move, the Ysletans "lived quietly, working at various jobs and continuing their tribal organization and family relationships."[275]

Between 1681 and 1691, the Spanish built a mission to serve the relocated Ysletans. By late 1684, the mission census counted 21 families and 188 people. The population grew, and the mission prospered until a flood washed away much of the mission and its surrounding buildings in 1740. The mission was rebuilt, and by 1788, the population had increased to 166 families with 733 people. The current mission has some of the original walls and is built on the same foundation as the original structure.[276]

One of the most curious facts about the Ysleta del Sur Pueblo is its shifting location. After moving south from northern New Mexico, the pueblo's land title shifted because the Rio Grande's channel moved. In 1831, it was an island in the river. The Treaty of Guadalupe Hidalgo of 1848 that concluded the Mexican War set the middle of the Rio Grande as the boundary between the United States and Mexico. Any confusion about which nation would claim the Ysletans was dispelled when the river's channel move southward in 1849. This placed the pueblo on the Texas side in land that was part of the United States.[277]

During the Civil War, President Abraham Lincoln

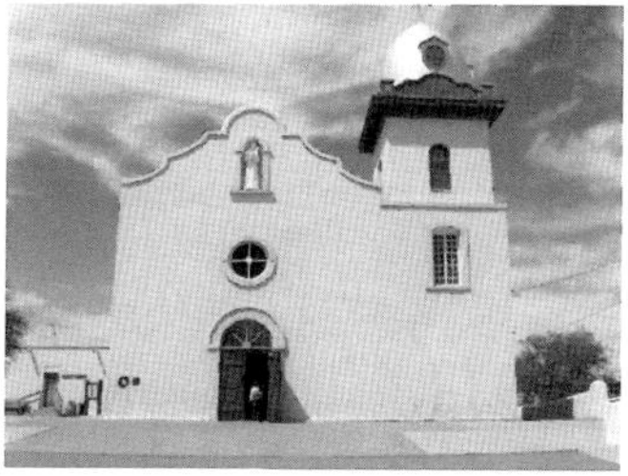

Ysleta del Sur Church (La Misión de Corpus Christi de San Antonio de la Ysleta del Sur). *Photograph by David, uploaded by PD Tillman (http://www.flickr.com/people/25876268@N05).*

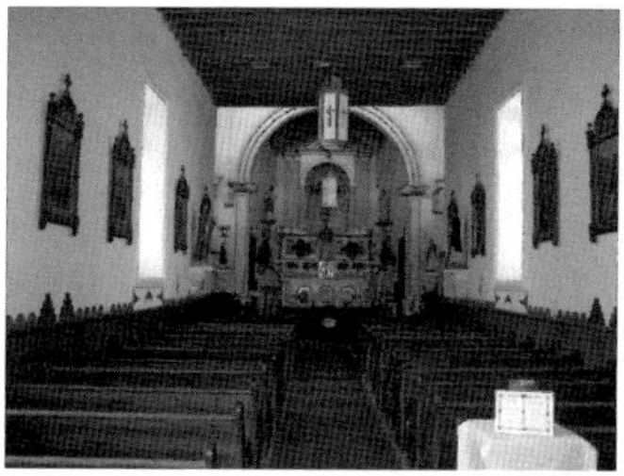

Interior of Ysleta del Sur Church (La Misión de Corpus Christi de San Antonio de la Ysleta del Sur). *Photograph and uploading by J Reyes at en.wikipedia.php.*

recognized the sovereignty of Native Americans living in the pueblos of New Mexico. This was one way to assert a firm claim on the area for the Union.

Since the Ysletans were in Texas, a state that had joined the Confederacy, the Ysleta del Sur Pueblo was not recognized by the U.S. government as a distinct and sovereign people until more than one hundred years later. President Lyndon B. Johnson signed a law in 1968 that recognized the tribe.[278]

In the early twenty-first century, the tribal enrollment is more than 1,600 citizens. The tribe operates many organizations, and information is readily available on the Internet. One of the most interesting sites is the quarterly newsletter on economic development on the website. The Ysletans also feature education and training programs in a quarterly newsletter about their empowerment program.

Z

LORENZO DE ZAVALA

Manuel Lorenzo Justiniano de Zavala y Sáenz was a well-educated, multilingual and widely traveled man of means and sophistication. He was a politician, diplomat, author and the first vice-president of Texas.

Zavala was born in 1788 in the Yucatán province of New Spain. Zavala had a reformer's approach, particularly in the newspapers he owned and edited. His democratic ideals were not favored by New Spain's governing authorities, and he was imprisoned for three years in an island fortress at Veracruz. While there, he studied English and read medical texts. Upon release, he qualified to practice medicine. After prison, he served as secretary to the Yucatán legislature, and in 1821, he joined the Spanish Cortes,

Spain's parliament, as Yucatán's representative. When Zavala returned to New Spain, it was independent and called itself the United States of Mexico. Zavala would spend the rest of his life working in favor of republican government.

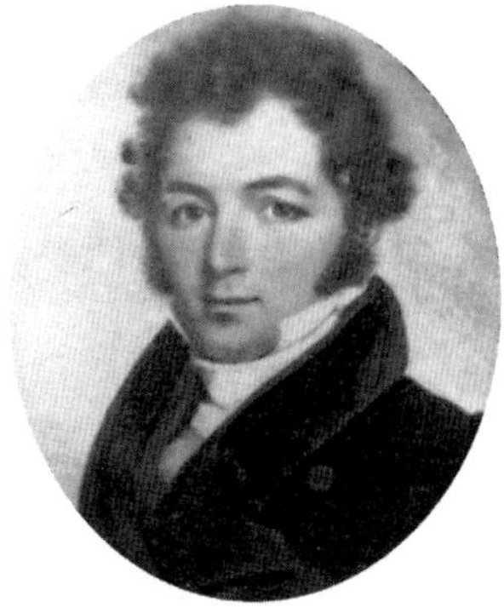

Painting of Lorenzo de Zavala, the first vice-president of the Republic of Texas. *Courtesy Texas State Library and Archives Commission, Prints and Photographs Collection, #001-102-135.*

Zavala was on the Federalist side of a struggle that tore Mexico in two. The Texas War of Independence unfolded during a civil war in Mexico with one side favoring a central government and another wanting a decentralized federation of states. Zavala served in various legislative and administrative posts, including governor of the state of Mexico, the federal district where Mexico City is located. President Vicente Ramón Guerrero named Zavala secretary of the treasury, where he served for most of 1829 until the conservative centrist Anastasio Bustamante became president.

At this juncture, Zavala despaired of having a decentralized federal government. He went into exile in New York City. He tried to find investors to buy his empresario grants that allowed him to settle hundreds of families in a vast area of southeast Texas. In late 1830, he sold the grants to the Galveston Bay and Texas Land Company. He took his profit and toured England and France for several months before returning to New York City and Mexico City in mid-1832. Once back in Mexico, Zavala retraced his previous life. Again he served as governor of the state of Mexico and a legislator for Yucatán in the national congress. In 1833, President Antonio López de Santa Anna appointed him ambassador to France. Zavala began this post in early 1834. He resigned his ambassadorship when he learned that López de Santa Anna had become a dictator, no longer the president of a republic. Zavala refused to return to Mexico as López de Santa Anna requested. Instead, he went to New York City and then to Texas, where he landed in July 1835.

Once in Texas, Zavala "despaired of reforming Mexico from within."[279] He joined the Texans who advocated independence from Mexico. He took leadership roles in framing the structure for the aspiring nation of Texas. He served on the Permanent Council and represented Harrisburg, now part of present-day Houston. The Permanent Council had two organizations that evolved into declaring independence for Texas, the Consultation and the Convention of 1836 at Washington-on-the-Brazos. Zavala's ability to work in three languages—Spanish, English and French—coupled with his work experience as a journalist, legislator, governor and secretary of the treasury gave him credibility and influence. His fellow

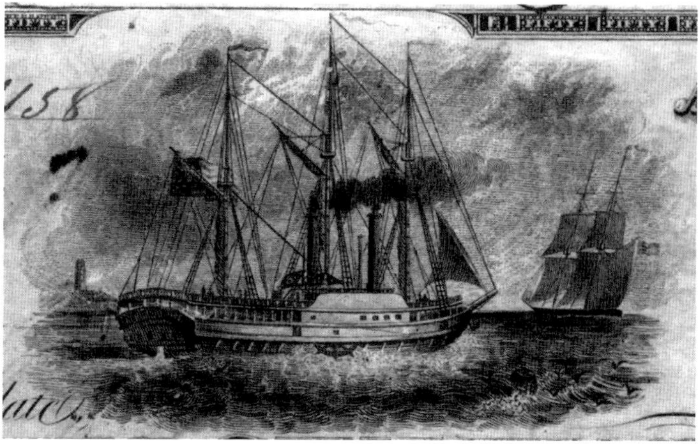

Texas navy ship *Zavala*, the first steamship in the Texas navy, found on the Republic of Texas fifty-dollar bill. *Courtesy Texas State Library and Archives Commission, Prints and Photographs Collection, #1989/84-16.*

delegates to the convention elected him vice-president of the newly independent nation of Texas.

Zavala tried to forge a peace with Mexico. He was not successful and became mortally ill after developing pneumonia following a soaking cold rain that overturned his boat in Buffalo Bayou in present-day Houston. He died on November 15, 1836, and is buried in a grave in Buffalo Bayou.

Lorenzo de Zavala exemplified the strength of the reforming liberals who brought about Mexico's independence from Spain. He is known not only for his political contributions to Mexico and Texas but also

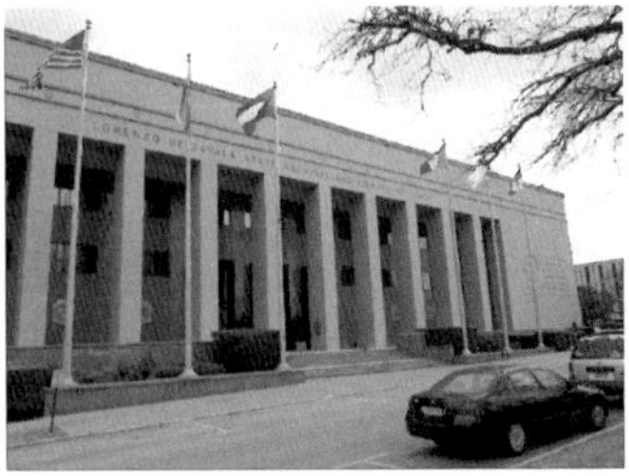

Lorenzo de Zavala State Archives and Library Building in Austin, Texas. *Photograph by the author.*

for his writing, especially the two-volume history of Mexico *Ensayo Histórico de las Revoluciones de México desde 1808 hasta 1830* (*Historical Essay of the Revolutions of Mexico from 1808 to 1830*) and his observations of the United States in *Viaje a los Estados-Unidos del Norte de America* (*Journey to the United States of America*).[280]

Zavala is remembered well. The Texas Republic named its first steam-powered warship, the *Zavala*, for him. He also has many schools and streets named in his honor. Texas has a city and county with his name. The Lorenzo de Zavala Texas State Archives and Library Building in Austin in named for him.

Lorenzo de Zavala was a powerhouse of energy and skill who contributed greatly to the creation of Texas.

JUAN DE ZUMÁRRAGA

In the early sixteenth century, Mexico was a place fraught with the upheaval of two cultures that differed in many significant ways. In addition to the usual differences of one culture from another that includes food, clothing, housing and other common attributes, the differences between the Spanish and Native Americans of Mexico were profound enough to influence every

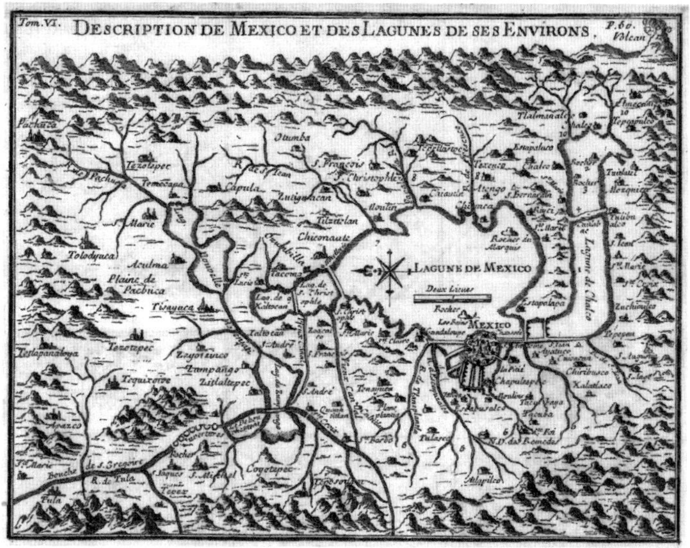

Description de Mexico et des Lagunes de Ses Environs (*A Map of Mexico and Its Surroundings* by Gemelli Careri, from a copy of a map by Charles Siguenza that he "derived from a copy of an original native map while Careri was in Mexico," published in his *Giro del Mundo* in a 1719 French translation, *Voyage du Tour du Monde* (Voyage around the World). The map depicts "Tenochitlán or Mexico City where an eagle is found standing on a cactus growing out of a rock," as shown in the coat of arms of Mexico. This is the land as it appeared during the early sixteenth century when Bishop de Zumárraga arrived in Mexico. *Photograph by Dottos.*

aspect of life. Generally, any invading group esteems its own values and structures. As with most people, the Spanish found more worth in their own approaches than in those of the Native Americans. Additionally, they overlooked what may have been useful, helpful and valuable to the Native Americans. Instead, as with most Europeans entering the New World, they strove to replace what they found with what they valued. They looked for what would benefit them immediately and their home country most in the long term. The Spaniards were in Mexico to claim land, exploit the natural wealth they found, profit from the labor of the Native Americans and convert the people to Catholicism.

In the midst of all this change and conflict, the Spanish had a system that tried to address the needs of safety and welfare of the Native Americans. The system did not succeed often. Sometimes it was ignored and put aside in the service of expediency and quest for further exploitation and the consequent increase of gold and silver being sent to Spain.

The Spanish monarchy had just recently emerged victorious in 1492 with the defeat of the last remaining Muslims in Spain. The victory in 1492 was the culmination of many battles over several centuries. With this in mind, it is understandable that Spain waged very ferocious campaigns and expensive wars in Europe. This mindset also influenced the Spanish in the New World. Curiously this warlike ferocity is embodied in the language differences between the English and Spanish. The English often called themselves explorers or colonists while the Spanish called themselves *conquistadores*, meaning "conquerors"—reminiscent of the *Reconquista* (the "reconquest") the 1492 defeat of the last Moors in the Iberian peninsula's southernmost province, Andalusia.[281]

In the midst of this time, came Juan de Zumárraga, who lived a long life of eighty years. He was born in Durango, Biscaya, in 1468 in the Basque area of what would soon become Spain. He died on June 3, 1548, in Mexico. His life spanned a time of great change, marvel and upheaval. As a young man, he became a Franciscan friar: "In 1527 he was custodian of the convent of Abrojo, where he received King Charles V." The king was favorably impressed. Soon afterward, Zumárraga was selected to be a judge in the trial of women to determine if they were witches. Zumárraga considered the accused to be women afflicted with hallucinations. On December 27, 1527, Charles V recommended he be named the first bishop of Mexico. Although he had not yet been consecrated bishop, he was sent from Spain and arrived in Mexico on December 6, 1528. Zumárraga was also titled "Protector of

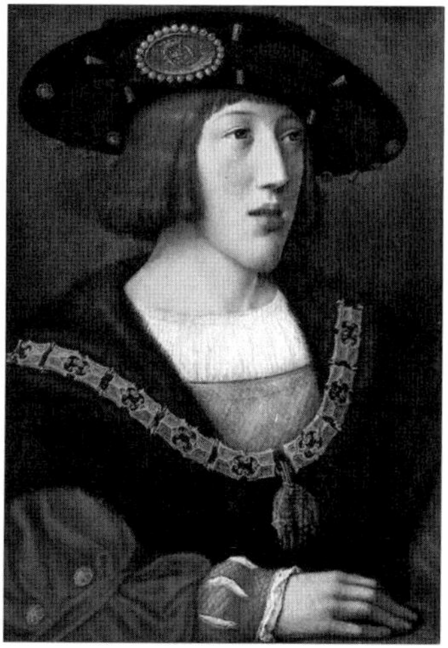

Charles V, King of Spain and Holy Roman Emperor (1500–1558). An oil painting by Barnaerd van Orley, after 1515. Charles V appointed Juan de Zumárraga bishop of Mexico and, later, the first archbishop of Mexico. *Photograph by Upload Bot.*

the Indians," as Bartolomé de Las Casas had been called before Zumárraga.

Accompanying the bishop-elect were the first civil officials whom Spain sent to Mexico, the *oidores*, meaning "judges." The men were to administer civil affairs, which included interactions with Native Americans. As the protector of the Indians, Zumárraga had a difficult time finding his way. He had no specific job description to guide him. As a bishop lacking the official sanction of the Church, not being consecrated, he lacked enough power or presence to affect much to benefit the Indians. Two of the judges died just after the party landed in Mexico. The remaining judges, Juan Ortiz de Matienzo, Diego Delgadillo and Nuño de Guzmán, were not sympathetic to Indian claims of injustice and maltreatment. Once Hernán Cortés returned to Spain, "no limits seem to have been placed on the auditors." It was an era of great strife and violence. The auditor-created civil order brought severe disorder for the Indians. "They impoverished the Indians by taxes, sold them into slavery, branded them with hot irons, sent shiploads to the Antilles, offered violence to Indian girls, and persecuted with incredible fury the followers of Cortés."

Despite having little leverage, Zumárraga tried to defend the Indians. They sought his protection while his fellow Franciscan friars urged him to end the abuse of the auditors. At the same time, some other religious orders countered the Franciscans, saying that the Indian claims were unfounded. Zumárraga tried to appeal for help form the Spanish court.

The auditors diverted some of his letters and censored others. In desperation, Zumárraga had a fellow Biscayan, a sailor, hide a letter in cargo being shipped to Spain. Zumárraga and the auditors struggled for influence at court. It was advantageous that Cortés supported Zumárraga's case.

A resolution emerged in December 1530, when the new judge of the high court, a man sent to administer the king's justice, arrived in Mexico. He heard and took action. Matienzo and Delgadillo were imprisoned and sent to Spain. Soon, they gained some influence and were released from prison, and Zumárraga was ordered back to Spain. Following more wrangling and contention, Zumárraga was believed and vindicated. He was consecrated as a bishop on April 27, 1533. He sought and received assurance that Indians would be treated better in the future and returned to Mexico in October 1534. Some teachers and mechanics accompanied him.

One of Zumárraga's most impactful actions centered on his involvement with Juan Diego Cuauhtlatoatzin who reported his encounters with the Virgin Mary. Zumárraga was skeptical about the truth and reality of these claims until December 12, 1532, when, at the bishop's request, Juan Diego Cuauhtlatoatzin opened his *tilma*, a cloak that peasants wore. Out of the *tilma* tumbled to the floor in front of them some Castilian roses. They were amazed to see the virgin's image on the *tilma*. Zumárraga's skepticism greatly diminished. He and Juan Diego believed they had experienced an apparition of the virgin.

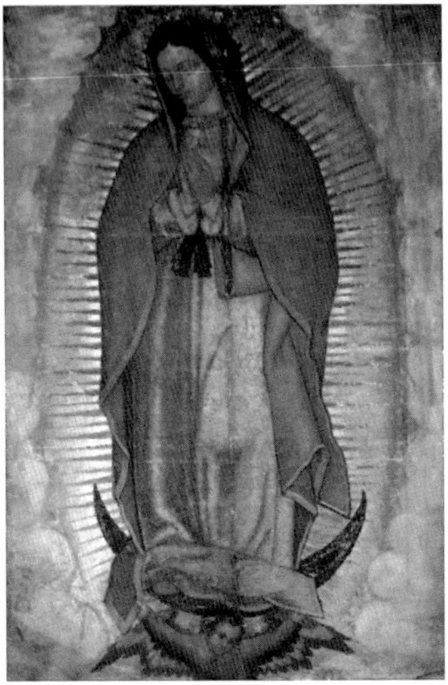

Original picture of Nuestra Señora de Guadalupe (Our Lady of Guadalupe), 1531, shown in the Basilica of Our Lady of Guadalupe in Mexico City. *Photograph by Anagoria.*

A church was built at the site, Tepeyac Hill, in present-day Mexico City. Today, the Basilica of Guadalupe is Mexico's most popular attraction. The Virgin of Guadalupe is revered worldwide, especially in Latin America, where she is venerated as "the patroness of the Americas."[282] In 1990, Pope John Paul II, at the Basilica of Guadalupe, announced Juan Diego Cuauhtlatoatzin's canonization. He is the first Roman Catholic indigenous American saint.

Zumárraga's title, protector of the Indians, was dropped as the king no longer believed it was necessary. Soon, the administrative structure for civil affairs changed. The auditors were disbanded and a king's representative system was established when Antonio de Mendoza became the first viceroy in Mexico. The Native Americans were converting to Catholicism in great numbers. A Franciscan friar, Toribio de Motolina, reported there were five million baptized Indians in 1536.

Conditions improved for the Native Americans, especially

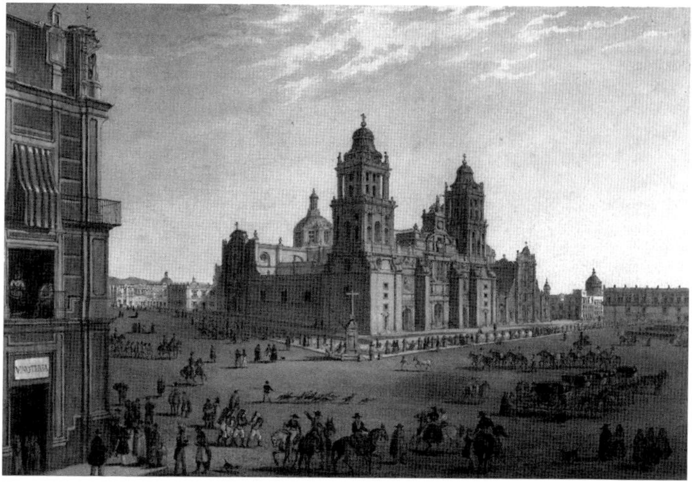

Plaza Mayor de México (the main square of Mexico City), a hand-colored lithograph highlighted with gum arabic by Frédéric Lehnert. The scene looks at Metropolitan Cathedral of Mexico City, where Archbishop Juan de Zumárraga is entombed in the crypt. Published in Carl Nebel, *Voyage Pittoresque et Archéologique Dans la Partie la Plus Intéressante du Mexique Par C. Nebel, Architecte. 50 Planches Lithographiées Avec Texte Explicatif.* Paris: Chez M. Moench, imprimé chez Paul Renouard, 1836. *Photograph by Lupo.*

after the institution of the Nuevas Leyes (new laws) that Bartolomé de Las Casas had negotiated in 1541–42. Slavery was no longer sanctioned. Indians received a new status, allowing more freedom of movement. Generally, they were now treated less frequently as European serfs. Much of this advance was temporary and fell aside when Mexico's ruling elite persuaded Emperor Charles V to rescind many of these measures. For the next four hundred plus years, the interactions between the descendants of the Spanish and the Native Americans of Mexico dealt with challenges, disputes, disruptions and even open warfare and revolution.

Bishop de Zumárraga was named the first archbishop of Mexico, a move to separate from the direct rule of the archbishop of Seville. Bishops would be consecrated in the new dioceses of Oaxaca, Michoacán, Tlaxcala, Guatemala and Ciudad Real de Chiapas. The pope sent out this appointment on July 8, 1548. Unfortunately, the bishop of Mexico, Juan de Zumárraga, had died the previous month.[283] He is entombed in the crypt of the Metropolitan Cathedral in Mexico City.

The struggles that Bishop Zumárraga had in Mexico informed what Spanish policy and actions would operate later in Texas. As the Spanish moved north toward Texas, they brought the same culture led by the two sources of authority and power, the military and the church. Texas became a territory of widely scattered settlements of presidios and missions. While most of the Spanish settlements did not last long in Texas, they did shape the development of land policy, civil administration and ecclesiastical presence defining the role of Native Americans as they related to the Spanish. Bishop Zumárraga left a lasting mark in the civil polity when he sought to protect the Native Americans he encountered and served in the church. Although this resulted in a paternalistic approach that may not be as self-fulfilling as modern people may desire, it was an improvement over a disregard of the most basic right, the right to life itself.

NOTES

Acknowledgements

1. Collins, *Story of America in Pictures*.

Introduction

2. "People: Alibates Flint Quarries National Monument."
3. "List of United States Cities by Population."

Marqués de San Miguel de Aguayo

4. Newton, "Aguayo, Marques de San Miguel de."
5. Ibid.

6. "Mission San José (Texas)."
7. Chipman, *Spanish Texas, 1519–1821*; Weber, *Spanish Frontier in North America*, in "José de Azlor y Virto de Vera."
8. "Canary Islanders," *Handbook of Texas Online.*

Agustín de Ahumada y Villalón, Marqués de las Amarillas

9. "Agustín de Ahumada."
10. Fehrenbach, *Lone Star*, 62.
11. "Agustín de Ahumada."

Lucas Ignacio Alamán y Escalada

12. "Lucas Alamán Biography," *Encyclopedia of World Biography*.
13. Fehrenbach, *Lone Star*, 45.
14. Letter of Manuel Mier y Terán to President Guadalupe Victoria, June 30, 1828.
15. Bishop, "Law of April 6, 1830."

Gabriel Minime, Sieur Barbier

16. Bruseth and Turner, *From A Watery Grave*, 34.
17. Ibid.

18. Ibid., 82.

19. Johnson, "Barbier, Gabriel Minime, Sieur."

20. Fehrenbach, *Lone Star*, 37, 39–41.

21. Weddle, "La Salle Expedition."

22. Ramos, "La Belle and Fort St. Louis," *Texas Almanac*.

23. Graczyk, "17th-Century Shipwreck to Be Freeze-Dried, Rebuilt."

Juan Antonio Bustillo y Ceballos

24. Taylor, "Bustillo y Ceballos."

25. Fehrenbach, *Lone Star*, 59.

26. "Canary Islanders," *Handbook of Texas Online*.

27. "Juan Antonio Bustillo y Ceballos."

Álvar Núñez Cabeza de Vaca

28. Fehrenbach, *Lone Star*, 23.

29. Chipman, "Cabeza de Vaca, Álvar Nuñez."

30. Ibid.

31. Fehrenbach, *Lone Star*, 23.

32. Chipman, "Cabeza de Vaca, Álvar Nuñez."

Charro

33. Fehrenbach, *Lone Star*, 75.
34. Ibid.
35. McMurtry, "Horseman, Goodbye," 60.

Teodoro de Croix

36. Weddle, "Croix, Teodoro de."
37. California State Military Department, California State Military Museum, "Teodoro de Croix."
38. "Teodoro de Croix."
39. Fehrenbach, *Lone Star*, 57.
40. Weddle, "Croix, Teodoro de."

Delaware Indians

41. Biles, "Susquehannah Company, 1750–1763, 105.
42. Hunter, *Forts on the Pennsylvania Frontier, 1753–1758*, 5.
43. Catlin, *Letters and Notes on the Manners, Customs, and Condition of the North American Indians*, 2:10.
44. Fehrenbach, *Lone Star*, 457.
45. Neighbours, *Indian Exodus*, 2.
46. Lipscomb, "Delaware Indians."
47. "John O. Meusebach," *Texas State Library and Archives Commission.*

48. Lipscomb, "Delaware Indians."
49. "Black Beaver."

Haden and Benjamin Edwards

50. Clark, "Beginnings of Texas, 1684–1718," 58.
51. Fredonian Declaration of Independence, Gammel, *Laws of Texas* 1:107–10, in Wallace, Vigness and Word, *Documents of Texas History*, 59–60.
52. Edwards, Haden, papers, 1836–1838, "Description, Special Info."
53. Fehrenbach, *Lone Star*, 163–64.
54. "Edwards County, Texas."
55. McCrain, "Edwards County."
56. "Edwards County, Texas."

José de Escandón y Helguera

57. García, "Escandon, Jose de."
58. Fehrenbach, *Lone Star*, 75–77.
59. "José de Escandón. 1st Count of Sierra Gorda."
60. "Order of Santiago."
61. Ibid.
62. García, "Escandón, Jose de."
63. Fehrenbach, *Lone Star*, 78.
64. Ibid.

François Marie Charles Fourier

65. Morison, *Oxford History of the American People*, 65.
66. Ryrie, *Ryrie Study Bible, King James Version*, 799, 1345.
67. Wilson, *To the Finland Station*, 86–89.
68. Fehrenbach, *Lone Star*, 291.
69. "La Reunion (Dallas)."
70. Davidson, "La Reunion."
71. "La Reunion (Dallas)."
72. Ibid.
73. "Texas Historical Markers in Dallas County, 2012."
74. Appleton, "La Reunion Cemetery's Upkeep an Eternal Problem."

Franciscans

75. Bolton, *Texas in the Middle Eighteenth Century*; Casteñada, *Our Catholic Heritage in Texas* in "College of Santa Cruz de Querétaro," *Handbook of Texas Online*.
76. Schoelwer, *Alamo Images*, in "Mission San Antonio de Valero."
77. Fehrenbach, *Lone Star*, 54.
78. "Francisco Garcés."
79. Habig, "Franciscans."
80. Fehrenbach, *Lone Star*, 54.

Padre Garza

81. Clark, "Beginnings of Texas, 1684–1718," 58.
82. McDonald, "Philip Nolan."
83. Fehrenbach, *Lone Star*, 66–69.
84. Blake, "Ibarvo, Antonio Gil."

Jared Ellison Groce

85. Jackson, "Groce, Jared Ellison."
86. Fehrenbach, *Lone Star*, 128, 140.
87. Marcom, "Beginnings of the African Diaspora in Texas."
88. Hazlewood, "Bernardo Plantation."
89. Jackson, "Groce, Jared Ellison."
90. Berlet, "Groce's Retreat."

Hape Indians

91. Campbell, "Hape Indians."
92. Logan, "Chapter Eight: Linguistics," in "Coahuiltecan People."
93. "Who Were the Coahuiltecans?"
94. Campbell, "Hape Indians."

Frances Cox Henderson

95. James L. Haley, *Passionate Nation* (New York: Free Press, 2006), 262, 280.
96. Fehrenbach, *Lone Star*, 263
97. Haley, *Passionate Nation*, 280.
98. "Visit San Augustine, Texas! Historic Churches."

Francisco Hidalgo

99. Chipman, "Hidalgo, Francisco."
100. "Los Adaes."
101. Weddle, "Chicken War."
102. Chipman, "Hidalgo, Francisco."

Antonio Gil Ibarvo

103. "Antonio Gil Y'Barbo."
104. Chipman, "Rubí, Marqués de."
105. "Rubí Report Recommends Reorganization," *Handbook of Texas Online*.
106. "Antonio Gil Y'Barbo."
107. Blake, "Ibarvo, Antonio Gil."

Independence

108. "Independence Baptist Church."

109. Haley, *Sam Houston*, 420.

110. Augustin and Pitts, "Independence TX (Washington County)."

Anson Jones

111. Caption of an engraving, "The Republic of Texas is no more—President Anson Jones, Annexation Ceremony, February 19, 1846."

112. Gambrell, "Jones, Anson."

Jumano Indians

113. Hickerson, "Jumano Indians."

114. "Jumano People."

Kadohadacho Confederacy

115. Clark, "Beginnings of Texas, 1684–1718."

116. Smith, *Caddo Indians*.

117. Fehrenbach, *Lone Star*, 11.

118. Ibid.

119. Pertulla, "Caddoan Area Prehistory and Archaeology," 65, in Wesson and Rees, eds., *Between Contacts and Colonies*, 49–66.

120. Aten, "Woodland Cultures of the Texas Coast," 82, in Davis, *Perspectives on Gulf Coast Prehistory*, 72–93.

121. Smith, *Caddo Indians*, 167–68.

122. Texas Historical Commission, "Caddo Mound State Historical Site."

123. Smith, *Caddos, the Wichitas, and the United States, 1846–1901*, xiv.

Karankawa Indians

124. Lipscomb, "Karankawa Indians."

125. "Karankawa People."

126. Lipscomb, "Karankawa Indians."

127. "Karankawa People."

128. "Juan Cortina."

Jane Herbert Wilkinson Long

129. Fehrenbach, *Lone Star*, 129.

130. "Jane Long (1798–1880)."

131. "Jane Herbert Wilkinson Long."

132. Ibid.

133. "Jane Long (1798–1880)."

Samuel McCulloch Jr.

134. Walker, "Black History under the Six Flags of Texas," in *Black History in Texas*, 1.

135. "Estevanico," *Encyclopedia of World Biography*, 200.

136. Walker, "Black History under the Six Flags of Texas," in *Black History in Texas*.

137. Ibid.

138. Ibid.

139. Institute of Texan Cultures. "African-American Texans, 2000," 1.

140. Thompson, "McCulloch, Samuel, Jr."

141. Ibid.

142. Ibid.

143. Ibid.

Athanase de Mézières

144. Clark, "Beginnings of Texas," 68.

145. Fehrenbach, *Lone Star*, 70–77.

146. Chipman, "Mézières, Athanase de."

Felipe Enrique Neri

147. Moore, "Bastrop, Baron de."

148. Frois, "On the Road, Bastrop Perspective, Around Louisiana: Northern."

149. "Felipe Enrique Neri, Baron de Bastrop."

150. "Baron de Bastrop: Diplomat, Legislator, Fraud."

151. "Antonio María Martínez."

152. "García, Luciano," *Handbook of Texas Online.*

153. Fehrenbach, *Lone Star*, 140–41.

154. Moore, "Bastrop, Baron de."

Philip Nolan

155. Letter from Thomas Jefferson to Philip Nolan, 308–11.

156. Texas Historical Commission, "Erected in Memory of Phillip Nolan, Hill County, Texas Historical Marker."

157. Fehrenbach, *Lone Star*, 116–17.

158. Pike, "Map of the Internal Provinces of New Spain."

159. *List of Staff Officers of the Confederate States Army, 1861–1865.*

160. Frazier, *Cottonclads!*, Appendix A, 116.

161. Texas Historical Commission, "Belton—Visionary Community."

Nuestra Señora del Espíritu Santo de Zúñiga Mission

162. Roell, "Nuestra Señora del Espiritu Santo de Zuniga Mission."

163. Fehrenbach, *Lone Star*, 50.

164. "Mission Espíritu Santo."

165. Roell, "Nuestra Señora."

166. Ibid.

Old San Antonio Road

167. "National Road."

168. "Old San Antonio Road," *Handbook of Texas Online.*

169. "History & Culture: El Camino Real de los Tejas Historic Trail."

170. "Mission Dolores, El Camino de los Tejas," *Texas Beyond History.*

171. "Old San Antonio Road," *Handbook of Texas Online.*

172. "Old San Antonio Road." http://www.en.wikipedia.org/w/index.php?title=Old_San_Antoni_Road&printable=yes.

Juan de Oñate

173. "Labor Omnia Vincit."

174. Wright, *Tiguas.*

175. Fehrenbach, *Lone Star*, 28.

176. Smith, *Wichita Indians*, 13–14.

177. Graffiti by Juan de Oñate.

Penateka Comanche Indians

178. Tetzlaff, "Meusebach-Comanche Treaty."

179. Neighbours, *Indian Exodus*, 90.

180. Texas Historical Commission, "Comanche Indian Treaty, Marker 991."

181. Tetzlaff, "Meusebach-Comanche Treaty."

Petroglyphs and Pictographs

182. Wickman, "Indian Rock Art."

Zebulon Montgomery Pike

183. "Battle of York."

184. Letter of Henry Dearborn, U.S. secretary of war, to General James Wilkinson, 193.

185. "Lieutenant Zebulon Pike's Diary."

186. "Zebulon Pike."

187. Letter of Thomas Jefferson to Secretary of State James Madison.

188. "Map of Zebulon Pike in Western Texas" and "Map of Pike in East Texas."

189. "Zebulon Pike Campsite: Alto, Cherokee County, Texas, Texas State Historical Marker No. 5073006962."

190. "Battle of York."

191. "Pike's Peak."

Quilting

192. Belcher, "Quilts Offer Bridge to Texas' Pioneer Past."
193. Yabsley, "Quilting."
194. Belcher, "Quilts Offer Bridge to Texas' Pioneer Past."
195. Texas State Library and Archives Commission, "Quilt expert Marcia Kaylakie analyzes 'summer spread' attributed to Margaret Lea Houston."
196. Yabsley, "Quilting."

Diego and Domingo Ramón

197. Weddle, "Ramón, Diego."
198. Weddle, "Ramón Expedition."
199. Weddle, "Paso de Diego Ramón."
200. Weddle, "Ramón Expedition."
201. Ibid.
202. Chipman, "Ramón, Diego."
203. Chipman, "Massanet, Damián."
204. Cunningham, "Domingo Ramón Diary," 62.
205. Ibid.
206. Chipman, *Spanish Texas, 1519–1821*, 18, in Cunningham, "Domingo Ramón Diary," 42.

Refugio Mission

207. Morison, *Admiral of the Ocean Sea*, 47.
208. Jackson, *From Savages to Subjects*, 4.
209. Ibid.
210. Fehrenbach, *Lone Star*, 46.
211. Robert M. Levine, "Foreword," in Jackson, *From Savages to Subjects*, ix.
212. Diocese of Corpus Christi, "Century of Tradition, Lifetime of Faith."
213. Benowitz, "Nuestra Señora del Refugio Mission."
214. Jackson, *From Savages to Subjects*, 58.
215. Our Lady of Refuge Church, Refugio, Texas, unpublished booklet.

San Fernando Cathedral

216. Gaines, "San Fernando Cathedral."
217. "San Fernando Cathedral: South and West Texas; A National Register of Historic Places."
218. Gaines, "San Fernando Cathedral."
219. "Cathedral of San Fernando."
220. "San Fernando Cathedral."
221. Gaines, "San Fernando Cathedral."
222. Ibid.
223. "Cathedral of San Fernando."

San Francisco de los Tejas Mission

224. "Driving Directions from Weches, Texas to Monclova/ MapQuest."
225. Fisher, *Spanish Missions of Sam Antonio*, 87.
226. Weddle, "San Francisco de los Tejas Mission."
227. "Mission San Francisco de la Espada."
228. Ibid.

Sisterdale

229. Biesele, "Texas State Convention of Germans in 1854," 24, in "Sisterdale, Texas."
230. Ibid.
231. "Funeral of German Patriots at Comfort, Texas, August 20, 1866."
232. Historical Marker Database, "Treue Der Union Monument Marker."
233. "Sister Creek Vineyards: Sisterdale Texas."

Texas Navy

234. Fehrenbach, *Lone Star*, 242.
235. Texas State Library and Archives Commission, "War with Mexico."
236. Fehrenbach, *Lone Star*, 243.
237. Kesting, "Invincible."

José de Urrutia

238. "Urrutia, José de."
239. "José de Urrutia," *Handbook of Texas Online.*
240. Ibid.

Uvalde

241. "Real y Militar Orden de San Hermenegildo."
242. Starnes, "Ugalde, Juan de."
243. Rogers, "Uvalde, TX."
244. Dolph, Briscoe Center for American History, "John Nance Garner Biography."
245. Hevesi, "Dolph Briscoe, Texas Governor in the '70s, Dies at 87."
246. "Happy Trails."
247. "Matthew McConaughey."
248. "Los Palominos."

Juan Martín de Veramendi

249. Allen, "Historic Veramendi Palace Fell on Hard Times."
250. "Veramendi, Juan Martín de," *Handbook of Texas Online.*
251. "Juan Martín de Veramendi."
252. Allen, "Historic Veramendi Palace Fell on Hard Times."
253. Ibid.

Wichita Indians

254. Smith, *Wichita Indians*, 2, 10.

255. Ibid., 1

256. Ibid.

257. Ibid., xi.

258. Ibid., 65–66.

259. "Letter of Robert S. Neighbors to his wife, September 14, 1859," in Neighbours, *Indian Exodus*, 13.

260. Smith, *Wichita Indians*, 15.

261. Ibid.

262. U.S. Fish and Wildlife Service, "Official Site of the Wichita Mountains Wildlife Refuge."

James Wilkinson

263. "James Wilkinson," http:www.history.army.mil.books/CG&CSA/Wilkinson-J.htm.

264. Wilkinson, *Memoirs of My Own Times*, 1:129, in Fischer, *Washington's Crossing*, 24.

265. W.W. Abbot, Dorothy Twohig, Philander D. Chase, Edward G. Lengel, Theodore J. Crackel and David R. Hoth, eds., *The Papers of George Washington: Presidential Series*, 15 vols. (Charlottesville: University of Virginia, 1985), 10:75, in Chernow, *Washington: A Life*, 31.

266. "James Wilkinson," http:www.history.army.mil.books/CG&CSA/Wilkinson-J.htm.

267. "James Wilkinson," http://www.en.wikipedia.org/wiki/James_Wilkinson.

268. Ibid.

269. Haggard, "Neutral Ground."

270. Weems, "Wilkinson, James."

Francis Xavier

271. Astrain, "St. Francis Xavier."

272. Supplee, "San Xavier Missions."

273. Chipman, "San Francisco Xavier Mission on the Guadalupe River."

Ysleta del Sur Pueblo

274. "Ysleta Del Sur Pueblo."

275. Wright, *Tiguas*, 4.

276. Ibid., 11, 1.

277. Ibid., 1.

278. Ibid., 4, 15.

Lorenzo de Zavala

279. Brands, *Lone Star Nation*, 38.

280. Estep, "Zavala, Lorenzo de."

Juan de Zumárraga

281. Fehrenbach, *Lone Star*, 20–21.

282. "Our Lady of Guadalupe."

283. Crivelli, "Juan de Zumárraga."

BIBLIOGRAPHY

Documents

Austin, Stephen F. *Translation of the Laws, Orders, and Contracts on Colonization*. Official translation. Columbia, Texas, 1837: 40–45, 56–57. In Wallace, Ernest, David L. Vigness, and George B. Ward, eds. *Documents of Texas History*. 2nd edition. Austin: Texas State Historical Association, 2002, 46–50.

Constitution of the Republic of Texas, Article VI, Schedule, Section 1. From *Laws of the Republic of Texas*. Printed by order of the secretary of state. 2 vols. Houston, Texas, 1838, 1:9–26. In Wallace, Ernest, David L. Vigness, and George B. Ward, eds. *Documents of Texas History*. 2nd edition. Austin: Texas State Historical Association, 2002, 100–06.

The Fredonian Declaration of Independence, December 21, 1826. Cited in Gammel, H.P N., comp. *The Laws of Texas, 1822–1897*. 10 vols. Austin, Texas, 1898, 1:107–10. In Wallace, Ernest, David L. Vigness, and George B. Ward, eds. *Documents of Texas History*. 2nd edition. Austin: Texas State Historical Association, 2002, 59–60.

"John O. Meusebach—Comanche Nation Treaty, May 9, 1847." Titled as *Between the Commissary General of the German Immigration Company and the Comanche Nation. Courtesy Texas State Library and Archives Commission, Prints and Photographs Collection, #1973/3-1-B.*

Letter of Manuel Mier y Terán to President Guadalupe Victoria, June 30, 1828. From Alleine, Howren. "Causes and Origins of the Decree of April 6, 1830." *Southwestern Historical Quarterly* 16 (April 1913): 395–98. In Wallace, Ernest, David L. Vigness and George B. Ward, eds. *Documents of Texas History*. 2nd edition. Austin: Texas State Historical Association, 2002, 65–66.

Letter of Thomas Jefferson to Secretary of State James Madison, August 30, 1807. Original in "Documents about Zebulon Pike and His Expeditions from the Library of Congress." http://zebulonpike.net.pike-docs.htm (accessed November 1, 2013).

List of Staff Officers of the Confederate States Army, 1861–1865. Washington, D.C.: U.S. Government Printing Office, 1891. Original copy in the James Verner Sciafe Collection of Civil War Literature, Cornell University Library, Cornell University, Ithaca, New York. Available at www.csatrainmen. com/PDF/CSA_StaffOfficers.pdf. http://www.archive.org/details/cu31924030921096 (accessed January 24, 2012).

"List of United States Cities by Population." 2010 United States Census. http://en.wikipedia.org/wiki/List_of_United_States_by_population (accessed June 26, 2012).

"Map of Zebulon Pike in Western Texas" and "Map of Zebulon Pike in East Texas." In *Zebulon Pike Educational Material–Pike National Trail Association and Membership*. http://www.zebulonpike.org.zebuloon-pike-route-maps.htm (accessed November 1, 2013).

Memorial to Congress Requesting Separate Statehood, April 1833. Signed by David G. Burnet, chairman of the committee. In Wallace, Ernest, David L. Vigness, and George B. Ward, eds. *Documents of Texas History*. 2nd edition. Austin: Texas State Historical Association, 2002, 76–80.

Mirabeau B. Lamar's Inaugural Address, December 10, 1838. In Gulick, Charles A., Jr., and Katherine Elliott, eds. *The Papers of Mirabeau Buonaparte Lamar*. 6 vols. Austin, Texas, 1922, 2:316–23, 346–369. In Wallace, Ernest, David L. Vigness, and George B. Ward, eds. *Documents of Texas History*. 2nd edition. Austin: Texas State Historical Association, 2002, 125–26.

Pike, Zebulon Montgomery. "A Map of the Internal Provinces of New Spain." 1807. *Courtesy Texas State Library and Archives Commission. Map Collection No. 1438.*

Proposed Constitution for the State of Texas, April 13, 1833. From the Constitution or Form of Government of the State of Texas. Made in General Convention in the Town of San Felipe de Austin, in the Month of April, 1833; New Orleans, 1833; Photostat copy, Archives, Texas State Library, Austin. In Wallace, Ernest, David L. Vigness, and George B. Ward, eds. *Documents of Texas History*. 2nd edition. Austin: Texas State Historical Association, 2002, 80–85.

Sam Houston's First Inaugural Address, October 22, 1836. In *Texas House Journal*, 1st cong., 1st sess., 84–88. In Williams, Amelia W., and Eugene C. Barker, eds. *The Writings of Sam Houston*. 8 vols. Austin, TX: 1938–43, 1:448–52. In Wallace, Ernest, David L. Vigness, and George B. Ward, eds. *Documents of Texas History*. 2nd edition. Austin: Texas State Historical Association, 2002, 123–124.

Stephen F. Austin's Address to the Convention of 1833, April 1, 1833. In Barker, Eugene C., ed. The Austin Papers. 3 vols. Washington, D.C., 1924 and 1928; and Austin, Texas, 1929, 2:934–40. In Wallace, Ernest, David L. Vigness, and George B. Ward, eds. *Documents of Texas History*. 2nd edition. Austin: Texas State Historical Association, 2002, 74–76.

Texas Historical Commission. "Comanche Indian Treaty, Marker 991." http://atlas.thc.state.tx.us/viewform.asap?_num=5411000991&site_name=Comanche% (accessed June 25, 2012).

Texas Parks and Wildlife Department. "Interpretive Guide to Hueco Tanks State Historic Site." www.tpwd.state.tx.us/park/hueco (accessed March 27, 2014).

Texas State Historical Association. Letter of Thomas Jefferson to Philip Nolan, June 24, 1798. In "Concerning Philip Nolan," *Texas State Historical Quarterly* 7 (April 1904): 308–11. http://books.google.com/?id=mNQAAAAIAJ&printsec=titlepage#PPA308.M1 (retrieved May 27, 2009). http://en.wikipedia.org/w/index.php?title=Philip_Nolan&printable-yes (accessed May 8, 2014).

Wallace, Ernest, David L. Vigness, and George B. Ward, eds. *Documents of Texas History*. 2nd edition. Austin: Texas State Historical Association, 2002.

Theses, Dissertations and Monographs

Aten, Lawrence E. "Woodland Cultures of the Texas Coast." In Davis, David E., ed. *Perspectives on Gulf Coast Prehistory*. Gainesville: University of Florida/Florida State Museum, 1984, 72–93.

Biles, Stephen P. "The Susquehannah Company, 1750–1763, a Study of Land Speculation and Conflicts of Sovereignty." Master's thesis, Midwestern University, 1970.

Catlin, George. *Letters and Notes of the Manners, Customs, and Condition of the North American Indians*. Vol. 2, 1841. Minneapolis, MN: Ross & Haines, 1965.

Clark, Robert Carlton. "The Beginnings of Texas 1684–1718." PhD diss., University of Wisconsin. Austin: University of Texas Bulletin No. 98, 1907. Reprint, Philadelphia: Porcupine Press, 1976.

Davis, David E., ed. *Perspectives on Gulf Coast Prehistory*. Gainesville: University of Florida/Florida State Museum, 1984.

Our Lady of Refuge Church, Refugio, Texas. Unpublished booklet available at the church's entrance. Author and date are not stated. Obtained January 16, 2013.

Pertulla, Timothy K. "Caddoan Area Prehistory and Archaeology." In Wesson, Cameron B., and Mark A. Rees, eds. *Between Contacts and Colonies, Archaeological Perspectives on the Protohistoric Southeast*. Tuscaloosa: University of Alabama, 2002: 49–65.

Wesson, Cameron B., and Mark A. Rees, eds. *Between Contacts and Colonies, Archaeological Perspectives on the Protohistoric Southeast.* Tuscaloosa: University of Alabama, 2002.

Articles

"Agustín de Ahumada." http://en.wikipedia.org/w/index.php?=Agust%C3%ADn_de_Ahumada&printable=yes (accessed October 31, 2013).

"Alibates Flint Quarries National Monument." http://en.wikipedia.org/wiki/Alibates_Flint_Quarries_Natinal_Monument (accessed March 27, 2014).

Allen, Paula. "Historic Veramendi Palace Fell on Hard Times." *San Antonio Express-News*, September 10, 2011.

"Amistad National Recreation Area (U.S. National Park Service)." http://www.nps.gov.amis/historyculture/howtorockart.htm (accessed March 30, 2014).

"Antonio Gil Y'Barbo." http://wn.wikipedia.org/w/index.php?title=Antonio_Gil_Y%27Barbo&printable=yes (accessed November 5, 2013).

"Antonio Gil y Barbo—Nacogdoches, Texas Attractions." http://www.allacrosstexas.com/texas-attractions.php?city=Nacogdoches&attraction+Antonio_Gil_y_Barbo.html (accessed January 3, 2013).

"Antonio María Martínez." http://en.wikipedia.org/wiki/Antonio_Mar%C3%AD_Mart%C3%ADnez (accessed November 19, 2013).

Appleton, Roy. "La Réunion Cemetery's Upkeep an Eternal Problem," *Dallas Morning News*, June 14, 2010. http://www.dallasnews.com/news/community-news/dallas/headlines/20100614-La=Runion (accessed February 16, 2013).

Astrain, Antonio. "St. Francis Xavier." *Catholic Encyclopedia*. Vol. 6. New York: Robert Appleton, 1909. http://www.newadvent.org/cathen/06233b.htm (accessed June 22, 2012).

Augustin, Byron, and William L. Pitts, "Independence, TX (Washington County)." *Handbook of Texas Online*. (Texas State Historical Association). http://www.tshaonline.org/handbook/online/articles/hli03 (accessed April 12, 2012).

Barnes, Michael. "Central Texas German's Tale." *Austin American-Statesman*, August 5, 2012, D1.

"Baron de Bastrop: Diplomat, Legislator, Fraud." http://myrahncilvain.wordpress.com/2012/10/12/baron-de-bastrop-diplomat-legislator-fraud (accessed November 1, 2013).

"Battle of York." http://www.en.wikipedia.org/wiki/Battle_of_York (accessed November 22, 2013).

Belcher, Helen. "Quilts Offer Bridge to Texas' Pioneer Past." *Huntsville Item*, January 11, 2012. http://www.itemonline.com/local/x1477837905/Quilts-offer-bridge-to-Texas-pioneer-past/print (accessed June 19, 2012).

Benowitz, June Melby. "Nuestra Señora del Refugio Mission." *Handbook of Texas Online*. (Texas State Historical Association). http://www.tshaonline.org/handbook/online/artices/uqn18 (accessed June 18, 2012).

Berlet, Sarah Groce. "Groce's Retreat." *Handbook of Texas Online*. (Texas State Historical Association). http://www.tshaonline.org/handbook/online/articles/ccg04 (accessed November 14, 2013).

Biesele, Rudolf L. "The Texas State Convention of Germans in 1854." *Southwest Historical Quarterly* 33 (April 1930): 24.

Bishop, Curtis. "Law of April 6, 1830." *Handbook of Texas Online* (Texas State Historical Association). https://www.tshaonline.org/handbook/online/articles/ng/101 (accessed May 8, 2014).

"Black Beaver." http://en/wikipedia.org/wiki/Black_Beaver (accessed December 28, 2012).

Black, Mary S. "Figures in White Shaman Shelter, Pecos Experience Day 4." http://marysblack.wordpress.com/2013/03/23/pecos-expereince-day-4/ (accessed March 30, 2014).

Blake, Robert Bruce. "Ibarvo, Antonio Gil." *Handbook of Texas Online.* (Texas State Historical Association). http://www.tshaonline.org/handbook/online/articles/fib01 (accessed August 17, 2102).

"Bucareli," *Handbook of Texas Online.* (Texas State Historical Association). http://www.tshaonline.org/handbook/online/articles/ueb05 (accessed August 17, 2012).

"Burro Mesa Archeological District." http://en.wikipedia.org/wiki/Burro_Mesa_Archeological_District (accessed March 27, 2014).

California State Military Department. The California State Military Museum. "Teodoro de Croix: Captain General of the Interior Provinces, 1776–1783." http://www.militarymuseum.org/Croix.html (accessed October 31, 2013).

Campbell, Thomas N. "Hape Indians." *Handbook of Texas Online.* (Texas State Historical Association). http://www.tshaonline.org/handbook/online/articles/bmh06 (accessed November 4, 2013).

"Canary Islanders." *Handbook of Texas Online.* (Texas State Historical Association). http://www.tshaonline.org/handbook/online/articles/poc01 (accessed November 4, 2013).

Caption of an engraving. "The Republic of Texas is no more—President Anson Jones, Annexation Ceremony, February 19, 1846." *Courtesy Texas State Library and Archives Commission, Prints and Photographs Collection #1977/62-8.*

"Cathedral of San Fernando." http://en.wikipedia.org/wiki/Cathedral_of_San_Fernando (accessed November 23, 2013).

Chipman, Donald E. "Cabeza de Vaca, Álvar Nuñez." *Handbook of Texas Online.* (Texas State Historical Association). http://www.tshaonline.org/handbook/online/articles/fca06 (accessed August 22, 2012).

———. "Hidalgo, Francisco." *Handbook of Texas Online.* (Texas State Historical Association). http://www.tshaonline.org/handbook/online/articles/fhi05 (accessed November 14, 2013).

———. "Massanet, Damián." *Handbook of Texas Online.* (Texas State Historical Association). http://www.tshaonline.org/handbook/online/articles/fma71 (accessed November 4, 2013).

———. "Mézières, Athanase de." *Handbook of Texas Online.* (Texas State Historical Association). http://www.tshaonline.org/handbook/online/articles/fme69 (accessed April 12, 2012).

———. "Ramón, Diego." *Handbook of Texas Online.* (Texas State Historical Association). http://www.tshaonline.org/handbook/online/articles/fra24 (accessed November 4, 2013).

———. "Rubí, Marqués de." *Handbook of Texas Online.* (Texas State Historical Association). http://www.tshaonline.org/handbook/online/articles/3215 (accessed November 15, 2013).

———. "San Francisco Xavier Mission on the Guadalupe River." *Handbook of Texas Online.* (Texas State Historical Association).

http://www.tshaonline.org/handbook/onlline/articles/uqslc (accessed June 22, 2012).

"Coahuiltecan People." http://en.wikipedia.org/wiki/Coahuiltecan_people (accessed November 14, 2013).

"College of Santa Cruz de Querétaro." *Handbook of Texas Online*. (Texas State Historical Association). http://www.tshaonline.org/handbook/online/articles/kbcut (accessed October 31, 2013).

Crivelli, Camillus. "Juan de Zumárraga." *Catholic Encyclopedia*. Vol. 15. New York: Robert Appleton, 1912. http://newadvent.org/cathen/15767a.htm (accessed November 1, 2013).

Cunningham, Debbie S. "The Domingo Ramón Diary of the 1716 Expedition into the Province of the Tejas Indians: An Annotated Translation." *Southwestern Historical Quarterly*, 110, no. 1 (2006): 65.

Davidson, Rondel V. "La Réunion." *Handbook of Texas Online*. (Texas State Historical Association). http://www.tshaonline.org/handbook/online/articles/ue101 (accessed April 11, 2012).

Dickerson, W.E.S. "Comanche Indian Reservation." *Handbook of Texas Online*. (Texas State Historical Association). http://www.tshaonline.org/handbook/online/articles/bpc10 (accessed June 27, 2012).

Diocese of Corpus Christi. "A Century of Tradition, Lifetime of Faith." http://acenturyoftradition.org/index.cfm?load=page&page=189 (accessed August 17, 2012).

Dolph Briscoe Center for American History. "John Nance Garner Biography." Austin: University of Texas–Austin, 2006–12. http://www.cah.utexas.edu/museums/garner_bio_two.php (accessed August 22, 2012).

"Driving Directions from Weches, Texas to Monclova/MapQuest," accessed November 26, 2013, http://www.mapquest.com/print?a=app.core.a097a78fdb113f9727de0a90.

"Edwards County, Texas." http://en.wikipedia.org/wiki/Edwards_County_Texas (accessed April 11, 2012).

Edwards, Haden, Papers, 1836–1838. "In Description, Special info." University of Texas Libraries Catalogue, University of Texas–Austin. http://catalog.lib.utexas.edu/record=b7816273 (accessed January 28, 2013).

"El Orcoquisac Archeological District." http://en.wikipedia.org/wiki/El_Orcoquisac_Archeological_District (accessed March 27, 2014).

Estep, Raymond. "Zavala, Lorenzo de." *Handbook of Texas Online.* (Texas State Historical Association). http://www.tshaonline.org/handbook/online/articles/fza05 (accessed June 22, 2012).

"Estevanico." *Encyclopedia of World Biography*. 2004. *Encyclopedia.com.* http://www.encyclopedia.com/doc/1G2-3404702043.html (accessed August 20, 2012).

Etchieson, Meeks. "Alibates Flint Quarries." *Handbook of Texas Online.* (Texas State Historical Association). http://www.tshaonline.org/handbook/online/articles/bba01 (accessed March 28, 2014).

"Farm-to-market-road." http://en.wikipedia.org.wiki/Farm_to_market_road (accessed June 20, 2012).

"Felipe Enrique Neri, Baron de Bastrop." http://wwww.en.wikipedia.org/index/php?title-Felipe_Enrique_Baron_de_Bastrop&printable=yes (accessed November 1, 2013).

"Francisco Garcés." http://en.wikipedia.org/w/index.php?title-Francisco_Gar%D3A9s&printable=yes (accessed October 31, 2013).

Frois, Jeanne. "On the Road, Bastrop Perspective, Around Louisiana: Northern." *myNewOrleans.com*. http://myneworleans.com/Louisiana-Lilfe/May-June2012/Around-Louisiana-Northern/ (accessed November 1, 2013).

"Funeral of German Patriots at Comfort, Texas, August 20, 1866." *Courtesy Texas State Library and Archives Commission Prints and Photographs Collection #1992/075-0.*

Gaines, Ann Graham. "San Fernando Cathedral." *Handbook of Texas Online*. (Texas State Historical Association). http://www.tshaonline.org/handbook/online/articles/ivs01 (accessed November 23, 2013).

Gambrell, Herbert Gambrell. "Jones, Anson." *Handbook of Texas Online*. (Texas State Historical Association). http://www.tshaonline.org/handbook/online/articles/fjo42 (accessed April 13, 2012).

García, Clotilde P. "Escandón, José de." *Handbook of Texas Online*. (Texas State Historical Association). http://www.tshaonline.org/handbook/online/articles/fes01 (accessed October 31, 2013).

"García, Luciano." *Handbook of Texas Online*. (Texas State Historical Association). http://www.tshaonline.org/handbook/online/articles/fga20 (accessed November 19, 2013).

Graczyk, Michael. "17th-Century Shipwreck to be Freeze-Dried, Rebuilt." *Austin American-Statesman*, August 19, 2012, B5.

Graffiti by Juan de Oñate written in 1605 on *El Morro* (the Headland), known to the Zuñi Indians as *A'ts'ina* (the Place of Writings on the Rock). Americans know the mountain as Inscription Rock. A 1934 Photograph by George A. Grant, chief photographer of the U.S. National Park Service. Public domain. http://en.wikipedia.org/wiki/File:1605_graffiti.jpg (accessed January 4, 2013).

Habig, Marion A., OFM. "Franciscans." *Handbook of Texas Online*. (Texas State Historical Association). http://www.tshaonline.org/handbook/online/articles/ixf01 (accessed October 31, 2013).

Haggard, John V. "Neutral Ground." *Handbook of Texas Online*. (Texas State Historical Association). http://www.tshaonline.org/handbook/online/articles/nbn02 (accessed November 29, 2013).

"Happy Trails." http://en.wikipedia.org/wiki/Happy_Trails_(song) (accessed June 20, 2012).

"Harrell Site." http://en.wikipedia.org/Harrell_Site (accessed March 27, 2014).

Hazelwood, Claudia. "Bernardo Plantation." *Handbook of Texas Online*. (Texas State Historical Association). http://www.tshaonline.org/hadbook/online/articles/acb01 (accessed October 31, 2013).

"Hermenegildo." http://es.wikipedia.org/wiki/San_Hermeneglido (accessed June 25, 2012).

Hevesi, Dennis. "Dolph Briscoe, Texas Governor in the '70s, Dies at 87." *New York Times*, June 28, 2010. http://www.nytimes.com/2010/06/29/us/29briscoe.html?_r=1&pagewanted=print (accessed June 20, 2012).

Hickerson, Nancy P. "Jumano Indians." *Handbook of Texas Online*. (Texas State Historical Association). http://www.tshaonline.org/handbook/online/articles/bmj07 (accessed November 4, 2013).

Historical Marker Database. "Treue Der Union Monument Marker." http://www.hmbd.org/marker.asp?marker=34985&Result=1 (accessed June 29, 2012).

"History & Culture: El Camino Real de los Tejas Historical Trail (U.S. National Park Service)." http://www.nps.gov/elte/historyculture/index.htm (accessed November 20, 2013).

"Hueco Tanks: Credits and Sources." http://www. texasbeyondhistory.net/hueco/credits.html (accessed March 28, 2014).

"Hueco Tanks: Crossroads through Time." http://www.texasbeyondhistory.net/hueco/index.html (accessed March 28, 2014).

"Hueco Tanks." http://en.wikipedia.org/wiki/Hueco_Tanks (accessed March 28, 2014).

"Hueco Tanks: Legacy on the Rocks: The Art of Hueco Tanks." http://www.texasbeyondhistory.net/hueco/rockart.html (accessed March 28, 2014).

Independence Baptist Church website. http:/www.independencetx.com/IndependenceBaptistChurch.htm (accessed December 28, 2012).

Institute of Texan Cultures. "The African-American Texans, 2000." San Antonio: University of Texas–San Antonio, Institute of Texan Cultures. http://129.115.219.13/publictions/texansoneandall/africanamerican.htm (accessed August 18, 2012).

Jackson, Charles Christopher. "Groce, Jared Ellison." *Handbook of Texas Online*. (Texas State Historical Association). http://tshaonline.org/handbook/online/articles/fgr70 (accessed October 31, 2013).

"James Wilkinson." http://www.en.wikipedia.org/wiki/James_Wilkinson (accessed November 1, 2013).

"James Wilkinson." http://www.history.army.mil.books/CG&CSA/Wilkinson-J.htm (accessed November 1, 2013).

"Jane Herbert Wilkinson Long." http://www.texanalivinghistory.org/longbio.html (accessed December 28, 2012).

"Jane Long (1798–1880)." http://www.lsjunction.com/people/long.htm (accessed December 23, 2012).

Johnson, John G. "Barbier, Gabriel Minime, Sieur." *Handbook of Texas Online.* (Texas State Historical Association). http://www.tshaotline.org/handbook/online/articles/fbaej (accessed January 7, 2013).

"José de Azlor y Virto de Vera." http://en.wikipedia.org/w/index.php?title=Jos%C3%A9_de_Azlor_y_Vitro_de_Vera&printable=yes (accessed November 5, 2013).

"José de Escandón, 1st Count of Sierra Gorda." http://en.wikipedia/w/index.php?=Jos%C3%A9_de_Escan%C3%B3n,_1st_Count (accessed October 31, 2013).

"José de Urrutia." http://en.wikipedia.org/wiki/Jos%C3%A9_de_Urrutia (accessed November 24, 2013).

"Juan Antonio Bustillo y Ceballos." http://en.wikipedia.org/w/index/php?title=Juan_Antonio_Bustillo_y_Cevallos&printable=yes (accessed October 31, 2013).

"Juan Cortina." http://en.wikipedia.org/wiki/Juan_Cortina (accessed November 17, 2013).

"Juan Martín de Veramendi." http://www.en.wikipedia.org/wiki/Juan_Mart%C3%ADn_de_Veramnedi (accessed November 1, 2013).

"Jumano People." http://en.wikipedia.org/w/index.php?_Jumano_people&printable=yes (accessed November 5, 2013).

"Karankawa People." http://en.wikipedai.org/w/index.php?=Karankawa_people&printable=yes (accessed November 5, 2013).

Kearney, James. "Moral Battles, During Civil War, German Settlers in Central Texas Had Hard Choice, One Paralleled in Days of Vietnam." *Austin American-Statesman*, July 29, 2012, F1.

Kesting, Robert W. "Invincible," *Handbook of Texas Online* (Texas State Historical Association). http://www.tshaonline.org/handbook/online/articles/qti02 (accessed May 7, 2014).

"*La Belle* Shipwreck." http://www.texasbeyondhistory.net/belle/ (accessed May 8, 2014).

"Labor Omnia Vincit." http://en.wikipedia.org/wiki/Labor_omnia_vincit (accessed January 29, 2013).

"Landergin Mesa." http://en.wikipedia.org/wiki/Landergin_Mesa (accessed March 27, 2014).

"La Réunion (Dallas)." http://en.wikipedia.org/wiki/La_Reunion_(Dallas) (accessed February 9, 2013).

Levine, Robert M. "Foreword, 2000." In Jackson, Robert H. *From Savages to Subjects: Missions in the History of the American Southwest.* Armonk, NY: M.E. Sharpe, 2002: ix–x.

"Levi Rock Shelter." http://en.wikipedia.org/wiki/Levi_Rock_Shelter (accessed March 27, 2014).

Lich, Glen E. "Sisterdale." *Handbook of Texas Online.* (Texas State Historical Association). http://www.tshaonline.org/handbook/online/articles/hns51 (accessed June 18, 2012).

"Lieutenant Zebulon Pike's Diary: New Mexico, Chihuahua & Texas, Lt. Pike in Spanish Texas." http://www.tamu.edu/faculty/ccbn/dewitt/pikejour.htm (accessed November 1, 2013).

Lipscomb, Carol A. "Delaware Indians." *Handbook of Texas Online.* (Texas State Historical Association). http://www.tshaonline.org/handbook/online/articles/bmd08 (accessed December 28, 2012).

———. "Karankawa Indians." *Handbook of Texas Online.* (Texas State Historical Association). http://www.tshaonline.org/handbook/online/articles/bmk05 (accessed November 4, 2013).

Logan, Jennifer L. "Chapter Eight: Linguistics." In *Reassessing Cultural Extinction: Change and Survival at Mission San Juan Capistrano, Texas*. College Station: Texas A&M University, 2001.

"Los Adaes." http://en.wikipedia.org/wiki/Los_Adaes (accessed November 14, 2013).

"Los Palominos." http://wwww.en.wikipedia.org/wiki/Los_Palominos (accessed June 20, 2012).

"Lubbock Lake Landmark." http://en.wikipedia.org/wiki/Lubbock_Lake_Landmark (accessed March 27, 2014).

"Lucas Alamán Biography." *Encyclopedia of World Biography*. Book Rags. http://.www.bookrags.com/printfreindly/?p=bio&u=lucas_alaman (accessed June 25, 2012).

Marcom, Robert. "Beginnings of the African Diaspora in Texas: A Brief Overview of the Bernardo Plantation Archeology Project." *March 2010 Newsletter, African Diaspora Archaeology Network*. http://www.diaspora.uiuc.edu/news0310.html (accessed November 12, 2013).

"Matthew McConaughey." http://www.imdb.com/name/nm0000190/ (accessed June 20, 2012).

McCrain, James B. "Edwards County." *Handbook of Texas Online*. (Texas State Historical Association). http://www.tshaonlline.org/handbook/online/articles/hce03 (accessed April 11, 2012).

McDonald, Archie. "Philip Nolan," *All Things Historical* (July 2003). http://www.texasescapes.com/AllThingsHistorical/PhilipNolanAM703.htm (accessed August 7, 2012).

McMurtry, Larry. "Horseman, Goodbye." *Texas Monthly* (February 2013): 58–60.

"Mission Dolores, El Camino de los Tejas." *Texas Beyond History*. http://www.texasbeyondhistory.net/dolores/camino.html (accessed November 20, 2013).

"Mission Espíritu Santo." http://www.texasbeyondhistory.net/espiritu/ (accessed October 31, 2013).

"Mission San Antonio de Valero." http://www.tamu.edu/faculty/ccbn/dewitt/adp/history/mission_period/valero.html (accessed November 13, 2013).

"Mission San Francisco de la Espada." http://en.wikipedia.org/wiki/Mission_San_Francisco_de_la_Espada (accessed November 5, 2013).

"Mission San José (Texas)." http://en.wikipedia.org/wiki/Mission_San_Jos%C3%A9_(Texas) (accessed November 9, 2013).

Moore, Richard W. "Bastrop, Baron de." *Handbook of Texas Online*. (Texas State Historical Association). http://tshaonline.org/handbook/online/articles/fbaae (accessed November 1, 2013).

"National Road." http://en.wikipedia.org/wiki/National_Road (accessed November 21, 2013).

Newton, Lewis. "Aguayo, Marques de San Miguel de." *Handbook of Texas Online.* (Texas State Historical Association). http://www.tshaonline.org/handbook/online/articles/fag02 (accessed November 4, 2013).

"Old San Antonio Road." *Handbook of Texas Online.* (Texas State Historical Association). http://www.tshaonline.org/handbook/online/articles/ex04 (accessed November 4, 2013).

"Old San Antonio Road." http://www.en.wikpedia.og/w/index.php?title=Old_San_Antonio_Road&printable=yes (accessed November 5, 2013).

"Order of Santiago." http://en.wikipedia.org/wiki/Order_of_Santiago (accessed March 20, 2014).

Osburn, Dodd S, "Petroglyph and Pictograph Site in the Finlay Mountains, 1941." SMU.edu/publication/Osburn1941.pdf (accessed March 27, 2014).

"Our Lady of Guadalupe." http://en.wikipedia.org/Our_Lady_of_Guadalupe (accessed March 17, 2014).

Owen, Sue. "DPS Patrol No Part of Texas Navy, Which No Longer Exists." *Austin American-Statesman*, April 8, 2012, B1.

"Paint Rock Indian Pictographs." http://texasfortstrail.com/plan-your-adventure/historic-sites-and-cities/sites/paint/-rock-indian-pictographs (accessed March 31, 2014).

"People: Alibates Flint Quarries National Monument (U.S. National Park Service)." http://www.nps.gov/alfl/historyculture/people.htm (accessed March 30, 2104).

"Petroglyph." http://en.wikipedia.org/wiki/Petrogylph (accessed March 25, 2014).

"Pike's Peak." http://en.wikipedia.org/wiki/Pike's_Peak (accessed March 12, 2014).

"Plainview Point." http://en.wikipedia.org/wiki/Plainview_point (accessed March 28, 2014).

Ramos, Mary G. "La Belle and Fort St. Louis." *Texas Almanac*. http://www.texasalmanac.com/topics/history/la_belle_and_fort_st_louis (accessed June 25, 2012).

"Real y Militar Orden de San Hermenegildo." http://es.wikipedia.org/wiki/Real_y_Militar_Orden_de_San_Hermeneglido (accessed June 25, 2012).

Richardson, Rupert N. "Neighbors, Robert Simpson." *Handbook of Texas Online*. (Texas State Historical Association). http://www.tshaonline.org/handbook/on;line/articles/fne08 (accessed June 27, 2012).

"The Rock Art Foundation." http://www.rockart.org (accessed March 30, 2014).

Roell, Craig H. "Goliad Campaign of 1835." *Handbook of Texas Online*. (Texas State Historical Association). http://www.tshaonline.org/handbook/online/articles/gdg01 (accessed August 18, 2012).

———. "Nuestra Señora del Espíritu Santo de Zuniga Mission." *Handbook of Texas Online*. (Texas State Historical Association). http://www.tshaonline.org/handbook/online/articles/uqn16 (accessed October 31, 2013).

Rogers, Freida R. "Uvalde, TX." *Handbook of Texas Online*. (Texas State Historical Association). http://www.tshaonline.org/handbook/online/articles/heu03 (accessed June 19, 2012).

"Rubí Report Recommends Reorganization." *Handbook of Texas Online*. (Texas State Historical Association). http://www.tshaonline.org/day-by-day/31215 (accessed November 15, 2013).

"San Fernando Cathedral." http://www.catholicearth.com/beta/profile/691san-fernando-cahtedral (accessed November 23, 2013).

"San Fernando Cathedral: South and West Texas; A National Register of Historical Places." http://www.nps.gov/nr/travel/tx32.htm (accessed November 23, 2013).

"Sister Creek Vineyards: Sisterdale Texas." http://www.sisterdalevineyards.com (accessed June 18, 2012).

"Sisterdale, Texas." http://en.wikipedia.org/w/index.php?title=Sisterdale_Texas&printable=yes (accessed June 18, 2012).

Starnes, Gary B. "Ugalde, Juan de." *Handbook of Texas Online*. (Texas State Historical Association). http://www.tshaonline.org/handbook/online/articles/fug01 (accessed June 19, 2012).

Supplee, Joan E. "San Xavier Missions." *Handbook of Texas Online*. (Texas State Historical Association). http://www.tshaonline.org/handbook/online/articles/uqs34 (accessed June 19, 2012).

Sutherland, Kay. "Rock Paintings at Hueco Tanks State Historic Site." http://www.tpwd.state.tx.us/...hueco (accessed March 28, 2014).

Taylor, C.H. "Bustillo y Ceballos." *Handbook of Texas Online*. (Texas State Historical Association). http://www.tshaonline.org/handbook/online/articles/fbu62 (accessed October 31, 2013).

"Teodoro de Croix." http://en.wikipedia.org/w/index/php?title=Teodoro_de_Croix&printable=yes (accessed October 31, 2013).

Tetzlaff, Otto W. "Meusebach-Comanche Treaty." *Handbook of Texas Online.* (Texas State Historical Association). http://www.tshaonline.org/handbook/online/articles/mgm01 (accessed June 25, 2012).

Texas Historical Commission. "Belton—A Visionary Community." http://www.thc.state.tx.us/visioninpres/vbelton.shtml (accessed August 19, 2012).

———. "Caddo Mounds State Historical Site." http://www.visitcaddomounds.com (accessed April 16, 2012).

———. "Erected in Memory of Phillip Nolan, Hill County, Texas Historical Marker." http://www.flilckr.com/photos/texasmarkers/6113234760/ (accessed August 19, 2012).

"Texas Historical Markers in Dallas County, 2012." www.dallascounty.org/.../documents/thcmarkerslist2012.pdf (accessed February 15, 2013).

Texas State Library and Archives Commission. "Quilt Expert Marcia Kaylakie Analyzes 'Summer Spread' Attributed to Margaret Lea Houston." *Speaker Series: Quilt Expert and Author Marcia Kaylakie—Texas State Library and Archives Commission.* http://www.tsl.state.tx.us/news/speakerseries/20110317/index.html (accessed June 19, 2012).

———. "War with Mexico: Texas State Library and Archives Commission." https://www.tsl.state.tx.us/exhibits/navy/war/html (accessed June 25, 2012).

Thompson, Nolan. "Ashworth Act." *Handbook of Texas Online.* (Texas State Historical Association). http://www.tshaonline.org/handbook/online/articles/mla03 (accessed August 18, 2012).

———. "McCulloch, Samuel, Jr." *Handbook of Texas Online.* (Texas State Historical Association). http://www.tshonline.org/handbook/online/articles/fmc36 (accessed August 18, 2012).

"Urrutia, José de." *Handbook of Texas Online.* (Texas State Historical Association). http:// www.tshaonline.org/handook/online/articles/fur03 (accessed October 31, 2013).

U.S. Fish and Wildlife Service. "Official Site of the Wichita Mountains Wildlife Refuge." http://www.fws.gov/southwest/refuges/oklahoma/wichita.html (accessed December 24, 2012).

"Uvalde, Texas." http://en.wikipedia.org/wiki/Uvalde_Texas (accessed June 19, 2012).

"Veramendi, Juan Martín de." *Handbook of Texas Online.* (Texas State Historical Association). http://www.tshaonline.org/handbook/online/articles/fve06 (accessed November 1, 2013).

"Visit San Augustine, Texas! Historic Churches." http://visit.sanaugustinetx.xom/churches/cce.html (accessed January 28, 2013).

"Waco Tribe." http://en.wikipedia.org/wiki/Waco_Indians (accessed June 25, 2012).

Walker, Juliet E.K. "Black History under the Six Flags of Texas: A Chronology, 2003." *Black History in Texas*. Austin: University of Texas–Austin. http://www.utexas.edu/world/texasblackhistory/Chronology.html (accessed August 18, 2012).

Weddle, Robert S. "Chicken War." *Handbook of Texas Online* (Texas Historical Association), http://www.tshaonline.org/handbook/online/articles/gfc02 (accessed April 10, 2014).

———. "Croix, Teodoro de." *Handbook of Texas Online*. (Texas State Historical Association). http://www.tshaonline.org/handbook/online/articles/fer26 (accessed October 31, 2013).

———. "La Salle Expedition." *Handbook of Texas Online*. (Texas State Historical Association), http://www.tshaonline.org/handbook/online/articles/up101 (accessed November 4, 2013).

———. "Paso de Diego Ramón." *Handbook of Texas Online*. (Texas State Historical Association). http://www.tshaonline.org/handbook/online/articles/rkp16 (accessed November 23, 2013).

———. "Ramón, Diego." *Handbook of Texas Online*. (Texas State Historical Association). http://www.tshaonline.org/handbook/online/articles/fra23 (accessed November 23, 2013).

———. "Ramón Expedition." *Handbook of Texas Online*. (Texas State Historical Association). http://www.tshaonline.org.handbook/online/articles/upr03 (accessed November 23, 2013).

———. "San Francisco de los Tejas Mission." *Handbook of Texas Online*. (Texas State Historical Association). http://www.tshaonline.org/handbook/online/articles/uqs15 (accessed November 1, 2013).

Weems, John Edward. "Wilkinson, James." *Handbook of Texas Online*. (Texas State Historical Association). http://www.tshaonline.org/handbook/online/articles/fwi87 (accessed November 29, 2013).

"Who Were the Coahuiltecans?" http://texasbeyondhistory.net/st-plains/peoples/coahuiltecans.html (accessed November 14, 2013).

Wickman, Melinda Arceneaux. "Indian Rock Art." *Handbook of Texas Online*. (Texas State Historical Association). http://www.tshaonline.org/handbook/online/articles/bqi03 (accessed March 30, 2014).

Wyatt, Tula Townsend. "Townsend, Everett Ewing." *Handbook of Texas Online*. (Texas State Historical Association). http://www.tshaonline.org/handbook/online/articles/fto32 (accessed March 31, 2014).

Yabsley, Suzanne. "Quilting." *Handbook of Texas Online*. (Texas State Historical Association). http://www.tshaonline.org/handbook/online/articles/liq01 (accessed June 190, 2012).

"Ysleta del Sur Pueblo." http://ysletadelsurpueblo.org/ (accessed June 19, 2012).

"Zebulon Pike Campsite: Alto, Cherokee County, Texas, Texas State Historical Marker No. 5073006962." http://www.9key.com/markers/marker_detail.asap?atlas_number=507006962 (accessed June 3, 2013).

"Zebulon Pike." http://en.wikipedia.org/index/php?title=Zebulon_Pike&printable=yes (accessed November 1, 2013).

Books

Bolton, Herbert Eugene. *Texas in the Middle Eighteenth Century*. Berkeley: University of California Press, 1915. Reprint, Austin: University of Texas, 1970.

Brands, H.W. *Lone Star Nation: The Epic Story of the Battle for Texas Independence*. New York: Anchor, 2005.

Bruseth, James E., and Toni S. Turner. *From a Watery Grave: The Discovery and Excavation of La Salle's Shipwreck*, La Belle. College Station: Texas A&M University Press, 2005.

Casteñada, Carlos E. *Our Catholic Heritage in Texas*. 7 vols. Austin: Von Boeckmann-Jones, 1936–58. Reprint, New York: Arno, 1976.

Catlin, George. *Letters and Notes on the Manners, Customs, and Condition of the North American Indians*. Vols. 1–2. 1841. Reprint, Minneapolis: Ross & Haines, 1965.

Chernow, Ron. *Washington: A Life*. New York: Penguin, 2010.

Chipman, Donald E. *Spanish Texas, 1519–1821*. Austin: University of Texas Press, 1992.

Collins, Alan C. *The Story of America in Pictures*. Garden City, NY: Doubleday, 1953.

Everett, Dianna. *The Texas Cherokees: A People between Two Fires, 1819–1840*. Norman: University of Oklahoma Press, 1990.

Fehrenbach, T.R. *Lone Star: A History of Texas and the Texans*. New York: Tess Press, an Imprint of Black Dog & Leventhal Publishers, Inc., 2000.

Fischer, David Hackett. *Washington's Crossing*. New York: Oxford University Press, 2004.

Fisher, Lewis F. *The Spanish Missions of San Antonio*. San Antonio, TX: Maverick, 1988.

Frazier, Donald S. *Cottonclads! The Battle of Galveston and the Defense of the Texas Coast*. Abilene, TX: McWhiney Foundation, 1998.

Haley, James L. *Passionate Nation*. New York: Free Press, 2006.

———. *Sam Houston*. Norman: University of Oklahoma Press, 2004.

Hamalainen, Pekka. *Comanche Empire*. New Haven, CT: Yale University Press, 2008.

Hunter, William A. *Forts on the Pennsylvania Frontier, 1753–1758*. Harrisburg: Pennsylvania Historical and Museum Commission, 1960.

Jackson, A.T. *Picture-Writing of Texas Indians*. Austin: University of Texas Press, 1938.

Jackson, Robert H. *From Savages to Subjects: Missions in the History of the American Southwest*. Armonk, NY: M.E. Sharpe, 2000.

Lindsell, Harold, ed. *Harper Study Bible, the Holy Bible, Revised Standard Version*. Grand Rapids, MI: Zondervan, 1985.

Malone, Dumas. *Jefferson, the President: Second Term 1805–1809*. Boston: Little Brown, 1974.

Morison, Samuel Eliot. *Admiral of the Ocean Sea: A Life of Christopher Columbus*. Boston: Little Brown, 1942.

———. *The Oxford History of the American People*. New York: Oxford University Press, 1965.

Neighbours, Kenneth F. *Indian Exodus: Texas Indian Affairs, 1835–1859*. San Antonio, TX: Nortex, 1973.

Ryrie, Charles Caldwell, ed. *The Ryrie Study Bible, King James Version*. Chicago: Moody Press, 1978.

Schoelwer, Susan Pendergast. *Alamo Images: Changing Perceptions of a Texas Experience*. Dallas, TX: Southern Methodist University Press, 1985.

Shafer, Harry J., ed. *Painters in Prehistory, Archeology and Art of the Lower Pecos Canyonlands*. San Antonio, TX: Trinity University Press, 2013.

Smith, F. Todd. *The Caddo Indians: Tribes at the Convergence of Empires, 1542–1854*, College Station: Texas A&M University Press, 1995.

———. *The Caddos, the Wichitas, and the United States, 1846–1901*, College Station: Texas A&M University Press, 1996.

———. *The Wichita Indians, Traders of Texas and the Southern Plains, 1540–1845*. College Station: Texas A&M University Press, 2000.

Webb, Walter Prescott. *The Great Plains*. Lincoln: University of Nebraska Press, 1981.

Weber, David. *The Spanish Frontier in North America.* New Haven, CT: Yale University Press, 1992.

Wilkinson, James. *Memoirs of My Own Times.* 3 vols. Philadelphia, 1816. Reprint, 1973.

Wilson, Edmund. *To the Finland Station.* Garden City, NY: Doubleday, 1940.

Wright, Bill. *The Tiguas: Pueblo Indians of Texas.* El Paso: University of Texas Press, 1993.

Design Glyphs

Beard, Frank, and Martha Van Marter. *Bible Symbols; Designed and Arranged to Stimulate a Greater Interest in the Study of the Bible by Both Young and Old.* Chicago: Hertel, Jenkins and Co., 1904.

Uncaptioned:

Lucas Ignacio Alamán y Escalada

José de Escandón y Helguera

Jumano Indians

Samuel McCulloch Jr.

Felipe Enrique Neri

La Feuille, Daniel De. *Devises et Emblemes Anciennes & Modernes.* Tirees de Plus Celebres Auteurs. Germany: Augspurg, 1699.

Uncaptioned:

Agustín de Ahumada y Villalon, Marqués de las Amarillas

Juan Antonio Bustillo y Ceballos

Haden and Benjamin Edwards

José de Escandón y Helguera
Antonio Gil Ibarvo
Kadohadacho Confederacy
Karankawa Indians
Penateka Comanche Indians
Philip Nolan
San Fernando Cathedral
San Francisco de los Tejas Mission
Francis Xavier

Wither, George; Rollenhagen, Gabriel. *A Collection Of Emblemes, Ancient And Moderne: Quickened with Metricall Illustrations, Both Morall And Divine And Disposed Into Lotterie.* London: Augustine Matthews for Henry Taunton, 1635.
Uncaptioned:
Franciscans

ABOUT THE AUTHOR

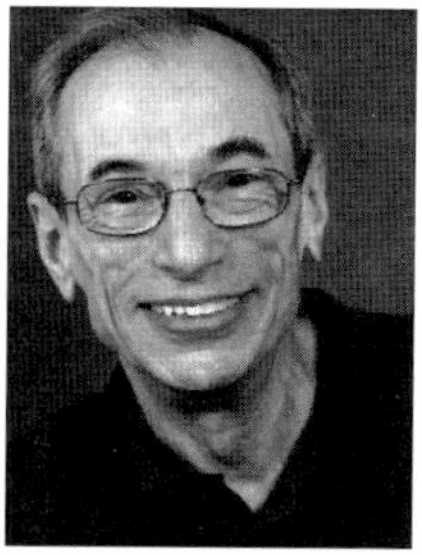

By Kelly Houston.

Stephen P. Biles is a naturalized Texan who came to Texas after completing high school. As a child, he moved with his father's U.S. Army assignments, growing up in San Francisco, Tacoma, San Antonio, Honolulu and Paris. Biles has studied the liberal arts and educational psychology earning an MA in history and a PhD in educational psychology. He is now retired after working in public and university administration, completing his career at the Texas State Library and Archives Commission in Austin. He lives in Austin with his wife.